COUNSELLING PARTNERS AND RELATIVES

OF INDIVIDUALS WHO HAVE SEXUALLY OFFENDED

A Strengths-Focused Eclectic Approach

Andrew Smith

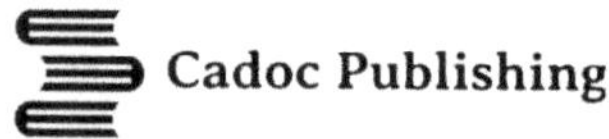 **Cadoc Publishing**

COUNSELLING PARTNERS AND
RELATIVES OF INDIVIDUALS WHO
HAVE SEXUALLY OFFENDED
A Strengths-Focused, Eclectic Approach
By Andrew Smith

Copyright © 2022 by Andrew Smith

Paperback ISBN: 978-1-8381965-3-0
eBook ISBN: 978-1-8381965-4-7

CONTENTS

ACKNOWLEDGMENTS

Once again, I would like to thank all the clients and colleagues with whom I work, who continue to expand my knowledge and understanding of this area. I would also like to acknowledge two individuals, specifically. The first person is my wife, Dr Ruth Smith, whose emotional support and proof-reading ability has been invaluable. I would also like to thank Dr Judith Earnshaw, a therapist and expert witness at the Lucy Faithfull Foundation of many years' standing, for editing the book and for her wise clinical input.

INTRODUCTION

My most emotionally draining experience as a worker has been co-facilitating groups for partners and relatives of men who had committed internet sexual offences. For group members, the disclosure that a loved one had committed a sexual offence had caused immense pain, often fracturing or severing family ties. The groups aimed to raise awareness of safeguarding issues and to offer support to individuals who, by the very nature of their stigmatized predicament, tended to be emotionally isolated. The degree of mental pain and internal conflict felt by the individuals in these groups seemed almost overwhelming. The reasons for such misery form a crucial component of this text. Attending to such distress, offering hope and, in the process, helping to safeguard children from sexual abuse, are the other main reasons for writing this book.

Why so much pain? Aren't these (mostly) women bringing it on themselves? If only they did the right thing and left these unconscionable men who engage with child abuse material online or, worse still, commit contact sexual offences against children and adults. Would not much of their pain be relieved, if they just walked away? This view is entirely understandable. However, it is an ill-informed one based, in part, on the fallacy that all individuals convicted of sexual offences will inevitably sexually offend again, including against their own or somebody else's children. Re-offending can undoubtedly occur, and some sex offenders should never be allowed contact with children. It should also be remembered that the prevalence of sexual abuse significantly exceeds the conviction rate. However, there are some sex offenders who will never re-offend, and other sex offenders who are at a low risk of re-offending. Even high-risk sexual offenders may not be a high risk forever (Hanson et al., 2014). Moreover, individuals who sexually offend on the internet but have no previous record of committing sexual or violent offences or anti-social acts pose a low risk of sexual re-offending, particularly to children offline (Seto and Eke, 2005: Krone and Smith, 2017).

All sex offenders and minor-attracted adults, regardless of the risk they pose, tend to be cast as monsters and beasts, rather than complex human beings who can also be caring partners and fathers. The love partners feel for these men is often automatically viewed as toxic, the result of being groomed by manipulative offenders. The attachment and dependency mothers feel towards partners who are sex offenders can be due to grooming (Still, 2016), and this will be duly explored. However, it does not happen in all instances and, when working with this client group, there is a tendency to discount the compelling pair-bonding instinct, which has a neurobiological basis (Young, 2003), an instinct which has evolved over millennia to keep couples and families together in order to facilitate the long haul of raising children. Philpot (2009) also depicts the conflicted responses of some non-offending partners who have experienced a positive relationship with their sexually offending partner, and where the sexual offending has occurred elsewhere.

In my first book, *Counselling male sexual offenders: A strengths-focused approach* (2017), I address the counterproductive stereotyping of sex offenders, and I will not rehash the same points here. This book is about counselling partners and relatives of individuals who pose a sexual risk; its purpose is to enable counsellors and child protection practitioners, generally, to assist partners in making informed choices and to empower them and other family members to better protect children.

The book takes a strengths-focused, but eclectic, perspective on counselling this client group, utilizing ideas from solution-focused therapy and motivational interviewing, while providing a strengths-focused slant on psycho-educational, psychodynamic, trauma and neurobiological informed therapeutic approaches. Also, a family system safeguarding model is presented, with partners of individuals who pose a sexual risk not viewed as autonomous actors, but relational protagonists within a family script. Transpersonal ideas also influence the text – sometimes referred to as the Perennial Philosophy (Huxley, 2009, first published 1945), or 'Soul' work, as such ideas are known in contemporary counselling and therapy circles, with this being the theme of the BACP annual conference in 2018.

As will hopefully be evident as this book unfolds, work with this client group is not about going for the quick fix, glossing over the long-term effects of trauma, avoiding problems or adopting a superficial view of risk issues which can put children and adults in increased danger - a naive, over-optimistic approach to child protection, termed 'professional dangerousness' (Dale et al.,1986). However, the approach offered does not merely focus on narratives of shame, stigma, and failure, but attempts to co-construct with clients robust, sustainable strategies to better manage challenging relational and safeguarding dilemmas.

The case studies and examples of interventions will include working with couples and with loved ones of offenders, including parents, grandparents, and siblings. Most of the partners in the fictional case studies are women. However, not all partners of sex offenders are women, and not all sex offenders are men. Hence, work with a non-offending male partner and a female sex offender is also featured. Much of the material in this book is also relevant to carers of children who are not family members or parents but who nevertheless have to protect children from sexual risk.

As with my previous book, the case studies are fictitious, containing composite themes taken from my professional practice in this area as a therapist, supervisor and my work as an expert witness in the family courts. I have taken pains to avoid any narrative details which could identify any clients or counsellors with whom I have worked. I will mainly use the term counsellor, although I will also employ the terms therapist, practitioner and worker, all interchangeably. The book is divided into three parts:

- *Counselling partners where there are no child protection safeguarding issues*
- *Counselling partners in order to improve their safeguarding ability to protect children from sexual abuse*
- *Counselling partners and other family members in a systemic way to consolidate and enhance family safety*

This book does not provide quantitative research data on how to work with partners and relatives of sexual offenders, but is designed to provide readers with insight into what commonly occurs behind the curtain of the therapy room, based on my own counselling and supervision practice. The text reveals typical inner processes of counsellors working with various clients, in order to explore how the emotional life of the practitioner in the here-and-now of the sessions, as well as how life outside work, impact upon therapy. This exploration will include excerpts from sessions between the various fictional counsellors and their fictional supervisors.

Part 1

The first part of the book looks at counselling partners where there are no child protection safeguarding issues. The four chapters in this section illustrate the many concerns partners may bring to counselling, not necessarily connected to child protection issues. A range of matters is explored, related to the crisis that happens in a couple's life when one partner discovers the other has been behaving sexually in secret and illegal ways.

Chapter 1 feature a woman in her mid-sixties, Margaret, who has been married to Dennis for almost 43 years. Both are committed Christians, with Dennis being a retired pastor. Unknown to Margaret, Dennis has viewed pornography for most of his adult life. He was arrested recently for viewing online illegal sexual images of teenage girls. The chapter charts how the counsellor helps Margaret to decide what she is prepared and not prepared to put up with and to come to an accommodation with what has happened, involving her developing a different perspective concerning trust in her husband and trust in God. The counsellor has to struggle not to allow her anti-Christian sentiments to get in the way of the therapy.

Chapter 2 features Anthony (31), a betting shop assistant, and Harry (49), an antiques and art dealer. As with Chapter 1, there are no immediate child protection issues. However, Harry has received a Police warning, after viewing a video online of two middle-aged men caning the bare buttocks of a number of South East Asian boys. The couple's relationship has a sadomasochistic element. The issues of relational power dynamics, when one person has sexually offended, is the core exploration of the chapter. In this case, the counsellor becomes aware of his current feelings about his irresponsible son and that he may be displacing these emotions onto his client, Anthony.

Chapters 3 and 4 feature a couple: Anna (39) and Greg (44). Before they met, Greg had been to prison for sexually assaulting a 15-year-old girl. They jointly run two busy florist shops, but Anna is worried about Greg's long-term pornography use and his flirtatious behaviour with the young, female florists. There are no current child protection issues. However, in this case, the offender has committed a contact sexual offence and conforms to somebody who could be termed sexually addicted. Transference dynamics are highlighted, with Anna reminding the counsellor of his sister, with whom he has a strained relationship. There is an exploration of co-dependency and an examination of treatment for sexual addiction.

Part 2

The second part of the book focuses on counselling partners in order to improve their safeguarding ability to protect children from sexual abuse. Part 2 depicts cases where partners of individuals who have sexually offended have to cope with child protection inquiries, and are expected to play their part in protecting their children from the risk posed by their (i.e. the mother's) partner.

The non-offending partner in Chapter 5 is Emily (36). Emily faces the common dilemma of wanting to remain in a relationship with her partner, Richard (49), a history professor who has committed sexual offending on the internet, with her choice perceived by Children's Services as indicative of a lack of ability to protect. They have two children: Jake (8) and Chloe (13). Richard is currently not allowed to live at home with them. Emily is isolated, due to the stigma attached to sexual offending, and needs to talk to somebody. The counsellor attempts to enlarge Emily's perspective, with regard to what good ability to protect means. A further complication is that the male counsellor finds himself attracted to Emily, feeling a rivalry with her academic husband, Richard.

Sian (34) is the protagonist of Chapters 6 and 7. Unlike Emily in the previous chapter, Sian is disadvantaged in many ways, including having been a victim of sexual abuse herself. Also, unlike Emily, Sian has to attend safeguarding counselling if there is any chance of her daughters - Taylor (8) and Lucy (7) - returning home from temporary foster care. Children's Services removed them from Sian's care after the children disclosed apparent sexually abusive behaviour by their father, Steve (46), a drugs dealer. The child protection social worker deemed that Sian did not take her daughters' disclosures seriously and has inadequate ability to protect them from the sexual risk posed by their father. The female therapist working with Sian is a caring, highly responsible person, but comes in and out of being judgemental about, what she perceives to be, Sian's irresponsible behaviour. Chapter 6 focuses on how the counsellor builds rapport with Sian, who is initially a somewhat hostile client. Chapter 7 presents an outline of a discrete course of one-to-one, psycho-educational safeguarding work that can be undertaken by counsellors, but also by other generic child protection workers.

Part 3

The third part of the book also deals with counselling partners where there are child protection issues to be considered, in order to consolidate and enhance safety in the family. In this final part of the book, the safeguarding counselling will involve other members of the family, in addition to the parents.

Chapter 8 features a couple: Yasmin (36) and Zara (38). Children's Services have worries that Yasmin might pose a risk to Zara's two children - Shona (7) and India (8) - because Yasmin has a history of mental health problems and a conviction for underage sex. The couple receives support from Zara's parents, who live nearby, so the grandparents of the children are also participants in the safeguarding work. The chapter explores the relationship between mental health problems and sexual crime, as well as female sexual offending. Also, the counsellor explores her insecurities about working with a client, Zara, who is a combative academic.

In Chapter 9, safeguarding counselling work with the Roberts family is illustrated. The father, Rhys (38) is a military veteran, who has suffered from PTSD. He is married to Viv (36), and they have 14-year-old twins, Rose and Alfie. Rhys has been in the Army since he was 18. He was given a dishonourable discharge from the Army, after being found guilty of raping an 18-year-old woman. The offence occurred on a drunken night out when he was home on leave to attend his mother's funeral. Rhys maintains that the victim consented to sex. Viv thinks there has been a miscarriage of justice.

The couple have had an open relationship and have been swingers in the past. Both parents and the twins undertake safeguarding counselling. The male counsellor considers himself non-judgemental. However, he is a pacifist, does not have much natural sympathy with military values and has not worked with 'swingers' before, all of which he finds challenging.

References

Dale, P., Davies, M., Morrison, T. and Waters, J. (1986) *Dangerous families: Assessment and treatment of child abuse.* London: Tavistock.

Hanson, R.K., Harris, A., Helmus, L.M. and Thornton, D. (2014) 'High-risk sex offenders may not be high risk forever', *Journal of Interpersonal Violence*, 29(15): pp. 2792-2813.

Huxley, A. (2009) *The perennial philosophy.* New York: Harpers Perennial Reprint Edition. First published 1945.

Krone, T. and Smith, R.G (2017) 'Trajectories in online child sexual exploitation offending in Australia', *Trends and issues in crime and criminal justice*, 524.

Peters, S. (2012) *The chimp paradox: The mind management programme to help you achieve success, confidence and happiness.* London: Ebury Publishing.

Philpot, R. (2009) *Understanding child abuse: The partners of child sex offenders tell their stories.* London and New York: Routledge.

Seto, M.C. and Eke, A.W. (2005) 'The criminal histories and later offending of child pornography offenders', *Sexual Abuse: a Journal of Research and Treatment*, 17(2): pp. 201–210.

Smith, A. (2017) *Counselling male sexual offenders: A strengths-focused approach.* London: Routledge.

Still, J. (2016) *Assessment and intervention with mothers and partners following child sexual abuse: Empowering to protect.* London and Philadelphia: Jessica Kingsley Publishers.

Young, L. J. (2003) 'The neural basis of pair bonding in a monogamous species: A model for understanding the biological basis of human behavior', in K.W. Wachter and R.A. Bulatao (eds.) *Offspring: Human fertility behaviour in biodemographic perspective.* Washington, DC: The National Academic Press, pp. 91-103.

PART 1

COUNSELLING PARTNERS WHERE THERE ARE NO CHILD PROTECTION SAFEGUARDING ISSUES

ONE
MARGARET

Introduction

This chapter focuses on the main topic of the first part of the book: counselling partners where there are no safeguarding or child protection concerns, but where the secret sexual behaviour of one partner has put the relationship into crisis. The case study in this chapter features a woman in her mid-sixties, Margaret, who has been married to Dennis for almost 43 years. Both are committed Christians. Unknown to Margaret, Dennis has been secretly viewing pornography for most of his adult life and has recently been arrested for viewing illegal online sexual images of teenage girls. The importance of establishing the goals of counselling early in the therapeutic process is explained. The topics of sexual addiction and sexual offending are then unpicked, and the nature of what constitutes trust discussed. These topics are relevant to Margaret and to many non-offending partners. Moral and risk issues with regard to legal pornography, sexual fantasy and masturbation are then explored, as is the importance of facilitating the client to come to an acceptable (for them) position with regard to their partner's sexual behaviour. The chapter also touches on transpersonal themes. The counsellor assists Margaret to reflect on the nature of her faith, as she comes to terms with the limited control she has over her husband's behaviour and, by proxy, over life in general. Suggestions for good practice are proposed at the end of the chapter.

Case study: Margaret and Dennis

Margaret (65) has been married to Dennis (68) for 43 years. Dennis is an ex-church pastor, having taken early retirement ten years ago on health grounds. He has recently been arrested for viewing indecent images of teenage girls. Fifteen underage sexual images were found, downloaded during an eight-week period. His wife, Margaret, knew nothing about his offending, or that he had secretly been viewing adult pornography for most of his adult life. The police contacted the church authorities and, to date, no allegations of sexual abuse or inappropriate behaviour have ever been recorded, in relation to Dennis. Dennis and Margaret met at Bible College, when they were both virgins, and have been soul mates ever since. They have one daughter, Deborah (39). Deborah is divorced and has no children. Child Protection Services are not involved with the family, as there are no children in the couple's life to protect. Margaret has come to counselling because she fears that she will never be able to trust her husband again. She also thinks he is brushing her concerns under the carpet. She tells the counsellor that Dennis takes the view that he has 'sinned' but has asked for, and received, God's forgiveness. He believes Jesus has set him free to 'sin no more' and to get on with the rest of his life. Margaret states that she wants to forgive her husband but is still very angry with him for 'making a mockery' of their life together. At the same time, she feels guilty for not being able to forgive him, and says that his behaviour has made her doubt her faith, wondering if she can rely on God to protect her any more. She wonders if her husband has suffered from a sexual addiction all these years, as this might explain his secret behaviour.

Therapeutic issues discussed in supervision

The counsellor experiences the case as challenging, bringing to the surface issues related to her own childhood experiences and subsequent world view. The counsellor was raised in a Pentecostal family, with a bullying father who was considered head of the house. When, as a teenager, the counsellor came out as lesbian, her family rejected her. As an adult, the counsellor has developed secular liberal values, with strong feminist sympathies. She did not reconcile with her father before he died but now sees her mother, who is in the early stages of dementia, from time to time. The two have an amicable, if perfunctory, relationship.

The counsellor finds it hard to consistently differentiate emotionally between her own parents and Margaret and Dennis. She has counselled Christians and people of faith before without any problems, but these have been younger people where the potential for counterproductive responses to transference and projection issues has not been so strong.

The supervisor compliments the counsellor on her self-awareness, discussing whether or not it would be better for the couple to see another therapist. There is no other therapist suitably experienced in sexual offending and sexual addiction problems living in the local area, and the counsellor has established a good rapport with Margaret. Hence, the counsellor decides it is best to keep the case.

The supervisor is intrigued by how the counsellor has managed to establish such a good rapport with her client, given the counsellor's negative feelings about Christianity. The counsellor reflects that, despite negative associations, she does know the world of the Church from the inside, which helps her to understand and empathize with many of Margaret's and Dennis's experiences.

The supervisor and counsellor agree that the counsellor will make a note after each session of instances when she experiences strong, negative feelings towards her client and how she responds. An exploration of such instances will then take place in supervision, providing a safety net against punitive practice and an opportunity to celebrate good practice.

Establishing goals of counselling

Completing the following therapeutic tasks early in the counselling process with partners and relatives of people who have sexually offended is as relevant and important as it is with all client groups. These initial tasks include:

- Collaboratively agreeing confidentiality guidelines
- Collaboratively developing a therapeutic alliance
- Collaboratively establishing initial goals of counselling

I have written extensively about confidentiality issues and the ethics of reporting or not reporting sexual risk in my previous book about counselling males who have sexually offended (Smith, 2017). The same principles broadly apply to working with non-offending partners, so I will not repeat the discussion here. Suffice to say that I would suggest agreeing the following basic confidentiality boundary with all clients:

I am aware as a counsellor of my primary responsibility for maintaining confidentiality between myself and the client. However, this general rule of confidentiality can be broken if you disclose information about a criminal offence or conduct that puts others or yourself at serious risk of harm. An attempt would be made to talk to you before disclosure if this does not further compromise anybody's personal safety.

I explored in my last book (Smith, 2017) the business of developing a therapeutic alliance, with the constituent aspects of building trust, engendering hope and increasing motivation to change. These key components will be germane to this text, too. I have also written in the past about negotiating initial goals of therapy with individuals who have sexually offended. However, this task warrants a separate, full discussion, in relation to working with partners and relatives.

As noted in the introductory chapter, counselling partners of offenders can be divided into three categories, which constitute the three separate parts of this book:

1. Counselling partners where there are no safeguarding or risk management issues
2. Counselling partners in order to improve their safeguarding ability to protect children from sexual abuse
3. Counselling partners and other family members in a systemic way to consolidate and enhance family safety

Regardless of the above specific categories, each partner or relative will have their additional personal reasons and goals in seeking therapy.

With regard to Margaret, she seemed to be initially seeking an external authority to tell her how to perceive her husband's behaviour. She appeared to be not only undergoing a crisis in her marriage, but also a developmental crisis of faith. For much of her life, her faith and trust in God had been interwoven with her faith and trust in her husband. This trust had now faltered. There is a body of literature about developmental stages of faith, which can include not just religious faith, but faith in any ideology or set of ideas, including faith in a favoured therapeutic approach (Fowler, 1979; Huxley, 1945, 1981; Scott Peck, 1987; Wilber, 2007).

Margaret was nobody's intellectual slouch. She had taken a great deal of responsibility as a pastor's wife, and was resourceful and competent in many areas. Neither was she naive about the world, having lived and worked in church settings where she had been involved in helping people with a wide range of social problems. An educated woman now in her sixties, she had lived through the second wave of radical feminism in the 1960s and 1970s, the influence of which had made its way, to some extent, into the Church. In her relationship with Dennis, she also tended to hold sway, being the more pragmatic, stable and forceful partner.

Nevertheless, as Margaret talked, the counsellor considered that she retained elements of a Christian belief system which subscribes to the following formative ideas: the husband is the spiritual head of the home, due a special respect independent of behaviour, and marriage is for life. Firstly, it was important for the counsellor to non-judgementally acknowledge Margaret's value base and not succumb to subtly privileging her own way of seeing the world over Margaret's. Secondly, it was crucial to bear in mind that this was not just a relationship crisis for Margaret, it was also a spiritual one, touching on Margaret's evolving understanding of her relationship to the divine.

As noted above, it was clear that for Margaret and Dennis there were no child protection issues. Their daughter was an adult. They had no grandchildren. Dennis no longer worked with children in a church context. With this in mind, the counsellor began the following interchange.

Counsellor: Margaret, if this counselling goes well and is of benefit to you, what will it achieve?
Margaret: That's difficult. Give me time to get things off my chest, time to think, maybe.
Counsellor: Anything else?
Margaret: (Eyes filling up) I'm sorry. It's silly - I can't think. I'm the one who's usually sorting out other people's problems.

The counsellor sensed that there was a body of emotion building up, like water behind a dam, waiting to be released. It was important to create a therapeutic space for this and, for the moment, to steer clear of the rational. Counsellor and client were sitting opposite one another. The counsellor left a period of silence, broken only by the hum of traffic outside. When the counsellor did speak, her words broke the tension and also the dam.

Counsellor: You must have felt very alone recently.

The counsellor was taken aback by the power of the emotional shock wave as a guttural sob came from Margaret, followed by a stream of tears.

Margaret: I've been so alone - for the first time in my life. I feel cut off from everyone - Dennis, Deborah, people in the Church, even God. It's the shame - the shame … I haven't been able to share it with anybody.

Counsellor: (The counsellor left space to honour the moment.) Take your time. You're safe here. Let's make friends with these very powerful feelings and learn what they have to say to you. What other feelings have you been keeping inside?

Margaret: It's the anger - I haven't been able to express it, not till recently. I was so frightened that he would do something to himself, or he would go to prison. I know he would never have survived it. I've done a lot of prison work. I know what it can be like inside.

Often partners and relatives of people who have sexually offended feel very conflicted. Like Margaret, they feel betrayed, humiliated, and that their whole world has been thrown into chaos. They are usually very angry with their partners for causing this hand grenade to go off in their lives. However, they often feel they cannot express this anger to their loved one, at least in the early part of the crisis, when sexual offending is first disclosed. At this early stage, the person who has offended is more likely than not very frightened about the possibility of going to prison and the social stigma of the offence, and is full of shame. The risk of self-harm or suicide is heightened at this point. Partners and relatives sense this and are wracked with fear and concern for the person. Hence, they feel unable to express anger, for fear of pushing the person who has offended over the edge. Counselling can offer the loved one a safe place to vent such anger.

Around ten minutes of the session had elapsed, in which Margaret alternated between crying and letting out an inchoate flow of negative feelings and thoughts. During this time the counsellor remained quiet, though the silence was not passive, but active. The key active element was not so much external empathic signifiers such as nods and 'ah has', but the healing quality communicated by the counsellor being fully present, and able to engage at a deep level with the stream of emotional material presented by the client.

Once the catharsis was complete, a peace descended upon the room. Margaret looked less burdened –younger even, it seemed to the counsellor. Margaret smiled.

> *Margaret*: I've never done that in front of anybody before. It felt good.
> *Counsellor*: It felt good to me, too. Sometimes when we let feelings and thoughts out that we have kept in for a long time, they can give us clues about the next step for us, or what seems right to do. Some people view this as the voice of God. Reflecting now on all the things you said earlier, can I ask you the same question that I asked a bit earlier. What do you want to gain from this counselling?

When talking about taking 'the next step', the counsellor allowed for the intuitive nudges we experience in life to be framed in terms of God speaking. The counsellor had no personal faith but was able to bracket her own views and to construct experience within the faith framework of another. This was mature functioning, given that the counsellor had experienced so much hurt within the church setting.

Haidt (2013) writes about how difficult such open mindedness is for all of us, including counsellors. Haidt contends that the political and spiritual beliefs and values we hold – even our consumer choices - form our cultural and tribal identity. We are evolutionarily disposed to stay loyal to and defend our tribe. For most of human history our very lives depended on it, as one tribe fought against another to obtain and secure resources. In modern society tribal conflict is no longer usually a feature, at least in developed countries, but the hardwiring persists.

Hence, the religious and non-religious, conservative traditionalists and liberal progressives, Brexiteers and non-Brexiteers, (currently in

2022, willing recipients of Covid vaccines and anti-vaxxers, supporters of the MAGA movement and those who oppose it), find it very difficult to maintain a genuinely rational understanding of the position of the opposing other. A pervasive irrational hostility is felt, expressed through virtue signalling and displays of moral superiority, with views and values becoming weaponized. Empathy is undermined, fuelling an urge to humiliate the other. Counsellors are not immune from 'us and them' instincts, when clients' views oppose our cherished values and beliefs.

Writing about 'Spiral Dynamics' Wilber (2007) describes various stages of human psychological and spiritual development. The further up the developmental ladder, the greater the capacity people have to escape dualistic 'us and them', tribal thinking and to non-judgementally appreciate the perspective of the other whilst, at the same time, holding on to their own value base and belief system. The counsellor in the case study was able to achieve this.

With regard to the counselling process, after a fruitful discussion, Margaret came up with the following counselling goals:

- To continue to be able to express and explore my emotions
- To find out if my husband is sexually addicted
- To explore if I will ever be able to trust my husband again

The first of Margaret's goals - *to continue to be able to express and explore my emotions* – would be an integral part of the therapeutic process, no matter what the subject under exploration, as is hopefully demonstrated throughout the case study. How the counsellor assisted Margaret to realize the second and third of her goals, constitutes the subject matter of the remainder of this chapter.

Are sexual offenders addicted?

Before describing how the counsellor dealt with this question, often asked by clients and one of Margaret's stated areas of exploration in therapy, the concept of sexual addiction and its relationship to sexual offending is examined. I write more extensively about the relationship between sex offending and sex addiction in *Counselling male sexual offenders: A strengths-focused approach* (2017). However, I will provide a summary here.

Sexual addiction can be defined as a pattern of compulsive sexual behaviour, causing harm to self or others and/or at odds with a person's stable value base. However, the degree of compulsion differs with regard to each individual.

Ward et al. (2004) propose a model of sexual offending involving four different pathways. The pathways describe processes of sexual offending, indicating that offenders can be at different motivational stages, and that not all offenders struggle with compulsive desires to act out at regular opportunities. According to the seminal model of sexual offending, proposed by Finkelhor (1984), there are four stages involved in a sexual offence: 1. *Motivation* (attraction to the victim or illegal sexual behaviour). 2. *Overcoming internal inhibitions* (using distorted thinking to bypass conscience). 3. *Overcoming external inhibitions* (getting the victim on their own). 4. *Overcoming the victim's resistance* (grooming the victim to give in and not tell). In the case of internet offenders, such as Dennis, the last two stages have been completed by somebody else i.e. creating the opportunity to take abusive photographs or videos and persuading or forcing the child to take part in the proceedings. Finkelhor suggests that all four stages must be completed for a sexual offence to occur. This cyclic process may happen frequently for some high-risk offenders who can reasonably be termed addicted to sexual offending. This cycle, however, can also be on a very slow burn for some individuals, perhaps taking years to activate. For other sex offenders, including some internet sex offenders, this cycle may be activated only once or over a limited period of time, with the consequences and remorse about committing a criminal act deterring future offending. It is difficult to conceive the latter two categories of offenders as being addicted to sexual offending.

From a social constructionist viewpoint (Milner and O'Byrne, 2002), concepts such as sexual addiction or sexual compulsivity can be viewed as arbitrary terms, created through the play of language by a

powerful constituency – in this case professionals who have ideological and commercial investment in the adoption of the terms. From the
social constructionist perspective, all non-negotiable categories used
by powerful experts and presented as non-negotiable truth claims can
be oppressive.

I like therapeutic models, have always found them useful in my
own development, and frequently utilize such models with clients.
However, I would consider them to be more or less useful guides to
human functioning, although always falling short of capturing the
fascinating complexity of any one individual. All persons evade
simplistic categorization. Hence, I try not to become too attached to
any one model or idea, attempting to notice when it is becoming
unhelpful and part of my ego identity.

Although I would basically adopt the social constructionist position
with regard to sexual addiction, I would summarize to a client what
being sexually addicted is like, according to relevant texts (Carnes,
2001; Steffens and Means, 2009). I might also suggest that clients take
a test (Hall, 2013: 28-9) to decide for themselves if they or a partner
fall into the category of being sexually addicted. As a strengths-
focused therapist, I want to do my best not to let my own therapeutic
biases overly influence my clients (ultimately an impossible task) and
would view part of the therapeutic journey as providing them with as
many ideas and courses of action as possible, hopefully enabling them
to make informed choices about their lives.

In practice, I find clients react differently to diagnoses, labels,
profiles, personality typing models, theories and categories of various
types. In the case of sexual addiction, it is no different. For some it
comes as a relief that they can place their own or their partner's
perturbing sexual behaviour into a clinically recognized category.
Others can object to being, from their point of view, pathologized,
finding terms such as sex addict stigmatizing and overly deterministic.
Thus, the term can increase hope, but can also reduce it. What I am
primarily interested in is what categories mean to individual clients,
and whether or not they help or hinder goal attainment. The counsellor
in this case study adopted a similar stance with Margaret.

Counsellor: Margaret, you said that one of the things you wanted out of counselling is to decide if Dennis is sexually addicted?

Margaret: Yes, well if he was, that might explain things. If it's a sort of disease, then maybe he couldn't help himself.

The counsellor at this point felt conflicted. She valued the idea that generally we are all responsible for our own behaviour. Margaret appeared to be suggesting the contrary, with regard to her husband's sexual behaviour, and using the term 'sexual addiction' to justify this view. However, was there anything wrong with this, if this construction of the past could enable Margaret and Dennis to salvage their relationship, and if this is what they both wanted? The counsellor decided to put her uncomfortable feeling on hold, and to show curiosity about how the term sexual addiction might be useful to Margaret.

Counsellor: OK, let's say that Dennis is – was - sexually addicted, what difference would this make?

Margaret: I think that I could find it easier to forgive him.

It was the counsellor's view that Dennis's behaviour did not conform to most descriptions of sexual addiction, as it simply was not compulsive enough over a period of time. However, his sexual behaviour was clearly problematic. The counsellor decided to provide Margaret with information regarding where she could find out more about sexual addiction, and different views on it. Below are some of the main contested views:

- Research suggests sexual addiction has a genetic component, as some individuals are more prone to becoming addicted to a range of things, including sex (Volkow and Li, 2015), lending validity to the concept of sexual addiction as a disease
- There is growing evidence, since the development of brain scanning technologies, that addiction can alter the

neurochemical balance of the brain (Barrett, 2010), again giving credence to the disease model

- The development of the disease model of addiction can be charted through the influence of the Alcoholics Anonymous (AA) 12-step model, with doctors and other practitioners promoting the belief that addiction is a largely degenerative disease over which the individual has no ultimate control, needing the treatment of the group. Sex Addicts Anonymous (SAA) promotes a similar view (Thompson, 2012)
- Thompson (2012) argues the SAA (Sexual Addicts Anonymous) approach can pathologize the individual, and does not account for people who succeed in managing addictions through their own efforts
- The disease model of addiction has also been criticized on moral and religious grounds for discouraging personal responsibility and self-control (Cherlin, 2009)
- Feminists have concerns that the notion of sexual addiction is a repressive social construction, medicalizing and hence excusing male misuse of power and sexual exploitation on one hand and, on the other hand, limiting free sexual expression (Irvine, 1995)

The counsellor did not expect that Margaret would go away and research all the controversies of sexual addiction, but she wanted to provide Margaret with the opportunity of discovering that sexual addiction has its proponents and detractors. Margaret came to the next session, having read around the subject. She and Dennis had also been talking about sexual addiction.

Margaret: Well, people say different things.
Counsellor: Yep, have you and Dennis discussed sexual addiction?
Margaret: Well, he accepts that he may have been sexually addicted. But he says that he has repented and been forgiven.

He has prayed for healing and we both believe that now he has been healed from his addiction.

Again, the counsellor felt inner resistance, as her personal value base was challenged. She had worked with individuals previously who said they had been forgiven by God, and now they just wanted to put everything behind them and move forward. Often the counsellor had suspected that this was a way of avoiding exploring the triggers which caused the problematic sexual behaviour. Despite her qualms, the counsellor was committed to the idea that therapy is far more effective when the practitioner can be flexible enough to work in the motivational and perceptual framework of the client. Therefore, she began working with the couple's construction of the problem, applying a strengths-focused approach, using the conceptual language of the client.

Counsellor: OK, let's say that Dennis has been forgiven and healed. Over the next few years, how will you know that this has happened?

Margaret: He wouldn't use the computer.

Counsellor: How would that work out over the long-term? So many things in life are done online these days. Would that be realistic?

Margaret: Well, he sees to all the bills, and writes the church's newsletter.

Counsellor: Yep, so he would have to use the computer. How would it feel for you to check what he's looking at on the computer?

Margaret: Oh, I wouldn't want to do that. That would feel like I didn't have faith in him or in God.

Counsellor: OK, that's part of how you might feel about checking up on Dennis. Any other feelings or thoughts?

Margaret: Well, we're all human, and I guess I would be worried about him doing it again.

Counsellor: Margaret, many clients I work with feel the same as you about checking up on their partner all the time. One solution - this might not work for you guys but it has worked for some clients I have counselled - is that the wayward partner proactively makes himself accountable. This would involve Dennis taking the initiative and every so often, maybe every month, bringing the online devices to you, and saying something like, 'I would appreciate you looking through my online history and checking there is nothing untoward there.'

Margaret liked this idea. She discussed the matter with Dennis and he was keen, too, saying that it was a way for him to demonstrate that he was serious about sanctification. From a Christian perspective, sanctification refers to the process of becoming holy, which can be seen as a sort of rehabilitative journey by which the person leaves destructive habits behind. This way of framing the problem and the solution seemed to work for Margaret and Dennis.

Trust issues

Margaret's third goal - *to explore if I will ever be able to trust my husband again* - is another common theme and dilemma many partners bring to therapy. However, what does the concept of trust actually mean? Below are a number of possible meanings counsellors may want to explore with clients:

- Trust the partner not to commit another contact sexual offence
- Trust the partner not to use online pornography
- Trust the partner not to have any (legal) sexual contact on or offline with another person
- Trust the person not to flirt with others
- Trust the partner not to fantasize about anybody/anything else
- Trust the partner not to masturbate about anybody/anything else

- Trust the partner not to lie
- Trust the partner not to be evasive or deceptive
- Trust the partner not to make autonomous decisions
- Trust the partner not to revert to habits and characteristics which have threatened the relationship in the past (e.g. substance misuse; debt; working away from home; emotional or physical abuse; lack of commitment to family time; lack of emotional and sexual intimacy etc.)

The above list is not exhaustive and each client will probably have their own unique trust issues, weighting each one differently with regard to importance. What complicates matters is that there is often a significant gap between rhetoric and psychological reality, with regard to what partners say they are prepared to put up with and what they are, in fact, prepared to put up with. Many clients, despite their protestations, would be prepared to live in a state of distrust because they are not yet ready to lose the hope that, one day, in an ill-defined future and undifferentiated way, they will be able to trust their partner. This position, whether within or outside the conscious awareness of the client should, in my opinion, be respected as a psychological survival mechanism that allows the client to cope with a painful reality - the best a person can manage at the time.

However, one drawback with this survival tactic is that the client's trust can be unrealistically transferred to the therapist, in the absence of being able to trust a partner. The hope can be that somehow the therapist can produce a magical diagnosis or cure, which will lead to the client's partner being transformed into the sort of person the client wants to be with i.e. a person they can trust. This is magical thinking and the therapist is not a magician. The real magic occurs when the therapist helps the client to identify their own untapped resources, which can enable them to solve problems.

Another challenge is that often the word 'trust' is used as if everybody knows and agrees what the word means. In reality, trust is a slippery concept, value-laden, and meaning different things to different people. From a philosophical and developmental perspective, placing too much trust in anybody would seem ill advised. People we love die or they leave us. They have their own weaknesses and foibles. They are bound to let us down sometimes. Hence, being appropriately non-attached (not putting too much trust in anything or anybody) can be seen as a sign of psychological and spiritual maturity, an adaptive response to the inevitable transience of life and relationships. From this perspective, trust in human beings or one significant human being is better replaced by trust in a benign God, or a benign Universe or the present moment, a largely benign unfolding 'Now' (Tolle, 1999).

However, the inability to trust people in general, a significant other specifically, or to trust oneself, can be seen as pathological. There is a wealth of research on attachment disorders (Bartholomew and Horowitz, 1991; Brennan et al., 1998; Salter Ainsworth et al., 1978), denoting how individuals with *avoidant/dismissive, ambivalent/preoc-cupied,* or *disorganized/chaotic* attachment styles can find it difficult to trust others. It is posited that those with a *secure* attachment style find it fairly straightforward to trust others, but also possess the security within themselves to separate from others and live independently when trust in a significant other proves misplaced over time. Whatever the theorized attachment history and attachment style of the client, the therapeutic task from a strengths-focused angle is to assist clients to maximize their potential for satisfying and mutually rewarding relating between self and others.

As is hopefully evident from the above discussion, trust is a complex concept, often a vague, unexamined idea, not grounded in everyday reality. One of the functions of counselling partners of sex offenders is to help clients define what trust in a partner actually means for them - and what the client is prepared and not prepared to put up with. Below, the counsellor continues her work with Margaret, exploring her goal: *to explore if I will ever be able to trust my husband again.*

Counsellor: Margaret, if sometime in the future you reach a
stage when you can trust Dennis again, what would this be
like?

Margaret: What do you mean?

Counsellor: Well, how would Dennis be behaving that would make you trust him?

Margaret: He wouldn't ever have sinful thoughts about women or young girls.

Counsellor: Anything else?

Margaret: He wouldn't look at pornography.

Counsellor: Anything else?

Margaret: He wouldn't, you know, play with himself.

Counsellor: Masturbate, you mean?

Margaret: (Embarrassed) Yes.

The counsellor considered that it was best not to use euphemisms, such as 'play with himself'. She suspected that to use straightforward terms for sexual behaviour might cause Margaret some discomfort. However, it was part of the counsellor's value base that counselling is not always an easy ride; human growth involves a degree of challenge, and it was important to develop a way of speaking about sex with Margaret that provided a clarity of discourse in which sexual themes could be constructively explored. After a while, Margaret lost her embarrassment around talking about sex in straightforward terms, which seemed to be a positive development, enabling Margaret to negotiate acceptable and non-acceptable boundaries more assertively with her husband.

With regard to Margaret's expectations concerning her husband's sexual behaviour, the counsellor was challenged. On one hand, she considered it unrealistic to think that Dennis would never view other females, including young females, sexually for the rest of his life, particularly as Dennis had been looking at pornography for so many years. On the other hand, she kept in mind that it was important to respect Margaret's expectations and view of such matters, and her right to say what she wanted. The counsellor decided to encourage Margaret to reflect further on her beliefs and values around legal pornography, sexual fantasy and masturbation.

Counsellor: Margaret, the couples I work with hold different positions about legal pornography, sexual fantasies and masturbation. The vast majority of people would probably see it as wrong to have sexual fantasies about behaviour that involves the abuse of others. However, some couples happily accept that their partner will have sexual thoughts about other people as long as it doesn't involve abuse, that they will even look at legal pornography, and will masturbate about other people. For some couples, sharing sexual fantasies about others is part of the erotic pleasure of their sex lives together. For other couples, one partner may not like the thought of this sort of thing but consider that it's not that big a deal. The partner who is not really into this behaviour merely accepts that their partner might watch pornography or masturbate about other people in private, but doesn't want to know too much about it. For other couples, the thought that a partner might secretly view pornography, find other people sexually attractive and have sexual fantasies about another person, accompanied by masturbation, is a deal breaker, and is considered totally unacceptable.
Margaret: Well, I would take up the last position. The Bible says that even to look sexually at another woman is being unfaithful.

In this case, the counsellor had a pretty good idea that Margaret would adopt the above position. However, she still thought that it was worth encouraging Margaret to consider that her personal view of pornography, sexual fantasy and masturbation is just one view amongst others. Whilst not minimizing Dennis's sexual behaviour and the hurt it had caused Margaret, encouraging Margaret to entertain the thought that her husband's behaviour is not untypical for many men may facilitate Margaret to have a larger perspective on matters, leading to a more rational response, less distress, and the opening up of new potentialities.

Clients may respond to such relativizing of sexual behaviour in two different ways. Some may gain comfort, finding the thought that couples take up different positions regarding fantasy and masturbation as a de-stigmatizing and freeing idea. Others, who are looking for a counsellor to take their side and state that pornography, sexual fantasy and masturbation about people other than one's partner is wrong, may be disappointed by and even angry with the counsellor, for not straight-forwardly supporting this stance.

Some forms of sexual addiction treatment suggest going 'cold turkey', a cessation of pornography use and masturbation in order to break the compulsion, and to re-wire the sexual hard drive (Carnes, 1991:248). Some clients I have counselled tell me this has worked for them. Other clients claim a gradual cessation has been more effective. I explore these issues in the chapter on fantasy management in my previous book (Smith, 2017).

However, when the sexual behaviour is not illegal, and does not constitute a trigger to illegal sexual behaviour, it is important, in my opinion, for the therapist to remain morally neutral, and not to foist any personal value bias on the client (i.e. pornography objectifies human beings, or pornography is a legitimate part of free sexual expression). The tack I take is to encourage clients to reflect on the following issues: the pros and cons of legal pornography and of continuing with their sexual fantasies, whether the values of each partner pertaining to sex are compatible or incompatible, and whether or not compromises are possible. The key question, for me, is what are the unique solutions for each couple? The counsellor adopted this approach with Margaret.

> *Counsellor:* Margaret, you said clearly what your bottom line is. You will not accept Dennis looking at pornography, mastur-bating or having sexual thoughts about other women. Let's take each of these one by one, and perhaps we can add viewing child abuse material.
> *Margaret:* Well that last one would be definitely out, but go on.
> *Counsellor:* OK, got that, but tell me, how would you react if you found out that Dennis had been viewing illegal material on the internet?
> *Margaret:* I would tell him to leave. I would not divorce him,

but it would be the end of the relationship and us living
together.

Counsellor:… And if he had been viewing pornography?

Margaret: The same.

Counsellor: How would this be? Where would he go?

Margaret: I don't know. He would not have anywhere to go, I
suppose.

Counsellor: Can I check with you; would you be angry
with him?

Margaret: Very.

Counsellor: Would you see him out in the street, homeless?

Margaret: Probably not. I would be worried about him.

Counsellor: Then what would you do?

Margaret: (After thinking for a while). I would arrange for him
to stay with my sister. She's a widow and a lovely Christian
woman. I wouldn't want him to stay with my daughter, as I
wouldn't want to burden her. But I know he could stay with my
sister until we sold the house. Hopefully, there would be
enough money from the sale for me and him to each buy a little
flat somewhere. He would have to find himself another church,
though. I wouldn't be prepared to give up all my friends at our
current place of worship, if he chose to do that again. After all
he has put us through, it would be up to him to find a new
Christian home.

Counsellor: Margaret, I am impressed with the rigour with
which you have thought this through.

What is the counsellor trying to achieve, here? Well, first of all, she
is trying to earth Margaret's future plans in potential reality. This might
both empower Margaret to put her plans into action and allow her to
reflect at greater depth on the new challenges her future choices could
bring about. In this case, the client was adamant about the course of
action.

Margaret: No, I know it would be difficult to separate after all these years, but if he ever did anything illegal again or looked at pornography - knowing the hurt it has caused me - then that would be it.

Counsellor: I respect your clarity.

At this point, the counsellor spent some time listening to how Margaret had been deeply hurt by Dennis's behaviour. To skip over Margaret's pain and immediately focus on strengths and solutions would have run the risk of seeming dismissive of the suffering Margaret had experienced. Moreover, human beings are fundamentally relational. It is possible that Margaret would never express the depth of her suffering to anyone else apart from the counsellor and, in my experience, it seems to help people to move on if time is allowed for their trials to be witnessed and honoured by the therapist.

In addition, helping Margaret to unpack her suffering might illuminate issues with which she may need help to come to terms. Frequently, partners and other relatives of sex offenders report that they need to reconfigure their view of themselves, their partner and the world in general, in the light of a loved one having committed a sexual offence. Partners of sex offenders frequently struggle with the following questions:

- Why did he do it?
- Is he sexually addicted?
- Can he be cured?
- Why didn't I know what he was doing?
- I used to think I knew him, but I was naive
- What is it about me that I chose a partner like that?
- What will I tell the children, family, friends, work colleagues, others?
- What will others think?
- What will people think if I leave him, or stay with him?
- What was he thinking about when we were having sex?
- Is it my fault that he did it?

- I used to think I was a good parent, but how could I be if I didn't notice what he was doing?
- How will we cope financially?
- How can I still respect him, if I am always on the lookout for signs that he might re-offend?
- How do I make sense of myself and the world now?

The above list is not exhaustive, and each client will have their own unique set of questions which are important to them. Many of the issues which underlie these questions will be examined in full in the forthcoming chapters. As noted above, for Margaret, the pertinent presenting issues related to whether Dennis was sexually addicted and whether she could trust him again.

With regard to trust, what seemed clearly to be the case was that Margaret would not be able to trust Dennis again if he committed a sexual offence or viewed pornography and, if he did this, she would separate from him. These lines in the sand established, the counsellor proceeded to explore with Margaret the issues of Dennis finding other females sexually attractive and lapsing into masturbation.

> *Counsellor:* OK Margaret, I get that your bottom line is that you could not live with Dennis if he ever looked at child abuse images or legal pornography again. Have you communicated this clearly to Dennis?
> *Margaret:* Yes I have, in no uncertain terms.

In this case, the client appears to have communicated her position about what her bottom line is. Sometimes a client may have decided upon a bottom line, but not communicated this to a partner. Ideally, it is best if the client can do this, as it can provide a partner with the motivation or deterrent to curb destructive behaviour, or at least to make an informed choice about future sexual behaviour, knowing the possible consequences.

However, a client who is intimidated by a partner may be afraid to be open about a bottom line. When a client is in an abusive relationship, the counsellor needs to be careful not to encourage the client to say something that may put them at risk. In such cases, the counsellor may need to explore with the client possible consequences of words and actions. It may be appropriate for the counsellor to plan with the client the safest way of exiting an abusive relationship. Victims of domestic abuse are most at risk of harm when wanting to end a relationship, as this can be the point when the abusing partner starts to lose control, control being a feature of domestic abuse.

Happily, there were no such abusive dynamics in Margaret's relationship with Dennis, and Margaret felt free to state her position unequivocally. Hence, the counsellor proceeded to explore with Margaret how she would react to Dennis behaving in sexual ways of which she disapproved.

Counsellor: Margaret, if Dennis happened to find another woman sexually attractive in the future, or sexually fantasized or masturbated about another woman, what do you think your reaction might be?
Margaret: I'd be very hurt. I'm not sure if I could go on.
Counsellor: So, does that mean we should extend your bottom line? If Dennis found any other woman or teenage girl sexually attractive, you would leave him?

The counsellor, here, is trying to encourage Margaret to reflect on the realism of her position.

Margaret: I don't know.
Counsellor: That's fine, not knowing. Can I put a question to you?
Margaret: Go ahead.
Counsellor: Can we help it if we find other people attractive? I don't know, perhaps it's a sort of instinctive thing?
Margaret: Well, we can all appreciate people's beauty but not, you know, focus on it lustfully and, as you call it, masturbate.

The counsellor noticed some internal annoyance with Margaret about her use of the phrase, 'as you call it' and the tone Margaret used in relation to masturbation. The counsellor experienced the throwaway comment as passive-aggressive, and suspected that Margaret was irritated by the focus on what was, for her, an uncomfortable and unpleasant subject - sexual fantasy and masturbation. The counsellor considered whether, in the name of congruence, to comment that she suspected that Margaret was angry with her. However, the counsellor desisted. She knew that Margaret would find such a challenge exposing. The counsellor was also sufficiently self-aware to know that she had experienced Margaret's comment as petty and prudish and that the motive behind calling out the comment would not be to facilitate the growth of the client, but to exact revenge. The counsellor allowed a brief period of silence, during which she took a few conscious breaths: accessing self-compassion on the in breath and silently transmitting compassion to Margaret on the out breath. Once composed and feeling free of judgement, she continued exploring with Margaret.

Counsellor: OK, if Dennis did find a woman attractive and had sexual fantasies about her, would you want him to tell you about it?

Margaret: No!

Counsellor: Would you want him to keep it to himself?

Margaret: No - take it to God.

Counsellor: (Smiling good-naturedly at Margaret) Let them sort it out between them.

Margaret: (Smiling back) Something like that.

Counsellor: How about masturbation?

Margaret: Tell a male Christian friend. I know that some men in the church hold themselves accountable to each other in that way.

Margaret and Dennis subsequently agreed that he would confess any sexual fantasies about women or teenage girls to God. Dennis also agreed with a member of the church leadership team that he would make himself accountable to him, if he lapsed into masturbation. The church leader said that he would do the same with Dennis.

During the last session, Margaret told the counsellor that she thought the counselling had been part of God's provision for her, through this difficult time. She said she had learnt that nothing is certain in life. Margaret stated that she understood now, at a deeper level, that although God wouldn't always protect her from trouble, He would provide ways for her to grow through any trial. She stated that she would rather trust in this than place complete trust in any one person, including her husband.

Conclusion

Through counselling, Margaret had been able to express the deep feelings of hurt and anger, concerning her husband's secret sexual behaviour. She had been helped to replace rather unconsidered notions about her husband's sexual behaviour and inner mental life, with a clear bottom line of what she would and would not be prepared to put up with and was able to clarify to herself and with her husband, the consequences if he crossed these lines in the sand. The client had been helped to find her own solutions to the potential problem of Dennis sexually fantasizing and masturbating about other women, in the future. The counsellor had facilitated Margaret to come to these solutions within her own Christian value system, utilizing the resources of her church community. Margaret had also developed as a person. She had replaced a relatively immature belief that she could trust in God to keep her safe from the sort of pain she had had to face due to Dennis's behaviour, with a more mature faith that, in her terms, God could be trusted to help her find a positive way forward, perhaps through the help of others, no matter what the problem.

Practice points from this chapter

- Collaboratively agree confidentiality guidelines

- Collaboratively develop a therapeutic alliance
- Collaboratively establish initial, evolving goals of counselling
- Partners of sex offenders are likely to have powerful, conflicting feelings including: shame, humiliation; trust; anger and concern for partner's wellbeing
- Allow space for non-rational expression of feeling
- Don't confront or challenge a client if you feel annoyed or angry with them
- Develop the ability to speak about sex in a straightforward, open way
- Allow space for non-rational expression of feeling
- Many sexual offenders are not sexually addicted
- Work within the perceptual and value framework of the client
- Explore client's values about sex, pornography, masturbation
- Inquire about the client's values around sexual offending
- Explore the pros and cons of any form of sexual expression
- The use of non-negotiable diagnostic categories by professionals can be oppressive
- Provide objective information on different views taken about sexual and offending matters
- Explore what trust means to the client, and different forms of trust
- Compassionately accept that the client may temporarily want you, as a counsellor, to cure their partner and make them trustworthy, but don't collude with such magical thinking
- Help the client to develop a bottom line, or a contract of behaviour with a partner
- Help the client communicate to a partner what the client wants from the relationship
- Attempt to earth the client's plan into their likely, future everyday 'reality'

- Gently encourage the client to reflect that it is impossible to have total trust in anyone, and that there can be no guarantees about a partner's future behaviour. To accept this is to grow as a person, with such development having a transpersonal or existential dimension

References

Barrett, D. (2010) *Supernormal stimuli: How primal urges overran their evolutionary purpose*. London and New York: W. W. Norton and Company, Inc.

Bartholomew, K. and Horowitz, L.M. (1991) 'Attachment styles among young people: A test of a four-category model', *Journal of Personality and Social Psychology,* 61: pp. 226-244.

Brennan, K.A., Clark, C.L. and Shaver, P.R. (1998) 'Self-report measurement of adult attachment: An integrative overview', in J.A. Simpson and W.S. Rholes (eds.) *Attachment theory and close relationships*. New York: Guilford Press, pp. 46-76.

Carnes, P. (1991) *Don't call it love: Recovery from sexual addiction*. New York: Bantam.

Cherlin, A.J. (2009) *The marriage-go-round: The state of marriage and the family in America today*. New York: Alfred Knopf.

Finkelhor, D. (1984) *Child sexual abuse: New theory and research*. New York: The Free Press.

Fowler, J. W. (1981) *Stages of faith: The psychology of human development and the quest for meaning*. New York: Harper and Row.

Haidt, J. (2013) *The righteous mind: Why good people are divided by politics and religion*. London: Penguin Books.

Hall, P. (2013) *Understanding and treating sex and pornography addiction*. London and New York: Routledge.

Huxley, A. (1945) *The perennial philosophy*. New York: Harper Collins.

Irvine, J. M. (1995) 'Reinventing perversion: Sex addiction and cultural anxieties', *Journal of the History of Sexuality*, 5 (3): pp. 429-450.

Milner, J. and O'Byrne, P. (2002) *Assessment in social work,* 2nd edition. Basingstoke: Palgrave Macmillan.

Peck, S. (1987) *The different drum.* New York: Simon and Schuster.

Salter Ainsworth, M.D., Blehar, M.C., Waters, E. and Wall, S. N. (1978) *Patterns of attachment: A psychological study of the strange situation.* Hillsdale NJ: Lawrence Earlbaum Associates.

Smith, A. (2017) *Counselling male sexual offenders: A strengths-focused approach.* London: Routledge.

Smith, A. (2018) 'Sex addiction and sex offenders', in T. Birchard and J. Benfield (eds.) *The Routledge international handbook of sexual addiction.* London and New York: Routledge, pp. 362-372.

Steffens, B. and Means, M. (2009) *Your sexually addicted spouse: How partners can cope and heal.* Far Hills, NJ: New Horizon Press.

Thompson, D. (2012) *The fix.* London: HarperCollins.

Tolle, E. (1999) *The power of now: A guide to spiritual enlightenment.* UK: Hodder and Stoughton.

Volkow, N. and Li, T.K. (2015) 'The neuroscience of addiction', *Nature Neuroscience*, 8: pp. 1429-30.

Ward, T., Bickley, J., Webster, S.D., Fisher, D., Beech, A. and Eldridge, H. (2004) *The self- regulation model of the offence and relapse process. Vol. 1: Assessment.* Victoria, Canada: Pacific Psychological Assessment Corporation.

Wilber, K. (2007) *Integral spirituality: A startling new role for religion in the modern and postmodern world.* Boston and London: Integral Books.

TWO

ANTHONY

Introduction

This chapter, like the previous one, focuses on a situation where there are no immediate child protection risk issues. The client, Anthony, discloses to the counsellor that his partner, Harry, has recently told him in a drunken argument that he received a Police warning a number of years ago. This was for viewing one video of illegal child abuse material. There is an age difference between the couple, and also sadomasochism in the relationship. Power differentials between partners are duly examined, particularly with regard to when sadomasochistic behaviour can become abusive. The male counsellor has a son the same age as Anthony, and transference issues consequently develop with his client, particularly around the issue of realizing personal potential.

Case study: Anthony and Harry
Anthony (31) works as a betting shop assistant. Harry (49) is an antiques and art dealer. They met at a party and have been in a relationship for three years. Six months ago, Harry told

Anthony that a number of years ago he received a Police warning, after viewing a video online of two middle-aged men caning the bare buttocks of a number of South East Asian boys. All the boys were in their late teens, but one or two of them were under 18, the age of consent on the internet. Harry said the caning was 'playful,' and did not cause the boys any serious pain. However, Anthony was shocked by his partner's disclosure. Anthony was also puzzled and hurt, having thought that the sadomasochistic part of their sex life, in which he would play the dominating role, had been something special and a unique gift he had given. Harry had told him that he had never wanted to experiment in this way with anybody else. When Anthony confronted Harry about this discrepancy, Harry became characteristically angry, accusing Anthony of being over-sensitive. He later calmed down and apologized, saying that he had only viewed the video on one occasion, after he had been drinking.

A couple of months after Harry's disclosure, Anthony discovered two online conversations between Harry and other men (six months apart), featuring conversations about fantasized sadomasochistic behaviour. Harry had taken the dominating role in these shared fantasies, in contradistinction to the passive role he played with Anthony. Although these conversations were clearly not criminal, Anthony again felt betrayed. Harry was unrepentant when Anthony challenged him about the conversation, telling Anthony to 'grow up'. He said that there was nothing criminal about his actions, and he did not know the men personally. He added, unapologetically, that he had chosen to act in this way when in a long-term relationship with his previous partner, who was sufficiently mature to think nothing of it. Anthony was shocked, but now thinks that Harry may have a point. Is he just being a prude? However, Anthony is becoming increasingly uncomfortable with Harry's drinking bouts and temper tantrums and is questioning whether he wants to be in a relationship with him, although he still says he loves Harry very much. He is also questioning whether he wants to continue with the sadomasochistic element of his relationship with Harry. The above areas were the main issues Anthony wanted to explore through counselling.

Therapeutic issues discussed in supervision

The counsellor, a heterosexual man, was father to a young man the same age as Anthony. In supervision, he explored the following issues which might impact on his facilitation of the therapeutic process:

- Was he concerned that Anthony was attracted to him?
- If so, why should this cause concern?
- Was any part of him attracted to Anthony?
- Were any such feelings driving him to emotionally distance himself from his client, or to become over-involved?
- Did he feel like a rival to Harry?
- Did he want to rescue Anthony from Harry?
- He had a son a similar age to Anthony. Were his feelings about his son (currently wanting his son to move out of the house and become more independent) getting mixed up with his feelings about Anthony?

From a psychodynamic perspective the above transference, counter-transference and projection issues are, in my view, always buzzing around a therapeutic relationship or perhaps around any relationship, like bees around a honey pot.

The counsellor did not consider that there were any unhelpful sexual dynamics between him and Anthony, but he was aware of other potentially contaminating dynamics. His youngest son (in his mid-twenties) was at a stuck point in his life: coming back to live at home with his parents, lounging on the settee looking at TV for large parts of the day. He seemed to have no direction in life. The counsellor acknowledged to his supervisor that he felt a bit of a failure as a father, but also helpless, disappointed and angry at what he saw as his son's fecklessness.

In supervision, the counsellor understood that his habitual reaction to feeling that people were not making the most of themselves was to first express anger, and then to emotionally detach, punishing the 'under-performer'. The counsellor was in a current battle not to repeat this script with his son. The counsellor had long ago worked out that his overreaction to people 'not coming up to scratch' was fuelled by the way his parents had, in his view, not 'come up to scratch' and how he had been powerless to do anything about it. In his lowest moments, the counsellor considered that his choice of profession was merely due to an unfulfilled desire to alter his parents - to make them the parents he would have ideally wanted.

The counsellor had worked through these issues in his own therapy. He had come to an accommodation that even if becoming a therapist was, in large part, motivated by an unconscious motivation to rescue and improve his parents, the wounded healer aspect of himself had been put to good use over the years. Nevertheless, like all of us, the counsellor knew that he would always have to be alert to when this old script was emotionally running him, making him overreact. He had to be careful to avoid this happening with Anthony.

Counselling clients engaged in sadomasochistic behaviour

A full examination of sadomasochistic behaviour is beyond the scope of this book. However, I will summarize some main points. BDSM stands for bondage, discipline/domination, sadism/submission, masochism. BDSM is actually described as a 'paraphilic disorder' in the DSM (Diagnostic and Statistical Manual, 2013). However, it is sobering to bear in mind that the DSM considered homosexuality a disorder until 1973. BDSM is more acceptingly categorized as an 'alternative sexuality' or 'kink' (Bettinger, 2003). Just as children enjoy role playing make believe, adults can gain pleasure from taking on certain unfamiliar roles while maintaining control (Pitch, 2014). When the body experiences pain it releases endorphins which make us feel good (Truscott, 2005). The thrill of knowing we are going to go through an intense visceral experience, even when it is going to be scary (e.g. watching a horror film, going on a frightening roller-coaster) is considered entertainment (Nichols, 2006). This has been related to BDSM. Hence, BDSM can be a harmless, enjoyable and fulfilling part of a person's sex life, involving an intimate trust of one's sexual partner.

One of the main issues for counsellors dealing with BDSM in the context of counselling can be whether or not BDSM crosses the line into abuse and who decides this. There are no easy answers. Sex, control and pain are emotive issues for most individuals, including counsellors and clients, engendering strong opinions. Those who disapprove and/or who are repulsed by such behaviour can be seen to be adopting an irrational, moralistic stance, perhaps motivated by religious or conservative considerations. Such individuals may be consigning repressed sexual desires, not consistent with their ego ideal, to their shadow. A process of projective identification then occurs, by which those who practice BDSM are judgementally viewed as deviant. When the BDSM is mutually consenting, causing no apparent harm, 'moral dumbfounding' (Haidt, 2001) can occur: a phenomenon whereby we struggle to explain the 'disgust factor' when acts are not obviously harmful.

It can also be conversely argued that the post-war idealizing of 'anything goes sex' can be traced to, among others, the work of Alfred Kinsey. Russell (1986) suggests that the Kinsey reports (1948, 1953), precursors to the sexual liberation movements of the 1960s and 1970s, ignored the misuse of power by males pressurizing women into having forms of sex women did not always desire. The more general point to be made is that vulnerable individuals of either sex can be pressurized into BDSM within exploitative and abusive relationships.

So how can a counsellor tell whether BDSM is abusive in a particular case or not? First of all, a counsellor's value base can make it difficult for them to acknowledge that BDSM may be abusive. This may be particularly the case if the counsellor is ideologically committed to promoting sexual liberation and/or has been repressed in the past, sexually or otherwise, resulting in anti-authority or anti-conventional sensibilities. Equally, it may be difficult for a counsellor who is ideologically or religiously opposed to BDSM to view such activity in a person's life as positive. As ever, the monkey of partiality is on our back, and can only be shrugged off by acknowledging it and exploring how it got there in the first place, through self-reflection and good supervision.

There are certain clues as to whether BDSM is non-abusive or abusive in any given instance. Firstly, BDSM needs to be mutually consensual at every stage of the sexual practice, with code words or signals agreed between the parties, which they can use if either partner wants to stop what is happening. Another area to explore is whether or not the choice to take part in BDSM behaviour seems to have been motivated by historical abuse issues. A further consideration is whether one partner has a history of being caught up in a cycle of abusive rela-tionships. The final area to explore is the overall power dynamic in the relationship between partners. The counsellor working with Anthony explored these issues as below, beginning with an exploration of Anthony's value base, concerning BDSM.

Counsellor: Tell me Anthony, what would you consider to be acceptable and unacceptable sadomasochistic behaviour?
Anthony: Well, it needs to be consenting and a person needs to stop when asked to. If it's not like that, then it's not acceptable.
Counsellor: OK. That seems clear. Has it always been like that between you and Harry?
Anthony: Yes, completely, apart from one occasion.
Counsellor: Can you tell me about the one occasion?
Anthony: It was a couple of months ago. I had won this award - employee of the year at the shop. A group of us went out to celebrate and Harry joined us later at a nightclub. Everyone was quite drunk. There was a guy there who obviously fancied me, and I guess I was a bit flirty back.
Counsellor: How old was the guy?
Anthony: About my age – anyway, Harry got jealous and

stormed out of the club. When I got home, he was in bed. I knew he wasn't asleep. I said I was sorry for behaving like a twat. We started to make love. It was very passionate. In the middle, he turned me around, reached for this big dildo he keeps in a drawer by his bed and tried to put it up my arse. He likes that particular dildo up him, but he knows I won't have it up me because it's too big. I was so drunk, I made a half-hearted attempt – something like, 'stop it, you know I don't like that one', but he put it a quarter way up anyway. I yelled and called him a 'cunt' and went off to sleep on the settee. We've never talked about it since.

Counsellor: Why do you think you've never talked about it?

Anthony: We both probably felt bad. Me for flirting, and him for doing something he knew I didn't like.

The counsellor kept this incident in mind, making a mental note to revisit it after he had explored two other areas with Anthony: power dynamics in relationships, and Anthony's own relationship history.

Power in relationships

Relationships are often conceived of in idealistic terms. Whilst not wanting to undermine the romantic element of a relationship between partners, relationships that endure and which are mutually satisfying tend to be ones where there is rough equality in terms of how power is shared.

Power is neutral. It can be used constructively or destructively. When counselling partners, I am always interested in power. Often people have not considered the different forms of power we bring to relationships. I am keen to raise clients' awareness of this matter. However, when I ask clients to think of different forms of relational power, the question often draws a blank, or at least a limited response. I then make a psychoeducational intervention, suggesting different types of power that partners can bring to a relationship. The list below is not exhaustive:

- Physical strength
- Force of personality
- Financial resources
- Control of the money
- Age
- Maturity
- Experience
- Education
- Intelligence
- Confidence
- Attractiveness
- Ability to drive
- Psychological maturity
- Support of family
- Support of friends
- Access to community resources

I then ask the client to draw a line down the middle of a piece of paper, making two columns. The client puts his name on top of one column, and his partner's name on top of the other column. The client then puts all the power he has under his name, and all the power his partner has under the partner's name. The power they both have or share is put down in the middle of the page. When the counsellor asked Anthony to do this task, he came up with the following:

Anthony's Power
Physical attractiveness
Family support

Shared Power
Friends

Harry's Power
Maturity
Physical strength

Force of personality
Financial resources
Life experience
Ability to drive
Education
Confidence

The relationship between Anthony and Harry did not seem equal.

Counsellor: What do you make of that, Anthony?
Anthony: Well, yeah (laughs ironically); it seems pretty one sided. He does seem like my father sometimes, always telling me I'm lazy and I could do a lot better for myself.
Counsellor: How does it feel, taking a bit of a step back, and looking at the relationship objectively?
Anthony: Well, is that bad, the power difference thing?

The counsellor was in a bit of a quandary as to how to respond. He was definitely beginning to formulate a hypothesis that Anthony's and Harry's relationship had an abusive element to it, and the power difference might be an aspect of this. However, he also knew that relationships between sexual partners aren't always equal. Sometimes one or both partners are at a stage of life where valuable experience and learning can occur when one partner has more power and maturity. The clue here is the word 'maturity'. In healthy relationships, where there is an imbalance of power, the person with the power tends to use that power benignly.

When I'm assessing whether a relationship is abusive, I try to gain some idea of what power a partner had when they first entered into the relationship. If the relationship is unhealthy and abusive, often the client will have been gradually stripped of power, in terms of resources and agency. They may have become less confident, more anxious and depressed, stopped working, tend to go out less, have fewer family members and friends in their life, be generally less happy. The opposite is likely to be the case if the relationship is healthy and non-abusive.

From a strengths-focused perspective it is the client, not the thera-pist, who is the expert on their own life. Hence, the counsellor did not want to fall into the trap of giving out advice, but rather to facilitate Anthony to make more reflective and informed decisions about his relationship with Harry. Also, the counsellor was significantly older than Anthony. If he did start pontificating paternalistically about whether the power imbalance in Anthony's relationship was 'bad', this would mirror the 'older man/younger man' dynamic between Anthony and Harry, repeating the same script inside the therapy room that might be occurring outside of the therapy room.

The counsellor reflected on the prescient view of existentialist psychotherapist, Irvin Yalom (1980), who remarked that a 'poor' life in psychological terms is one in which the same relational stuff happens again and again (i.e. problematic scripts repeated). On the other hand, a 'good' life is one in which variation and change are embraced, resulting in growth. Hence, the counsellor considered it was an impor-tant part of the therapeutic process not to repeat the wiser older man act and provide Anthony with a different experience of what relating to an older guy could be like. Thus, in response to Anthony's invitation to say if the power difference in his relationship with Harry was 'bad', the counsellor replied as follows:

Counsellor: Search me if it's bad or not – what do you think?
Anthony: (Looking hurt) I dunno.

In the here-and-now of the therapeutic moment, the counsellor reflected on the tone of his response to Anthony's question about whether or not the power differential in his relationship with Harry was bad – 'search me if it's bad or not'. It was important for Anthony to come to his own conclusions, but the counsellor concluded that his response did have a tinge of punitive over-detachment about it: prob-ably a reaction to and a defence against his felt powerlessness to make young men in his life 'grow up' (see section on counsellor's supervi-sion issues, above).

Counsellor: (More conciliatory) Well, let's look at the pros and cons. What are the pluses of Harry having more power than you?

Anthony: Well, I've always been attracted to older men, but he keeps on saying that he knows young people - in the trendy art galleries in London - who have gone to university but they're no brighter than me, and I could do much better for myself than working in a shop. But I like my job, probably more than Harry likes his. Sometimes, he sounds just like my fucking Dad.

Counsellor: (Gentle and engaged). Can you tell me more about your relationship with Harry; maybe the good things?

Anthony: I like living in a nice house and Harry gives me that. He has introduced me to loads of things like food and music and plays and stuff. He took me to New York before Christmas.

Counsellor: Anything else?

Anthony: He's very generous, and at times he can be a good listener – at times that is.

Counsellor: Anything else?

Anthony: Um, I guess he can also be a good laugh, in a bitchy sort of away, slagging people off. He's a good mimic. Some of his impressions of people we know are brutal - hilarious though.

Counsellor: Friends, you mean?

Anthony: Well, that's it. We haven't got any mutual friends really. We tend to have separate friends because of the age difference. Most of his are older, - arty bods. Mine are younger - mostly from the betting shop and around town. He finds them immature and chavvy.

Counsellor: Tell me about the other cons in the relationship, particularly in terms of Harry having more power than you.

Anthony: Well, he makes me feel foolish sometimes. He laughs when I say something stupid and says, 'I can't believe you don't know that'. He's always correcting me about things.

Counsellor: How do you feel when that happens?

Anthony: Stupid, I suppose. But then other times he goes on

about how bright I am. To be honest I don't care about how bright I am. I just want to be me and be happy.
Counsellor: Sounds a good place to be.

At this point the counsellor drifted off a bit, thinking about his son. Did he communicate acceptance and approval to his son, just for being himself, not for what he achieved? Perhaps his client might be reminding him of a valuable truth in connection with his son, about the importance of communicating acceptance and approval of the essential valuableness of his son's being, rather than his son's doing. The counsellor caught himself drifting and refocused his attention back to the client.

Counsellor: That sounds good that you can maintain that positive view of yourself. How do you do that in the light of being put down by your partner? Are you comfortable with me using that phrase, 'put down'?
Anthony: Sure, I guess that's what it is, and it does bother me, but I simply don't care about being brainy. Now, if he put me down about my looks, that would be another thing altogether. I guess I'm vain (laughs). I care about my looks.
Counsellor: And does he put you down about your looks?
Anthony: No, he keeps on telling me how beautiful I am - which I like. He's always saying he doesn't know what I'm doing with a fat old bastard like him. I keep on telling him it doesn't matter and I love him, but he doesn't believe it. In fact, he's still quite handsome really, although he's let his body go a bit. But I guess in this area, I have the power. I'm fairly good looking, and I work out at the Gym five times a week.
Counsellor: And in your sex life, who has the power there?
Anthony: Well, that's the strange thing. With us I have always played the dominating role, and Harry has always played the passive role.
Counsellor: So, it's like the reverse of the power dynamics in the rest of your relationship?

Anthony: Yeah, that's right. But what really got to me was the video with the young boys. They were obviously the submissives, and it was the same in the online stuff with the other men – Harry was taking the dominating role.
Counsellor: Can you explain why this upset you?
Anthony: I don't really know.
Counsellor: Sometimes it helps a client, if I deliberately leave about five minutes of silence for them to think about the problem. Do you want to try that?
Anthony: Yeah, I'll give anything a try.
Counsellor: All right, sit comfortably in what is the best relaxing position for you. Close your eyes or focus on a point in front of you. Sometimes it helps to take deep breaths from your solar plexus, rather than from your chest, feeling your rib cage expand and retract and, as you follow the breath, imagining all of the tension leaving your body. OK, as you get into the flow, keep following the breath and open your mind, becoming receptive to whatever insights emerge. If you just continue doing this, following the breath, I'll tell you when the five minutes are up.

During the five minutes, the counsellor also meditated, wishing good things for the client and envisaging passing on streams of universal love to Anthony and also to Harry.

Counsellor: (In a soft, gentle tone) OK, five minutes are up, Anthony. Just re-orientate yourself to the room and this moment and when you are ready, tell me where you got to?
Anthony: Yeah, I'm always on the go. It's nice to sit and just chill.

In my experience, some clients take to this sort of exercise and some do not. When there appears to be motivation for meditative reflection, I ask the client's permission to explain about mindfulness and meditational practice, providing them with relevant information about helpful resources. Some clients then take up regular mindfulness or meditative practice to help manage problems and improve quality of life.

Counsellor: So, did anything emerge in that time out, Anthony?
Anthony: Well, it felt strange. On one hand I felt really relaxed, but then I felt sort of angry and sad, all at the same time.
Counsellor: Can you say more?
Anthony: It's hard to put into words, really.
Counsellor: Just take your time.

A number of minutes elapsed.

Counsellor: All right, how about if I come up with some words, or suggestions? You can tell me if anything resonates with you - hits the nail on the head - or is really wide of the mark. Or we can just carry on enjoying the silence or talk about something else, if you like.
Anthony: No, I like the first idea. Let's go with that.

Some therapists, especially client-centred ones, would balk at the idea of the counsellor making suggestions, and solution-focused practitioners would generally posit that clients have the means to solve their own problems. I find the notion that all answers, understandings and solutions can be found within the client, limiting. Sometimes a client's awareness can be raised by the counsellor suggesting things. What prevents paternalistic advice giving or the practitioner casting themselves in the expert role is how suggestions are made. If the suggestions are made lightly, in the spirit of mutual exploration, meaning-making can remain a collaborative process.

Counsellor: Did you feel jealous perhaps? Or excluded or betrayed that your partner was sexually acting out with other men without telling you?
Anthony: Jealous definitely, and excluded and betrayed, but

something else as well.

Counsellor: A sense perhaps that Harry didn't trust you, or trust himself maybe, to play the dominant role?

Anthony: Something like that, like he didn't think I was up to it somehow. Yeah, that he needed to treat me with kid gloves. That's it - like he still sees me as a kid.

Counsellor: OK, so let's explore this more. Is it that it feels that you are being excluded from the world of grown-ups? As you say, treated like a child?

Anthony: That's it, I'm mad because he still sees me like a kid, and when he put the big dildo in me, it felt that he was angry about losing control and punishing me like a kid for flirting. It wasn't an adult decision made by the two of us.

Counsellor: From what you say, he put the sex toy inside you without your consent. Do you want to report that to the police?

Anthony: God no! I don't have to, do I?

Counsellor: As nobody seems to be at immediate risk, this is up to you.

Anthony: No, I don't want to.

The counsellor decided to privilege client confidentiality over reporting an alleged sexual offence. Nobody appeared to be at risk, and the client was adamant that he did not want to report what had happened. Moreover, the counsellor and Anthony had co-constructed a narrative around the problem, rather than the counsellor making his own interpretation of events. If the counsellor had fallen into the latter paternalistic trap, Anthony would have likely felt like a 'kid' yet again, with the counselling process having imitated life. Below, it becomes apparent how feeling like an inadequate 'kid' was an early script in Anthony's life.

Anthony's life history and forming an abusive relationship

Anthony was the younger of two brothers. His parents were caring, but strict. His father was a policeman, his mother a nurse. Both were sporty. His mother was a long-distance runner and his father was a football referee. Stuart, Anthony's brother, studied sports science at university. His father also continues to struggle with Anthony defining himself as gay, with his relationship with Harry never talked about in Anthony's family of origin.

Anthony hated sport and, as a child, had some health problems. As a teenager he rebelled against the sport ethic of the family, taking up smoking early and spending his spare time lazing around with friends, listening to music all day. He was also obsessed with reading comics, which he used to get from a friend. He recalled in one counselling session how his father would often say, 'all he does is read those damn comics', and his mother would respond, 'well, at least he's reading, Rob'.

As a teenager Anthony got into fashion, dyeing his hair different colours and changing his image frequently. His one interest at school was drama; he enjoyed acting in school plays. As he got older, he would often abscond from school with friends, although he was never delinquent.

His parents realized that Anthony was not a sporty child and tried to accept this. However, what frustrated them was his lack of 'get-up-and-go', as his father would put it. This tension mounted in Anthony's teenage years, when he opted out of school work altogether, and his parents were called in to see the Head. When Anthony was 15, his relationship with his father more or less broke down, after his father caught him smoking cannabis in the lane outside the house. His mother remained supportive, although disapproving of the drug.

In counselling, Anthony talked about a period when he was around 8 or 9 years old. His parents were in the middle of having their own house built. He and Stuart would go with their father to the building site at weekends, just the three of them, as Anthony's mother worked weekend shifts at the hospital. Anthony came to dread these days. His brother, older and more practical, would be given jobs to do. He would sit on the floor, reading comics. One day, he asked if he could saw a piece of timber. His father reluctantly agreed, demonstrating the proper technique. When Anthony took over, the saw slipped, deeply gashing his finger. The cut was bleeding profusely and Anthony screamed. His father shouted, 'you can't trust that bloody boy with anything'. Later, his father apologized when they sat together in casualty, waiting for the finger to be stitched. However, subsequently, whenever his father and brother went to the house at the weekend, Anthony would be left at home to read his comics, with a neighbour keeping an eye on him, as he was too young to be left alone.

As Anthony related this story, his eyes welled up with tears. The counsellor reached over to hand him a tissue, realizing that this incident had been deeply shaming for Anthony. It seemed emblematic of the family's psychodrama, in which Anthony was cast into the role of the inadequate brother, too weak to be trusted with anything demanding or risky.

Counsellor: Anthony, do you think that there might be any link between this incident and how you felt about yourself generally in your family of origin, and your strong reaction to Harry's interest in taking up the dominant sexual role with the other men he was talking to online?

Anthony: I don't understand.

Counsellor: Well, in both cases, it may have felt that a significant male in your life, your father and Harry, didn't think you were up to scratch. The hard stuff, as it were, is only for other, tougher guys.

Anthony: (Breaks out into sardonic laughter). You mean, I've been fucking my father then?

Counsellor: (Laughs) Not quite, but maybe you have been looking to Harry to provide you with the sort of affirmation that you didn't get from your father. Hasn't Harry fallen short, leaving you feeling betrayed, humiliated and enraged, just like your father? It's just a theory.

The above is not a typical strengths-focused intervention. It has more in common with a psychodynamic therapist inviting a client to consider an interpretation. In my experience, this works sometimes, if the intervention is not too dogmatic, and offered tentatively as one possible explanation amongst others. Providing a client with a take on an experience that they have not considered before can lead to a cognitive shift in the way the client perceives themselves and their situation, leading to constructive change.

In the case of Anthony, his parents were not knowingly abusive or neglectful. Nevertheless, their lack of attunement to, and prizing of, their son's unique individuality seemed to have produced a shame-prone identity, with gaps in self-esteem which Anthony was looking to Harry to fulfil.

DeYoung (2015) relates shame not only to serious abuse and neglect, but to the less dramatic failure of caregivers to recognize children as separate, valuable persons in their own right. Taking a psycho-analytical and neuro-scientific perspective, Schore (2012) posits how 'good enough parenting' inculcates a positive 'ego ideal', hardwiring the message that *I should give myself a bad time if I fall short, but not that bad a time*. The ego ideal, Schore argues, is predominantly located in the right brain hemisphere, made up of pre-rational impulses. Guilt is located in the left hemisphere, dealing with cognitions. The brain is probably more complex than this dualistic notion. That aside, if shame is linked to early developmental problems, such as lack of parental attunement (which seems to have been the case with Anthony), the client might be unable to engage with rational, informed decision making. However, once attachment wounds are tended through the limited re-parenting function of the therapeutic relationship (encouraging brain plasticity growth), then improved left brain functioning in terms of rational consideration as to best options in life can be worked towards, or might follow naturally. In this case, the counsellor managed to provide this limited re-parenting work to Anthony over many months.

Gradually, Anthony became less tolerant of Harry's dismissive and abusive behaviour, having grown out of the need to be affirmed by his older partner. As for sadomasochistic behaviour, Anthony decided that he enjoyed playing about with different power roles in his sex life — after all he liked acting. Towards the end of counselling, Anthony joined an amateur dramatics society and said that he might consider going back to college to gain the qualifications needed for drama college, sometime in the future. Anthony eventually ended the relationship with Harry, after a particularly nasty drunken outburst, explaining to the counsellor that he was fed up with Harry's behaviour and that he wanted to experiment sexually with people his own age for a while, which he thought might well include some S and M, with consenting partners.

The issue that brought Anthony to counselling was discovering that his partner had committed sexual offending behaviour on the internet. However, the more pertinent matter for the client was the unequal power dynamic between him and his partner. The glue that kept the client stuck in this increasingly abusive relationship was wanting something that his partner could not give him – parental affirmation and relief from a shame-prone identity. The limited re-parenting capacity of the therapeutic relationship facilitated the client to rationally reflect that he was trying to repair parenting deficits through this relationship, repeating an unsatisfactory script. It was this dynamic which led to the abusive elements in the relationship, not the sado-masochism *per se*. Emotionally and cognitively freed from the dysfunctional dynamic, the client was freed to pursue relationships with men more on his terms, becoming empowered to make his own informed choices about sex and partners.

Practice points from this chapter

- When considering whether any sexual practice in a
  relationship is abusive, consider the power dynamics
  between partners
- When considering whether any sexual practice is abusive,
  consider the wider context of power and possible abuse
  issues in the client's background
- If making interpretation or suggestions, do so in a
  respectful, collaborative fashion

- The therapeutic relationship at its best and over time can offer a limited re-parenting experience to clients
- Sometimes pre-rational emotional deficits need to be partially healed through the therapeutic relationship, encouraging the growth of new neural pathways, before rational, left brain consideration of best options can kick in.

References

Bettinger, M. (2003) 'Sexuality, boundaries, professional ethics and clinical practice', *Journal of Gay and Lesbian Social Services*, 14(4): pp. 93-104.

DeYoung, P.A. (2015) *Understanding and treating chronic shame: A relational/neurobiological approach.* New York, London: Routledge.

Diagnostic and Statistical Manual of Mental Disorders (5) (2013). American Psychiatric Association.

Haidt, J. (2001) 'The emotional dog and its rational tail: A social intuitionist approach to moral judgement', *Psychological Review*, 108 (4): pp. 814-34.

Nichols, M. (2006) 'Psychotherapeutic issues with 'kinky' clients: Clinical problems, yours and theirs', *Journal of Homosexuality*, 50 (2-3): pp. 301-324.

Pitch, N. (2014) 'Working with and understanding clients with BDSM desires and behaviours: A guide for the inexperienced therapist', In G.Hudson-Allez (ed.) *Sexual diversity and sexual offending: Research, assessment and clinical treatment in psychosexual therapy.* London: Karnac Books Ltd, pp. 65-78.

Russell, D. (1986) *The secret trauma: Incest in the lives of girls and women.* New York: Basic Books.

Schore, A. N. (2012) *The science of the art of psychotherapy.* New York and London: W.W. Norton.

Truscott, C. (2005) 'S/M: Some questions and a few answers', In M. Thompson (ed). *Leatherfolk: Radical sex, people, politics and practice.* Los Angeles, CA: Daedalus, pp. 15-36.

Yalom, I. D. (1980) *Existential psychotherapy.* USA: Basic Books.

THREE
ANNA

Introduction

This chapter, again, focuses on a situation where there are no current child protection issues. However, the case study here involves an historical contact sexual offence, rather than an internet offence. Anna's partner, Greg, conforms to the profile of a person who can reasonably be termed sexually addicted, as his behaviour is damaging, compulsive and seemingly out of his control. The chapter begins, as usual, with the background to the case scenario. Transferential dynamics are highlighted, with Anna reminding the counsellor of his sister, with whom he has always had a strained relationship. The issue of co-dependency is explored, with the counsellor exploring Anna's early experiences of life, which might be influencing how she views her relationship and future with Greg. In addition, a summary of some orthodoxies regarding counselling partners of those deemed sexually addicted is provided, below.

Case Study: Anna and Greg

Anna (39) has been married to Greg (44) for five years. He has a daughter from a previous relationship whom he never sees. His ex-wife stopped any contact with his daughter, after Greg was found guilty of sexually assaulting an underage 15-year-old girl. He met the girl in a pub, when he was working away from home. He gave her a lift home and the next day she accused him of attempting to rape her in the back of his car. The charge was reduced to sexual assault. Greg maintained his innocence but was found guilty and received a 5-year prison sentence.

This is Greg's only offence. However, he has a long history of pornography use. Anna does not mind him using pornography, as long as he is open about it, and they continue to have an enjoyable sex life together. Both are very busy, running two successful florist shops. Greg manages the shops and the business side of things, and Anna is responsible for the floristry, creating the products and training the staff. Their relationship is at breaking point, due to Greg's constant flirting with the female florists. Anna has also found flirty text messages between Greg and one of the florists on his smartphone, which he described as 'innocent fooling around'. In addition, Anna has discovered that on three occasions in the last couple of years he has used sexual chat lines. Each time he has promised that he will stop doing this but has reneged on his promise. A couple of weeks ago, Anna discovered he had been using chat lines for a third time and decided to seek counselling. Greg is now saying that he recognizes that he has a sexual addiction and will do anything to keep the relationship. He says he has joined SAA (Sex Addiction Anonymous) and has gone cold turkey on all pornography use and masturbation.

Therapeutic issues discussed in supervision

'Some people provoke threat in others', the counsellor told his supervisor. 'They don't have to say or do anything particularly threatening, it's usually something about the way they look or how their carry themselves: just who they are, intrinsically, as people. They make other people wary'. His new client, Anna, was such a person, the counsellor said. Morag, his supervisor for many years, raised an arched eyebrow.

The counsellor had a fascination for people like this, although he usually ended up finding fault with them. He put this down to his relationship with Marion, his elder sister, the drama queen of the family. Both siblings are now in their sixties and live in the same town. Marion has progressive multiple sclerosis, no partner and few friends. She is increasingly reliant on her brother and his wife Jenny, a peace-lover like him. The counsellor told his supervisor that he resents his sister's demands, but also feels guilty because she needs him, and it is Jenny who takes up most of the slack.

Anna did not look anything like Marion, but there was the same imperious air about her. He hypothesized that a partner would not find it easy to be concerned about this woman – she took up too much power. The counsellor told his supervisor that he was shocked by his own judgementalism. He was sufficiently aware to understand that it would take more time to understand if he was picking up on an enduring theme in Anna's life, or if he was simply bringing his sister into the therapy room.

Opening interchanges

When Anna arrived at the counselling session, she looked angry.

Anna: I couldn't find anywhere to bloody park. I'm soaked through. Have you got somewhere to hang this up?

Anna's army coat was drenched. It was raining heavily and the branches of the large beech tree, which could be seen out of the window, swayed precariously in the wind. Tall, with close-cropped black hair, Anna cut a dramatic figure. She was attractive in an Amazonian sort of way. The counsellor felt on his guard. He was feeling threat rather than interest and concern - what would she say or do next?

This did not stop him responding in a professional manner, telling Anna in a sympathetic tone to hang her coat up on a hook on the door and offering her a hot coffee. He didn't usually offer clients a drink, apart from the obligatory glass of water, as it takes up valuable time and runs the risk of putting the encounter on a chatty rather than a therapeutic basis. In this case the client was cold and wet. He intuited that Anna needed looking after and deliberately responded with sympathy, perhaps because of his gut reaction to do the contrary.

> *Anna:* As you know from my email, my partner, Greg, says he's sexually addicted. I think he is and it's come as a relief that somebody has called it out at last. But now I'm worried that he's found a peg to hang his problems on – something he can use as an excuse, as usual.
> *Counsellor:* I can understand your concern.
> *Anna:* Oh well, that's all right then.

The counsellor felt that Anna was dismissive of his attempt at empathy, and was putting him down. Rather than just blanking this and moving on, he brought his observation into the room, whilst trying not to sound defensive.

> *Counsellor:* (Leaving a gap) Does that sound a bit pat, saying I understand?
> *Anna:* Just a bit. Well it does sound like something a counsellor is supposed to say. You know, like a waitress saying 'enjoy' when she serves you a meal.

The counsellor felt belittled, irritated for a second.

Counsellor: A waitress, hey?

Anna: (Smiling) Sorry. Oh, don't take any notice of me. I just
don't know what to do. The business is going great, our lives
are completely bound up with each other - and anyway I like
and love the bloke – but my life's a fucking mess. If only he
didn't have this problem.

The counsellor saw the intelligence in her eyes and a warmth and
vulnerability he had not seen before, like the sun breaking through the
mist. He felt himself softening towards her and smiled back.

It can be constructive to lance a wound, to encourage the expression of negative thoughts and feelings, as long as this is not likely to
prove inflammatory. Such honest exchanges can lead to more authentic
relating, improving and deepening the therapeutic relationship. Once
negativity is expressed and given due space, clients (and sometimes
counsellors) can move forward positively.

Counsellor: So, you want to remain in the relationship because
you love Greg, but also because your working lives are bound
up together. Anything else you value in your relationship?

Even when a client comes to counselling because of an unsatisfactory relationship, they have usually invested a good deal of themselves
in their partner and the commitment is part of their identity. Asking
about strengths not only helps serve the purpose of stimulating a client
to weigh up the pros and cons of remaining with or leaving a partner, it
also honours the life led, promoting self-esteem.

Anna: We have a giggle together. He lets me boss him about
(laughs). His parents have invested in the business, not that that
would stop me leaving him. But that's what makes me mad.
He's in danger of throwing all that away.

Counsellor: OK, tell me about the worst part of the relationship, for you.

Anna: Well, it's his sexual addiction, obviously.

Counsellor: Can you say how you've come to view his behaviour as sexual addiction?

The subtext of this last question is to gently challenge the fixed notion that such a thing as sexual addiction exists. If the concept of sexual addiction, or any large concept such as 'trust' - a concept deconstructed in the first chapter - becomes less fixed, this can open up possibilities for negotiating new solutions. As explained elsewhere, as a therapist, I am not chiefly concerned about whether any one narrative related to a problem is necessarily true as most truths, from a social constructionist perspective, are contingent positions constructed through language. What I am focused on is whether or not the client's story of the problem hinders or facilitates the achievement of desired goals.

Anna: Before I came to see you, we went to see a couple counsellor. We only had two sessions. Greg didn't get on with her. She said that Greg was sexually addicted and he was minimizing the problem. Greg thought that the counsellor was on my side so he wouldn't go again.

Greg had seemingly viewed the couples' counsellor as biased against him. Anna's counsellor was alert to the possibility that within his relationship with Anna, notions of counsellor bias had the potential to flow the other way. As noted above, the counsellor was aware of negative transferential dynamics connected to his sister. He needed to find a way of using this transference constructively or at least preventing it from infecting the client relationship. He also harboured critical thoughts about the couple's previous counsellor - probably professional rivalry, in part. He considered the previous counsellor had been hasty with an overly deterministic diagnosis of sexual addiction and was beginning to feel consequential sympathy with Greg.

Whether counselling a couple, or one half of the couple, the other partner is always in the room: both in the client's experience and in the therapist's imagination. Hence, it is important to be even handed. In this case, aware of his potential biases, the counsellor wanted to remain genuinely open minded to Anna's view of the problem and her related motivational framework, in order to find ways forward. Like Margaret in the first chapter, the notion that her partner was sexually addicted appeared to offer her hope.

Counsellor: Tell me about hearing that Greg might be sexually addicted.
Anna: Well, for me, when the counsellor said Greg had sexual addiction something just clicked. I just thought, 'that's it'. The pieces sort of fell into place. Now we've got something to work on.
Counsellor: OK, Anna, so something clicked for you, the pieces sort of fell into place, and now you've got something to work on. Can you say more?
Anna: Well, now we know that he has an addiction, I know he's not just being selfish and mean to me and not caring about our marriage, or our whole life together, sort of thing. He can't help it, well he can, but he can't in another way. At least he can get treatment, now I know what the problem is. At least, that is, if I can get him to see another bloody counsellor.

The counsellor and Anna both laughed at Anna's quip about 'another bloody counsellor'. Humour was clearly a way to both of their hearts. However, behind the moment of light- heartedness, a flock of troubling thoughts was gathering in the counsellor's mind. *Anna felt totally committed to the idea of Greg being sexually addicted. What if Greg did not want to accept this idea? Anna seemed to have a strong paternalistic agenda to sort Greg out. Greg probably resented this. She might want to co-opt him* (her counsellor) *onto her side to sort Greg out and to provide a treatment and cure for Greg. The counsellor considered that the straightforward medical process of assessment, diagnosis, treatment and cure rarely applied to complex relationship problems. How would Anna react if she discovered this for herself?*

The counsellor felt that he might end up disappointing Anna, as Greg had done.

The counsellor did not resist these anxiety-provoking thoughts. He simply breathed deeply, concentrating on his breath, acknowledging his anxiety and reminding himself that, for him, counselling was about the Buddhist notion of 'right action', having faith that there will be an appropriate next step to take or intervention to make. He just needed to trust what felt right, whilst at the same time employing compassionate, critical reflection in the here-and-now of his own practice.

Feeling more at peace now, the counsellor experienced a relaxed sensation throughout his body, which tended to manifest when he was not resisting the situation in front of him or his feelings about it. He found himself able to see with clarity the wonderful interconnectedness of life and relationships. Sure, he feared disappointing his client, just as he feared disappointing his needy sister, whom he didn't happen to actually like very much. Sure, Anna might eventually feel let down by him, just as she felt let down by her partner. He saw all four of them struggling with life. He imagined them all as children in a nursery: imagined himself trying to kick a yellow ball and falling over in the process; his sister crying in the sandpit because a sandcastle she was trying to build had collapsed; Greg trying, without success, to climb over the barrier and escape the nursery; Anna with a plastic hammer, struggling to hammer plastic shapes into sections of a plywood box. All would eventually grow and mature. He brought to mind the intuition of the medieval Christian mystic, echoing down the centuries: 'All shall be well and all shall be well and all manner of things shall be well' (Julian of Norwich, 2015: 74).

> *Counsellor:* So, let's say Greg is sexually addicted. Can you say a bit more about how viewing Greg in this way helps?
> *Anna:* Look, I believe anything can be sorted – just as long as you know what you're dealing with. I'm a fighter, and I intend to fight for this relationship. I know what you and other people are probably thinking – *Just leave him*. But I believe in him, and we've got too much to lose to just throw it all away.

Co-dependency

The counsellor began to entertain the hypothesis that Anna was displaying co-dependent characteristics. The notion of co-dependency has its roots in the AA movement, where loved ones of alcoholics are often viewed as playing the rescuer role, sustaining the addiction by protecting alcoholics from the consequences of their behaviour. The non-addicted partner continues in a toxic relationship because of their own dependency needs. The term co-dependency has been popularized by authors including Beattie (1986), Cermak (1998), Lancer (2014), Norwood (1986) and Woititz (1990). Co-dependency is seen as having roots in childhood. The child may have filled in the caring gaps for absent or incompetent parents. This script is continued into adulthood with dysfunctional partners. The carer looks for someone to care for and the addict is looking for a rescuer - a match definitely not made in heaven.

Co-dependency has been criticized for being overly diagnostic or pathologizing the natural instinct in people to care for people they love (Katz and Liu, 1992). As a strengths-focused therapist, I have sympathy for this view. Yet I do frequently observe what can be called co-dependency dynamics in relationships, some of which constitute subconscious secondary gains for the non-addicted partner. Below are common ones I observe:

- Thinking they are the cause of their partner's addiction because of something they have or have not done
- Thinking that they can fix their partner
- Waiting forever for a magical diagnosis and related cure
- Thinking that if they are sufficiently vigilant and investigative, they can prevent any lapses (leading to constant checking)
- Thinking that if they are sufficiently angry or appalled their partner will change
- Hoping that their partner will finally see the light and

realize what they have to lose if they continue with their behaviour

- Subconsciously being gratified by the secondary gains of feeling needed by or superior to their partner
- The drama of having an addicted partner giving meaning and significance to life
- Being afraid of losing the social context and status that the relationship provides
- Being afraid of losing financial provision
- Being afraid of being a single parent
- Being afraid of loneliness
- Being afraid of living as an independent adult person
- Being afraid of facing the fact that some people do not change, and this undermining their existential faith in a just, benign universe

I tend to view these dynamics as indications that clients need to develop a wider range of life skills or develop different aspects of personality. If a person has played a caring role as a child, they have likely developed valuable caring capacities such as empathy, problem solving, self-sacrifice, hope and sheer stickability. These attributes need to be acknowledged and affirmed, not just written off as dysfunctional aspects of co-dependency. Nevertheless, clients may benefit from developing alternative ways of feeling good about themselves: releasing untapped potential for fun, independence, and letting people learn from their mistakes, or fulfilling legitimate needs for power, significance and competence in more ultimately rewarding ways.

Texts by Davis Kasl (1990), Steffens and Means (2009), and Hall (2015) offer a plethora of valuable advice, acrostics, thinking errors and thinking solutions, with regard to partners living an independent life and coming to realize that the only thing they can change is themselves. I find that this good advice works if the partner undergoes profound cognitive shifts with regard to how they perceive and experience themselves and the world – often brought about by light bulb moments. The penny drops and they see the counter-productiveness of efforts to control the addict. A different bargain with life is then made. For example: *I'll lose the hope that I can change him, for the peace of mind of knowing that I can only change myself.*

It is a mystery of the therapeutic process as to what brings about such profound changes in perception and feeling. It can be something that is said in therapy, an event outside of therapy, and/or the experience of being partially re-parented through the therapeutic relationship - usually a long-term endeavour - in order to heal the wounds which caused the co-dependent symptomology in the first place.

Anna's early life

Counsellor: You seem pretty confident that things or people can be fixed, and that you can play an important part in the fixing. Do you base this on life experience?
Anna: Well, I guess I've always had to look after people. My Dad was an alcoholic, cured now, the bastard, after he left my mother for Shirley, a younger model. My Mum is harmless, but hopeless. My younger sister, Gracie, had profound learning disabilities and a serious congenital heart disease. She was confined to a wheelchair, could hardly speak. We knew she wouldn't last that long.
Counsellor: What happened to her?
Anna: She died when she was just 11. I was 17. It was a blessing really, and it meant that I felt free to go to university.
Counsellor: What did you study?
Anna: Sociology. Couldn't find a job. Always loved flowers, so trained to be a florist. My teachers said I had a gift.
Counsellor: Did you enjoy it at university?
Anna: Had a wild time.
Counsellor: Sounds as if you deserved it.

The counsellor and Anna exchanged smiles and sat in silence for a minute. The silence was not uncomfortable. The branches of the beech tree outside were still swaying and the counsellor followed a rain drop as it trickled down the window pane. Another storm was forecast for that night. He had sat in the same room a few months before, on a balmy August afternoon, when it seemed that the summer would never end. He breathed deeply from his belly and smiled, wishing for his client to know that everything has a season, everything changes, there is meaning, the universe is ultimately benign.

Above, the counsellor asked factual questions about how old Anna's sister was when she died, what Anna studied at university, whether or not she enjoyed her time there, in order to understand the context. However, asking such factual questions can be overdone. Counsellors can ask mundane questions out of idle curiosity or to fill up space because they cannot think of where to go next, playing for time until they can think of something. If one is stuck, it is usually better to leave a silence. Eventually, a productive way forward will present itself, often coming from the client. If nothing emerges, it's usually best to be congruent, and say something like, 'I'm not sure where we go next': 'Have you got any ideas?': 'What would be useful?'

An important area of competence for therapists is to know why we are asking a question, making an intervention, or leaving a silence. What are we trying to achieve in terms of therapeutic outcomes? In the case above, the counsellor is trying to build rapport. He also suspects that facilitating Anna to talk about her obviously troubling background will likely prove intense. As they both sit, listening to the wind, she may also sense this. It is sometimes good to allow respite. As a therapist, I notice that there is an ebb and flow in counselling. It can feel right to turn down the intensity, if this does not dishonour the gravity of what is being said; humour employed sensitively is a prime example.

> *Counsellor:* How many of you were in your family?
> *Anna:* Just me, Mum and Dad, and Gracie.
> *Counsellor:* Tell me about your parents and life at home, when you were growing up.

Anna: Where do you want me to start?
Counsellor: Anywhere you like.

Anna related the following story from her childhood.

*Anna:*I grew up in a working-class area of Liverpool. My Dad
was an Everton supporter. He would take me to matches sometimes. He was good then, not drinking. He also had budgies in
the shed out the back, and we would feed them together. I
remember him and Mum laughing a lot. They both liked bingo.
He worked in the docks before he was made redundant. Gracie
was born soon afterwards, and that's when he started drinking.
When he was drunk he could be really mean. He slapped my
mother a couple of times.
Counsellor: Did he hit you?
Anna: He wouldn't dare. Even as a kid, I wasn't afraid of
anybody. Besides, he was a bit of a wimp really, not physically
so much, but emotionally. We also had a very strong bond
together. I know it sounds daft but he was my hero when I was
little, still is really, even though he's a twat.

The counsellor self-observed that, at some level, he felt jealous.
Nobody had ever thought of him as a hero. He also felt irritated that
Anna's hero-worship of her father seemed so undeserved. A fantasy
flashed into his mind: Anna looking at him with admiration, after he
had set her free from her trouble. He felt needy, foolish and ashamed.

Therapists experience all kinds of thoughts and feelings during
sessions: attraction, repulsion, interest, boredom, to name a few. Any
sustained pattern of problematic thoughts and feelings in relation to a
client should be taken to supervision. However, if responses are fleeting, it is usually best to view them as part of the essential egocentricity
and absurdity of the human condition and observe them with detached
amusement.

Counsellor: And where was your mother in all this?

Anna: She lives in Turkey now, with a waiter half her age. She was - still is - a good looking woman - more curves than me (Anna seems to be enjoying drawing the counsellor's attention to her body. He declines the invitation to flirt). She's always been one for the men and having a good time. My father has told me since that she was having it away with blokes when she was with him, after Gracie was born.

Counsellor: Did you realize this as a child?

Anna: No, but I sensed it, I think. Always felt protective towards my father, but angry with him at the same time.

Counsellor: It sounds like you have similar feelings towards Greg?

Anna: (Looking adamant) No, it's different with Greg. He's nothing like my father.

At this point Anna is not ready to make the connection between her relationship with her father and her relationship with Greg, although this connection seemed fairly clear to the counsellor. In the previous chapter, there was also a crucial link between Anthony's father and his partner, Harry. The client, Anthony, identified the link more or less immediately. This did not occur with Anna.

It is pointless for a therapist to work outside the motivational and conceptual framework of a client, by trying to get beyond the client's psychological defences. Defences are there for good reason, to protect us from pain we cannot yet cope with. Arguing the toss about a counsellor's favoured interpretation, no matter how subtly, is likely to counterproductively undermine the therapeutic alliance (the most important component of therapy), even if the interpretation is valid. Here, the counsellor 'rolls with the resistance' and leaves the possibility of a connection to percolate within Anna's mind at a subliminal level. As with all clients, if and when Anna is ready to make a cognitive shift in how she perceives 'reality' this will happen naturally, as part of the therapeutic flow, rather than being forced by the therapist.

Counsellor: OK, you say that your father was your hero. Tell me about what made him special to you?
Anna: My first memory is waiting for a bus with him at the crossroads close to our house. It was a Saturday morning. The sun was shining and everything seemed fresh - like the world was new, you know? I held his hand and remember him smelling nicely of aftershave. He used to slick his hair back with gel – jet-black it was. I think he had a white shirt on, with sleeves rolled neatly up to his elbows. Looking back, I think he was a bit obsessive back then. He used to put all his shaving things in a row. He even used to insist on doing his own washing and ironing, so my mother told me.

Anna had an almost beatific look on her face. The counsellor's stable, rational mind was telling him that it was important to value what Anna was saying. This was his ego ideal: how he wanted to be. Another part of him despised Anna's sentimentality. The counsellor made an effort to remember that, like his client, he had different selves vying for attention. He thanked his sceptical self for helping to keep him from being taken in but told this self to relax and allow his innocent self to hold the reins for a while.

Counsellor: Anna, that sounds like a precious memory of your father.
Anna: Yeah, the trouble was … (Anna laughs sardonically) that he didn't stay that way for very long.

The counsellor felt relieved that the more hard-bitten Anna was back. However, he knew his relief was not the main issue here. To have more choices in her relationship with Greg, Anna needed to understand how her own defence against being left vulnerable as a child might be restricting her choices with regard to her current partner. Hence, it was important for her to get in touch with and express, at a pre-rational level, the ideal and the innocence that had been lost.

Counsellor: Tell me more about your good memories of your father.
Anna: (A smile returns and her face softens). It's bits and pieces really. I remember him sawing some wood in the kitchen. Again, it seems like a sunny Saturday morning …
Counsellor: When the world was new?
Anna: (Laughs) Yeah. I remember how big the muscles were in his arm. He wasn't a macho man or anything like that, and that's why I think I was surprised.
Counsellor: What did you feel, when you looked at the muscles in his arm?
Anna: Proud of him, I suppose.
Counsellor: Anything else?
Anna: (Pauses) As if he could take care of us (Anna begins to weep).

The counsellor reached over to the table beside Anna, handed her a tissue and waited for her to stop crying. Sitting in silence, he imagined the tears as a balm, healing Anna's emotional wounds.

Counsellor: How did it change with your father?

Anna blew her nose, rolled the tissue up, and dropped it nonchalantly into the waste paper bin by the side of her chair.

Anna: Well, he changed after Gracie was born disabled. Everything changed. My mother couldn't cope and began chasing men. He hit the bottle and he became a right slob and a loser.
Counsellor: When you think of all this happening - your father hitting the bottle, being a slob, your mother chasing men, your father becoming a loser - what day is it? What's the weather like?
Anna: Oh! That's easy. It's still Saturday, but late afternoon, early evening. It's drizzling outside. I hate fucking Saturdays around that time. Hate it when all the young florists are excited

about going home, giggling and acting like air-heads, excited about Saturday night out on the town. Greg's just having a laugh with them, rather than helping me sort things at the shops.

Counsellor: What used to happen on Saturday evenings at home?

Anna: My father would be drinking cans, ready to go out to the pub, and my mother would be titivating herself in front of the mirror, ready to go out with her mates. Plumes of lacquer stinking the place out. She used to have a frizzy mop perm. (The counsellor notices again that Anna's hair, by contrast, is cropped into a bob). My mother always had friends around the house, drinking tea and talking crap all day, or she would be around theirs. That's how my Dad met Shirley. My mother was a lazy cow - an 'anything goes' sort of person. But Saturday would be the big night out. I would be left to look after Gracie, right up until I was 17, really, and then I left home.

Counsellor: How did you feel about that?

Anna: OK, actually. It gave me plenty of time to study for my GCSEs and A-Levels. I don't think that I would have gone to Uni if my Mum and Dad had been proper parents. None of my friends went to Uni. I was always the hard-working one.

Counsellor: It sounds as if you feel that you missed out?

Anna: Not really. If I did, I made up for it at Uni, like I said. Besides, I liked looking after Gracie, and even Dad. I used to do the washing and ironing for him when he stopped doing it himself.

Counsellor: Tell me more about your mother in all this.

Anna: I guess she would look after Gracie in the day. Dad got hopeless after he lost his job. He would stay up late at night and not get up till the afternoon, when he would go down the off-licence. I don't think he could cope - seeing Gracie there, stuck in the chair and having everything done for her. She couldn't talk, only grunt. But she always had a happy disposition. I would come home from school and more or less take over from

Mum. Dad would be watching telly with his cans in the living room and Mum would go around to the neighbours, or perhaps out to meet men - I don't know. I expect she needed a break after looking after Gracie all day. I would sit in the kitchen with Gracie, and do my homework and try out Delia Smith recipes, casseroles and soups and stuff, that I would put in the fridge for us all to eat through the week. Mum wasn't interested in cooking. Gracie was content as long as we had music playing. Sometimes my friends would come around and sit with us in the kitchen, and sometimes we would take Gracie out to the park.

The counsellor felt close to tears as he listened to Anna. He was struck by her commitment to her family, her lack of self-pity, her sheer sensible practicality and 'can do' spirit. In comparison he felt like a heel, being so parsimonious about his sister's health problems and her neediness. He tried to calm the critical voice in his head and be compassionate to himself, reminding himself that there were different power dynamics at work between him and his sister. Nevertheless, he realized once again how much he learned from his clients. He refocused on Anna.

Counsellor: It sounds like you were holding things together
back there.
Anna: (Looking embarrassed) Yeah.

Anna's monosyllabic response did not give much away on the surface. However, the counsellor sensed that, underneath, Anna felt affirmed by the genuine admiration invested in his comment.

Counsellor: Sounds like you are still holding things together,
not at home any more, but at the flower shops.
Anna: But I like holding things together.
Counsellor: And that's fine. You holding things together was a
great blessing for your family and for Gracie. Your ability to

hold things together meant that you were able to get over all the challenges of your background and still go to university, get a degree, open your own business.

Anna: Yeah, but so?

Counsellor: Well, I wonder if there might be something else at play in you sticking with Greg, no matter how many times he lets you down. This is just an idea and you may think it's a load of tosh, Anna, but can I share it with you?

Anna: (Looking slightly uncomfortable). Go for it.

Counsellor: Well, maybe why you want to rescue Greg is not just because you're good at caring for people. Perhaps you are looking for that Saturday morning feeling again, when the world was new, and your father was strong and he could look after you, and you didn't have to take up the slack. Perhaps you are not prepared to give up the hope that, one day, Greg will be strong for you, in the way your father once was, before Gracie was born. Maybe, what you really want is for Greg to make life like those sunny Saturday mornings.

A silence descended on the room. Outside there seemed to have been a break in the weather. The wind was no longer howling. A ray of sunshine was breaking through the clouds.

Anna: But he's not ever going to … is he, probably not with me? Even my father didn't give up drink for me. He only did that after Gracie died and he met Shirley.

Anna paused and the counsellor was happy not to break the silence.

Anna: All of a sudden, I feel quite light. Right, I'm going to give the bastard one more chance and if he blows it, that's it, I'll make my own sunny Saturday morning.

After the above session, Anna went home and said to Greg that she was going to give him one more chance of not acting out sexually behind her back. She told him that, in addition to attending the SAA group, she wanted him to attend couple counselling with her new therapist. She said that she had seen how her past was impacting on the relationship and she now wanted them to establish, with the therapist, how they wanted their lives to be in the future. Anna had moved on but was still organizing proceedings. The next chapter focuses on how the counsellor processed and undertook this joint work with Anna and Greg.

Conclusion

The case study, above, demonstrates how childhood experiences of lack of security and care can be transferred to adult relationships, causing co-dependency dynamics. If an individual has taken on a premature caring role in childhood, there will be many resources and strengths gained from this experience, which should be validated. However, the person may be stuck in a pattern where they are continuing the caring role with a sexually addicted partner because this role is familiar, and it provides unacknowledged secondary gains. Nevertheless, there will be other needs and desires unfulfilled as the rescuer hopes, usually in vain, for a partner to fill the gaps left by inadequate nurturing as a child. In order to be released from this trap, the individual needs to gain insight into such dynamics, which can be helped by corrective nurture provided within a therapeutic relationship with a counsellor or therapist.

Practice points from this chapter

- When meeting a client note first impressions, but do not be overly guided by them
- When feeling strongly about a client when first meeting them, check for transference issues
- Sometimes it can help to sensitively call out negative

dynamics, as long as this is for the client's benefit and not the counsellor's

- It is important for the counsellor to be aware of their own process, no matter how irrational, in order to avoid being emotionally driven by unacknowledged egocentric impulses
- It is equally important for the counsellor to be compassionate about the vagaries and inconsistencies of their own humanity
- Perceiving self and others as having competing selves vying for attention can reduce shame and open up therapeutic possibilities
- Be curious about and affirm the positive aspects of dysfunctional relationships
- It can be helpful to focus on whether or not clients' narratives and interpretations are working for them, rather than on whether or not they are likely to be true
- Consider co-dependency dynamics, whilst not pathologizing the instinct in people to want to remain loyal to and care for people they love
- Be alert to feeling biased in favour of one partner if working in relationship therapy, even if the other partner is not attending therapy
- In times of silence, positive visualization or silent prayer for a client may be beneficial (although the efficacy of this can never be proven and is a matter of faith)
- Consider the ebb and flow of the session. Sometimes the client needs respite from intensity
- If you genuinely are impressed or admire the way a client has coped or acted, communicating this can have a significant therapeutic effect
- Clients often have to undergo profound cognitive shifts in the way they conceptualize past and current events and relationships, before discovering how to better cope with losses and lacks
- Co-constructing metaphors for what is lost and desired (i.e.

sunny Saturday mornings, when the world was new) can release subconscious material into rational consciousness, opening up new potentialities

References

Beattie, M. (1986) *Codependent no more: How to stop controlling others and start caring for yourself.* Minnesota: Hazelden.

Cermak, T.L. (1998) *Diagnosing and treating co-dependence: A guide for professionals who work with chemical dependents, their spouses, and children.* Minnesota: Hazelden.

Davis Kasl, C. (1990) *Women, sex and addiction: A search for love and power.* Great Britain: Mandarin Books.

Hall, P. (2015) *Sex addiction: The partner's perspective.* London and New York: Routledge.

Julian of Norwich (trans. B. Windeatt) (2015) *Revelations of Divine Love.* Oxford: Oxford University Press.

Katz, S.J. and Liu, A.E. (1992) *The co-dependency conspiracy: How to break the recovery habit and take charge of your life.* New York: Grand Central Publishing (formerly Warner books).

Lancer, D. (2014) *Conquering shame and codependency: 8 steps to freeing the true you.* Minnesota: Hazelden.

Norwood, R. (1986) *Women who love too much.* London: Arrow Books.

Steffens, B and Means, M. (2009) *Your sexually addicted spouse: How partners can cope and heal.* Far Hills, NJ: New Horizon Press.

Woititz, J. G. (Rev ed. 1990) *Adult children of alcoholics.* Florida: Health Communications Inc.

FOUR
ANNA AND GREG

Introduction

This chapter continues with the case study which featured in the previous chapter. The counsellor has decided that, having provided individual counselling to Anna, he will agree to counsel Anna and Greg as a couple. The pros and cons of the same counsellor providing individual counselling to one partner and then to both partners as a couple, are discussed. Some good practice tips are illustrated, related to the counsellor moving from one-to-one counselling to couple counselling, with the same partners. Treatment options for individuals who are sexually addicted are summarized and the issue of disclosing details of the addictive sexual behaviour to the partner is also explored. Some favoured ideas and methods used by the author when counselling couples, where one partner has committed a sexual offence and may be sexually addicted, are demonstrated throughout the chapter.

Pros and cons of counselling a couple, and also seeing each one separately

Some counsellors and agencies take the view that it is not good practice for the same counsellor to conduct counselling with two partners together and also separately. One concern is that working with a couple separately as individuals, and then as a dyad, is too much for one counsellor to process, potentially leading to loss of perspective and balance. Partners in conflict often invite the counsellor, in subtle and not so subtle ways, to take their side. Add to this, the complex transference dynamics which can occur with one client, let alone two, and it can be a lot for one therapist to hold.

Partners have different needs. One partner, for instance, might have profound childhood challenges to address, perhaps related to attachment and trauma issues. This may require long-term therapy, with the client needing to feel that the therapist's focus is on them alone and not divided between the two partners.

On a practical basis, if one partner requires longer-term therapy, a stronger therapeutic alliance is liable to be built up with the client seen for a more extended period. In such circumstances, it can be difficult for the counsellor to be even-handed or, at least, for the partner with less history with the counsellor not to feel that the counsellor is unbiased.

Confidentiality can also be challenging. One partner may reveal information in a single session that they do not want repeated in joint sessions. An example of this might be when one partner discloses to the counsellor that they are having a secret affair. This can put the counsellor in an uncomfortable position. The counsellor and one partner might know things of which the other partner is unaware. This can feel like collusion, with the unaware partner being placed at a disadvantage.

Despite the above challenges, there can be distinct advantages in counselling partners separately and together. Firstly, there may not always be another sufficiently suitably experienced counsellor in the local area to work with couples impacted by sexual offending and sexual addiction issues. This tends to be a niche area. The work is also highly sensitive, and couples often have enough trouble summoning up the courage to see one counsellor, let alone having to build rapport with more than one.

Above, I have pointed to the problem of the counsellor's sympathies being split between two partners when providing different configurations of counselling. However, splitting can also occur with different counsellors: typically, when each counsellor displays partiality to the partner they are seeing. Couples can also become confused by the varying approaches taken by the different counsellors, and the related communication of sometimes contradictory messages.

The advantage of one counsellor providing therapy for each individual and for the couple is that they can take a more systemic approach (see Part 3 for a further discussion of this). It is arguably easier to focus on, and attend to, the couple's relationship, rather than just the specific issues each individual brings to therapy, although the two domains are interconnected. The same counsellor can also get to know the intricacies of each partner's history and functioning, and how such issues impact on the relationship, at significant depth.

In my experience, some counsellors are more comfortable with counselling only one partner, or only the couple. Other counsellors are happy to work with all three configurations: each partner and the two partners as a couple. I am in the latter category.

A generic, comprehensive exploration of how to conduct couple counselling is outside the purview of this book. Any counsellor embarking on couple counselling with this, or any other, client group should have undertaken training in, and have experience of, providing counselling to couples. There has been little written about couple counselling, when one partner has committed a sexual offence. However, Hall (2019) and Schnarch (2009) offer ways of counselling couples, where one partner has a sexual compulsivity problem. Below are a number of salient good practice tips:

- If any risk of domestic abuse is apparent, consideration should be given to whether any control or power loss (actual or perceived) through participation in couple counselling might trigger further abuse

- The counsellor should be aware not to take up invitations to take sides
- Ideally, the couple should spend significant time relating to each other in the sessions, rather than taking it in turns to engage with the counsellor, in binary fashion
- Counselling should afford the couple the structured opportunity to practise discussing difficult issues with each other in a constructive way
- Prepare the room by putting the couple's seats at an angle to encourage them to interact with each other and not just with the counsellor, as individuals.

Before seeing a couple together, I am keen to check out with one partner, or with the two partners if they refer as a couple, the pros and cons of different ways of working, and what each wants to achieve from the counselling. If I have been counselling one partner for some time, and they want the other partner to attend, or the other partner wants to attend, I will repeat the same process in order to help each partner make informed choices.

If seeing the couple together first, I will negotiate a number of sessions with each of them separately. This allows me to build a thera-peutic alliance with both. Before embarking on these separate journeys, I tell each partner that I will not generally inform the other of any infor-mation that they have not agreed can be disclosed. However, I also discuss with them what they would like to happen if one of them revealed a major secret to me, such as having an affair or lapsing into secret sexual behaviour which they want to remain hidden from the other. I ask each of them how they would feel if I and their partner knew something of this magnitude that they were ignorant about, and state that I would not personally be prepared to work with them and keep such a secret. We then agree the sort of information that will need to be shared.

By the end of this second stage, I will also renegotiate afresh the goals of counselling, which may have evolved. This renegotiation of goals is important, as the frame of mind of one or both partners may have altered considerably, through their respective experiences of having individual counselling with me.

In the third stage, I see the couple together. We begin by discussing the respective goals set by each partner in the individual sessions, in order to ascertain if they are compatible and acceptable to both parties. We then come up with shared goals for the joint counselling. Alongside the joint counselling process, it may seem useful for one or both parties to have separate time with me to explore a particular issue. This can be productive, as long as it does not result in one partner feeling left out in the cold, as it were.

Once the confidentiality boundaries are established, then some ground rules can be agreed:

- No generalization (i.e. 'you always do that')
- The use of 'I' statements (i.e. 'I feel, I want, I think')
- Be kind and considerate when making difficult points
- Whatever else the couple and counsellor agree

Below are some general questions which can be used throughout the above process to encourage mutual discussion. As with all questions and prompts suggested throughout this book, the therapist can rephrase to suit his or her own personal style, and clinical judgement should be made regarding the timing and the appropriateness of any input.

- Can you say what first attracted you to one another?
- Can you say what you appreciate about your partner?
- At what times are things good between you?
- How would you have wanted your partner to make that point?
- Can you give more detail?
- If somebody waved a magic wand or a miracle happened

and your partner became as you would like them to be, what would be the changes?

- What could your partner do in order to reassure you that things will be better in the future?
- In what ways can risk be monitored? What would be the pros and cons of this?
- Could we prioritize the most important things you want from your partner?
- Could you say that again, but this time to your partner?
- Could you say to your partner how you think it felt for them to say that?
- Could you say to your partner what you'd be thinking or feeling if you were in their shoes?
- Have I got this right, are you trying to say to your partner that …?
- Maybe you could say to your partner what you really meant
- Can I stop you there? It's becoming a bit of a battle
- How do you think your partner feels when you say that?
- Can you tell your partner how you felt when they said that?
- Is there any way in which you could have made the same point in a kinder way?

Individual Counselling with Greg

At the end of the last chapter, Anna told the counsellor that Greg now wanted to have couple counselling, to supplement the input he was getting from the SAA (Sexual Addicts Anonymous) group he was now regularly attending. The counsellor suggested that if Greg wanted to attend counselling, then he should contact himself and they could arrange for an introductory couple session with him and Anna to ascertain if joint work would be likely to prove constructive. The counsellor considered it was important for Greg to make contact off his own back, as he was aware that Anna was a forceful personality. It was important to establish that Greg was motivated to attend counselling himself and was not just being pressurized into it by Anna, thereby repeating a familiar unproductive pattern in their relationship. In order to remain congruent and transparent, the counsellor explained to Anna his reasoning, which she took with good grace.

In the joint session, the following initial goals were agreed for joint work, with all agreeing that these goals might change and evolve as the counselling process progressed:

Anna's goals

- To stop checking up on Greg
- To be assertive rather than aggressive: to stop shouting, swearing and throwing things at Greg
- To show Greg respect in front of staff
- To go swimming twice a week
- To go out with her friends once a week
- To inquire about undertaking an MA in environmental studies

Greg's goals

- To desist from any secret sexual behaviour
- To stop flirting with the young florists
- To proactively make himself accountable to Anna and the SAA group
- To be more open about his thoughts and feelings
- To stop sulking
- To initiate acts of care and concern for Anna
- To be more assertive with Anna
- To start going to the gym three times a week

In addition to the above goals, the counsellor suggested that he would like to have six sessions with Greg, in order to build a separate therapeutic alliance with him, and to understand how he thought his life and sexual behaviour impacted on the relationship with Anna. Both agreed to this.

I will not provide an in-depth account of the six sessions with Greg, as this book is concerned with working with partners, rather than individuals who have sexually offended and who have sexual compulsivity problems. I address treating sexual offending in my previous book (Smith, 2017), and provide a brief summary of some of the main rehabilitative issues when working with clients who are sexually addicted, later on in the chapter. However, immediately below is a précis of the work conducted by Greg in his individual sessions with the counsellor.

Greg told the counsellor that he was raised in a liberal, middle-class family, in which there had been subtle expectations to perform. His father was emotionally absent, working long hours as a corporate lawyer. His mother remained at home looking after him and his older brother (now an eye surgeon), until his mother trained to be a psychotherapist. She had always been into 'good works.' She had the philosophy of never actually sanctioning her sons for 'bad behaviour', instead repeating to them: 'If you behave badly, you will know inside, and it's up to you to make good choices'. Greg was assessed as dyslexic at school, and has always had difficulty with self-discipline, only ever really persevering with cooking. He recalled being at his happiest as a child, cooking with his mother in their large kitchen, his mother being a great cook. As a teenager he felt guilty about opting out of school and getting into the 'wrong crowd', drinking heavily and taking drugs, mainly cannabis and speed. He talked about feeling a failure in relation to his brother and his father - both high earners - and feeling 'bad' because they helped him with money to set up a restaurant, which failed. The word 'bad' cropped up frequently in Greg's discourse. He described getting into looking at online pornography around the age of 13 and, before meeting Anna, living a promiscuous lifestyle. Many of his relationships were with girls from troubled, disadvantaged backgrounds. With the help of the counsellor,

Greg saw he had gravitated to risk-taking groups, compensating for feelings of inadequacy in relation to higher achieving peers.

With regard to his sexual offence, Greg maintains that the girl in question made a false allegation. He accepts that Anna maintains an open mind about this, consistent with the account Anna gave the counsellor. He thinks that Anna is worried about him re-offending against one of the young florists, or one of them making an allegation and this sticking because of his past. The counsellor informed Greg that he would share Anna's concerns. Greg stated that he would never commit a sexual offence but admitted feeling 'bad' about 'sexually acting out' - saying he had learnt this term in the SAA group – and that he was afraid of losing Anna. He reflected that, in one way, Anna was like some of the girls he had gone out with previously, from a 'rougher background', a 'bit mouthy', which he liked, but also intelligent and reliable.

Through one-to-one counselling, Greg began to consider new ways of constructing his life experiences. Liking 'mouthy' women may compensate for the absence of emotion in his family and his own stunted emotional expression. Due to the premature maternal message that he must be his own moral judge, he may have developed a strong inner critic, telling him he is 'bad'. But he also rebels against moral constriction and plays out this internal drama with Anna taking on the role, in his mind, of moralizing mother.

What helped Greg to understand the above dynamics was the counsellor introducing him to transactional analysis ego states, proposed by Eric Berne (1961), and elucidated further by Harris (1970):

Parent - Parent
Adult - Adult
Child - Child

The counsellor explained that in a functional relationship, partners spend a lot of time interacting in the adult ego states, relating as peers. However, if one is ill or feeling down, it can be comforting for the other to take up the parental role, taking care of the other partner. This is healthy as long as the arrangement is reciprocated when the other is feeling down. When relaxing, it is fun for both to be in the 'child' ego state. Without this capacity, a relationship can become staid and lacking in passion. Nevertheless, if one or both remain in the child state for too long, this can lead to substance misuse, debt, sexual addiction and sexual offending, as means and results of escaping responsibility. In some relationships an imbalance develops where one partner, often the addict, becomes like a rebellious teenager, with the other partner taking up the space of nagging parent. Greg instantly recognized this dynamic in his relationship with Anna, and stated that he would like to be more of an adult in the relationship.

In addition to the above focus on the dynamics of the relationship, Greg wanted to know about treatment options, with regard to sexual addiction. The counsellor provided a simplified summary, which is outlined below.

Treatment options concerning sex addiction

Sex addiction can be seen as a pattern of compulsive sexual behaviour causing harm to self or others and/or at odds with a person's stable value base. There is no one recommended treatment model for sexual addictions. Therapists use a range of counselling methods, often within an integrative method (combining different approaches together) or an eclectic style (selecting the best approach for the client).

Early attachment deficits and trauma can sometimes lead to addictions, including sex addiction, with the addictive buzz being used to soothe and regulate unwanted emotional states related to past deficits (Kohut,1977; Holmes, 1996; Flores, 2011). A psychodynamic approach can be employed, using long-term psychotherapy. With this approach, the therapeutic relationship, with its roots in humanistic psychotherapy, is seen as a way of partially re-parenting and healing attachment and trauma wounds, lessening the need to use sex as a coping method. The interaction between therapist and client can be a potential means by which the client can experience, learn and practise more productive ways of relating to others and being happier in the world, as well as facilitating the client to have greater insight into their functioning.

If working holistically, what it means to be human and to live what Ward et al. (2007) call a 'Good Life' often involves exploring existential and transpersonal issues - apparent with Margaret in Chapter 1. There has been a particular focus upon the spiritual with regard to working with addictions, including sexual addictions. The roots of this lie in large part in the AA (Alcoholics Anonymous) creed of the addict having to accept his powerlessness to fix his addiction without the help of a greater power, whether it be God or other people, expressed through the support and accountability offered by a group of fellow addicts. This therapeutic philosophy has crossed over into the work of sexual addiction, with groups such as SAA (Sex Addicts Anonymous) working in similar ways.

As already noted, the belief that addiction is a disease over which the individual has no control is criticized for pathologizing the individual, removing personal responsibility and not accounting for those who manage addictions through their own efforts (Cherlin, 2009; Thompson, 2012). The disease model has also been seen as a repressive social construction, limiting free sexual expression (Irvine, 1995).

However, it is strongly argued that sexual addiction does have a genetic component – with certain individuals being more prone to addictions generally, including to sex (Volkow and Li, 2015). Brain scanning technologies indicate that preoccupied, compulsive use of pornography can alter the neurochemical balance of the brain, especially in relation to dopamine (Barrett, 2010). Hence, sexual addiction is viewed by many of those writing on it as a disease to be treated.

With increasing numbers of young people being exposed to cybersex from an early age, individuals are presenting with the symptoms of addiction, without any obvious serious dysfunction in their backgrounds. Repeated exposure to sexually explicit material results in needing to seek out more frequent and extreme forms of sexual stimulation in order to gain the same satisfaction that otherwise is gained from more modest sexual experiences with partners.

Barrett (2010) points out how for most of human history we have lived in small groups and only had a small selection of potential sexual partners, with whom to mate. Urbanization, mass media and now the internet have surrounded us with a wide range of idealized and extreme sexual forms – supernormal stimuli. Barrett argues that, as with food, our primitive brains have been evolutionarily adapted to seek variation in order for the species to have the best chance of survival. Hence, online fantasy sex, the world of frequent, impersonal sexual encounters, can easily become addictive. 'Supernormal' sexual activity, like substance misuse, can artificially raise the levels of the feel-good neurotransmitter dopamine, while inhibiting the natural production of the substance, fuelling sexually addictive behaviour. High-level dopamine production also inhibits executive brain function, seriously undermining self-control and rational, consequential thinking. Providing a client with a simple rational explanation of the neurobiological roots of sexually addicted behaviour can reduce shame and increase motivation to change addictive sexual patterns.

As noted in Chapter 1, some would argue that the most effective way to treat sexual addiction is for the person to go 'cold turkey', as one would with alcohol or drug addiction: i.e. not engaging in any sexual activity, not sexually fantasizing and not masturbating (Carnes, 1992). This allows neural pathways connected to sexual arousal to cool down. As one client put it, 'it (temporary abstinence) rebooted my sex life'.

Once the addictive cycle has been broken, the sexual arousal pattern can be reconditioned to be triggered by sexual thoughts and behaviour about a long-term partner, merging emotional intimacy with sexual fulfilment. This allows sex to take up a proportionate rather than a disproportionate place in a person's life – although what is proportionate will be a value judgement for each person. Exploring tantric sex practices is often recommended by sex therapists (Lorius,1999), to help deepen and mature the sexual and emotional life of a couple. With people who have sexual addiction problems or who have sexual offending difficulties, sex therapy is an often, underused resource. Addiction and forensic practitioners often know a lot about 'bad' sex, but not so much about 'good' sex, being more focused on likely problems rather than possible solutions.

There are different views about the necessary period of abstinence. Whereas some, as noted above, argue that a period of abstinence is necessary, others would argue that complete abstinence counter-productively builds up tension, running the risk of the person acting out sexually in more extreme and destructive ways. The sheer difficulty of total abstinence for some clients can also set people up to fail, potentially undermining hope and motivation. Hence, some therapists opt for a gradual decrease in sexual preoccupation, agreeing with the client a bottom line concerning sexual behaviour which should never be crossed. This was the case with Margaret and Dennis in Chapter 1.

People with sexual addiction problems can be treated on a one-to-one basis, or in a group setting, such as in SAA groups. The advantage of individual counselling is that it proves less intimidating for some clients, than sharing personal material in a group. Counselling, at its best, offers the opportunity to explore personal issues at focused, concerted depth, that can be difficult to achieve in a group. Clients also benefit from close bonds with individual therapists, which is of particular value if a client's issues are more about one-to-one relationships, rather than groups. There may also be no SAA-type groups close to where a person lives; counsellors tend to be more widespread.

Nevertheless, there are distinct advantages with groups. Participants learn from others with similar problems, allowing themselves to observe their behaviour through seeing it in others. If an individual finds groups difficult, being a valued group member can offer a powerful corrective experience. A group of peers can also offer significant support and accountability. Some clients are more willing to accept challenges from somebody who 'has been there' than from a counsellor who hasn't.

Leaving the above controversies and different views on sexual addiction and treating sexual addiction aside, the majority of therapeutic methods for tackling sexual addiction in counselling involve cognitive-behavioural and psycho-educational approaches, (Hall, 2012; Birchard, 2015). Such approaches usually involve the following:

- Establishing initial rapport and goals for counselling
- Helping clients to understand theories of why people become sexually addicted
- Exploring past lifeline issues contributing to sexual dependency
- Assisting the client to understand their own cycle or pathway of addiction
- Holistically helping the client to develop healthy life habits
- Agreeing a Relapse Prevention Plan or Safety Plan, consisting of negotiated ways of managing risk of relapse
- Sometimes sharing the Plan with significant others

The disclosing process

A common tenet of working with individuals who have sexual addiction and sexual offending problems is that their partner or significant others need or want to know about their partner's sexual acting out. There are various reasons for this:

- To re-establish honesty in the relationship
- To repair trust
- To help the other person understand the problem
- To help the other person understand risk triggers
- To help the other person identify and respond to signs of risk, especially if there are child protection concerns

The disclosing process can take various forms. Everything can come out unexpectedly, often if the Police are involved or if the secret sexual behaviour is suddenly discovered in some other way. The extent of the covert behaviour can seep out gradually, either because the person discloses bit by bit, or the significant other perseveres in trying to find out the truth through constant questioning, investigating phones, computers, bank accounts and talking to mutual friends etc.

The person who has acted out sexually may want to control the flow of information as a way of managing shame, or as a means of maintaining control and continuing the sexual behaviour. They may fear hurting a partner, or that the relationship will end if they disclose the entirety of their secret sexual behaviour. The situation can be even more complex as the partner may be giving subtle, or not so subtle, signs that they do not want to know what has gone on, or at least not the grisly details of it.

For some partners, knowing everything can bring a sense of control and relief. Their mental pictures may be worse than what has actually occurred. However, for others, knowing the details may prove traumatizing and counterproductive, and they can never get the disturbing vision of their partner's sexual behaviour out of their minds.

Disclosure can also take various trajectories. It can be part of a planned process, with therapist and couple agreeing that disclosure will occur in a particular session. Below are some good practice guidelines for this sort of work.

Disclosure work with partners separately

- Going through with each partner separately the pros and cons of disclosure
- Establishing what each partner separately wants to gain from disclosure, and exploring whether expectations are realistic
- Exploring with each partner their preferred ground rules for disclosure
- Exploring with each partner when and how they would like you, as the counsellor, to intervene

Disclosure work with partners as a couple

- In the light of the above work with the partners on their own, establishing with the couple how they would like the disclosure session/s to run
- If any discrepancies have become apparent through working with the partners separately about specific expectations, facilitating a discussion about these
- As with couple counselling generally, facilitating the couple to speak to each other, rather than addressing the counsellor in turn
- At pertinent points, asking each how they think the other has felt or is feeling about the matter in question
- If necessary, intervening to leave space to honour the feelings being expressed

Counselling Anna and Greg together

In the case of Anna and Greg, neither wanted a structured disclosure session. Greg insisted that he had already told Anna everything about his sexual acting out, or she had found out about it herself. Anna said she doubted that Greg had told her everything, but she thought she knew enough and now wanted to move on.

When Anna and Greg had their first session together, the counsellor was keen to observe the power dynamics between the couple in action. Couples utilize power in different ways, related to the basic fight/flight/freeze responses. Schnarch (2009) describes how, both generally and related to specific issues like sex, there is a 'Low Desire Partner' and a 'High Desire Partner'. One partner can have a tendency to use power to assert, which can flow over into aggression, whilst the other can be in the habit of using power to resist, which can turn into passive aggression. This results in road blocks in a relationship when values, priorities and goals differ, with each partner deploying their favoured interactional weaponry in endless arguments about the same contested issues.

Individual partners can talk about such power dynamics separately, although not necessarily conceptualizing the relationship in these terms, in individual sessions with a counsellor. However, it is often not until the counsellor sees the couple together that the interactional power dynamics clearly emerge. Who speaks the most? Who is the louder of the two? Who interrupts more often? Who tends to talk over the other? Who has more emotional energy? Who takes up power passively through sarcasm, sulking, silence?

It became fairly obvious that Anna was the partner who took up more active power, with Greg taking up power in a passive, resentful way. The counsellor drew the couple's attention, in a light-hearted manner, to how these interactional dynamics were playing out in the here-and-now of the sessions. He would frequently ask how each experienced and felt about the habitual combative tactics employed by the other and if they could express their feelings and thoughts in kinder, more assertive ways, rather than resorting to aggression, sulking or passive aggression. Often counsellors can underestimate the importance of the sometimes repetitive, hard slog of this ongoing communication training which can, in some cases, be as important as tackling the big issues. Some relationships are improved not by differences necessarily being resolved, but by learning to discuss differences in more considerate ways.

Having talked about the importance of communication, Anna and Greg nevertheless had issues to re-negotiate. As the result of the preparation work completed with them individually, both had gained insight into how Anna played the rescuing role to Greg's rebellious child. However, despite Anna agreeing to the goal - *to stop checking up on Greg* (see above) - she had checked his phone and found what she considered to be a number of flirtatious texts, between him and one of the young florists, Chloe (22). This appeared to run counter to Greg's stated goals: *to desist from any secret sexual behaviour* and *to stop flirting with the florists* (see above).

Anna: You said in this room, only a few weeks ago, you would stop any fucking flirting with the florists and you start flirting with Chloe. (She looks at the counsellor). He didn't want to come today because he didn't want to be caught out.

Greg: And you said you wouldn't check my phone, and you did. And you're over- reacting. It was just innocent messing about.

Anna: Right, she texts you at 1.30 in the morning, saying she's out with her friends in a club pissed - what has that got to do with it? - and she can't remember if she's got a shift the next day. One, why didn't she contact me? And why contact you when she's obviously drunk, and why did she sign off as 'Chloe, pissed and horny?'

Greg: She was just pissed. They (the florists) come to me because they're afraid of you, and I manage the shops.

Anna: Then you replied - I've written it down here for Mark (the counsellor) to see – 'You're in tomorrow. Don't do anything I wouldn't do, with all those studs sniffing about'. Then she says, 'I need you here to save my virtue'. What's all that about?

Greg: It was just banter, messing around for goodness sake!

Anna: But we've talked about Chloe before, and me thinking it's out of order talking to you about her break-up with her boyfriend.

Greg: You know he was a bastard to her. You wanted her to her get shot of him.

Anna: But that's not the point. What sort of relationship have you got with her, that she feels free to text you like that?

The counsellor found himself on Anna's side, irritated with Greg's evasions. He had clearly been flirting with the florist and was now trying to normalize it, suggesting that Anna was making a fuss about nothing. What should the counsellor do? Should he remain neutral or act as some kind of arbitrator of common sense; the judge and jury pronouncing if Greg was out of order and whether or not Anna had a right to feel aggrieved? The counsellor responded as follows:

Counsellor: OK Greg, if you had ten people in this room and they were given a vote as to whether or not your communication was flirtatious and breaking the previous agreement you made with Anna in counselling, what do you think the majority verdict would be?
Greg: It would depend if they were men or women.
Counsellor: (In a gentle voice) Greg, I need to be honest with you at this point. It seems to me that you were flirting with the young florist and your communication with her clearly breached your part of the agreement.

At this point, the counsellor came off the fence. He was aware that siding with Anna might be perceived by Greg as another therapist being on Anna's side, and that Greg might see him as just another parental or authority figure disapproving and trying to curtail his freedom. However, the counsellor considered that it would be too incongruent and simply not genuine to remain neutral on such a blatant matter.

I find that I am able to say tough, uncompromising things to clients, to seemingly useful effect, once a good therapeutic alliance has been established, and if the client considers or experiences me as having their best interest at heart. Greg seems to feel this way about his counsellor.

Greg: OK, I've obviously messed up.

Greg's admission came towards the end of the session. In the time left, Anna said little, looking deflated, as Greg made promises that nothing like this would happen again. The following day, Anna phoned the counsellor, saying that she wanted to have a couple of sessions on her own to discuss her options. Concerned that Anna might be under the impression that she could attend sessions on her own without Greg's knowledge, the counsellor asked if Greg knew of her plans. She confirmed that she had informed him, and he was content with this.

In my view there can be no hard and fast rules about seeing partners coming for couple therapy, separately. As noted above, counsellors and therapists hold different views about this. However, generally, if I have commenced couple therapy, I like to even out the number of single sessions I have with each partner, in order to avoid any bias, real or imagined. Nevertheless, if there is an obvious risk of domestic abuse in the relationship, then I am prepared to see the partner at risk of abuse separately, in secret, if this is absolutely necessary to help keep the client safe, and to agree a risk management strategy.

There were no domestic abuse issues in this case, so the counsellor asked Anna if Greg would phone to say if he was also prepared to attend two sessions on his own. Greg phoned and the counsellor suggested that the sessions could be used to explore his underlying motives for breaching the agreement by flirting with the florist, and Greg's own options concerning his relationship with Anna. Greg agreed.

The individual work with Greg consisted of Greg exploring the pros and cons of flirting with the florist. Often counsellors fail to significantly explore the rewards of seemingly destructive behaviour, missing the opportunity to help clients face up to the cost of changing their ways. In the single sessions, Greg reflected that he wanted to remain faithful to Anna, but he also wanted to be free and not constrained. He talked of life not seeming worthwhile if he could not flirt with women or talk sexually to them. He even admitted that the thought of not having sex with anybody apart from Anna for the rest of his life seemed, to him, a very depressing one.

Greg reflected how he liked being a manager. At the end of the shift, he was often high or exhausted or both and was looking for some way to celebrate, relax or console himself when he had a bad day in the shops. Often Anna just wanted to chill after the shops had closed, watching her soaps and going to bed early. It was at these times that he would be particularly tempted to act out. Greg reflected further that he had always known how to 'talk to' and 'joke about' with women, and women had always found him attractive. At one point, close to tears, he stated that giving all this up felt like an 'early death'. Yet, he loved Anna and was prepared 'to give it another go'.

Sex addiction, like other compulsive habits such as substance misuse, can be viewed as a learnt way of emotional regulation: *I feel bored, I turn to my addiction; I feel depressed, I turn to my addiction; I feel angry, I turn to my addiction; I want to relax, I turn to my addiction*. From a psychodynamic perspective, poor attachment and trauma experiences may be factors in the sustaining of this pattern. From a strengths-focused viewpoint, a client can develop ways of meeting such needs and desires in rewarding ways, acceptable to a partner. However, this usually involves a time of grieving for the lost pleasure.

In Celia Walden's book, *Babysitting George*, the journalist writes about being with the notorious footballer, George Best, in the last days of his life. He explains to her that what people never understood is that alcohol gave him more pleasure than football or relationships. This may, of course, be partly rationalization, although it is also probably a valid admission. Often recovering addicts, whether the addiction is to alcohol, drugs, gambling or sex, have to accept that they are giving up something that has provided them with the best highs or feelings they have experienced in life. Some people are prepared to do this because of valuing something more than personal pleasure and satisfaction, such as the welfare of loved ones, self-respect, adherence to a faith, all of which can intrinsically involve existential and transpersonal considerations.

Regardless of Greg's motivations, it turned out that Anna would not allow him any more chances to change his life, at least not with her. Anna told the counsellor that in the previous session with Greg, she had felt numb when Greg talked about his latest behaviour with the young florist, even slightly bored. She had gone home and that night had a dream about being in a gelateria somewhere in Italy. A good-looking young man in a white shirt with slicked back black hair was serving ice-cream to a group of attractive women in colourful polka dot dresses and high-heeled shoes. The man was a conflated version of Greg and her father. She was sitting at a table in the shop, wearing a brown boiler suit, stirring a cup of coffee in a desultory fashion. In the dream she had wanted to get up out of the chair, walk out of the shop and change into some nicer clothes, but she was stuck to the chair.

Anna said that soon afterwards she packed her bags and moved in with a friend, enrolling on the MA in environmental studies that she was interested in. She told Greg that she wanted to end the relationship and put the florist business up for sale. She wanted to conduct the sale of the business and end the relationship with him amicably. They would both be free to see anybody they wanted.

Anna told the counsellor that Greg had phoned her the following night, obviously drunk and in tears, saying he could not live without her. Anna told Greg that she was not going to speak to him when he was drunk but, if he was desperate, he could phone the Samaritans. She texted him the number after she came off the phone. Anna explained how she was worried about Greg all night and could not get any sleep. That night she made the decision that even if Greg decided to take his own life, she could not rescue him from this. This was a watershed moment for Anna, as it brought back the memory of not being able to prevent her sister from dying. She told the counsellor that she had remembered his words that 'pain either makes people grow or shrink and no one adult can protect another from making the choice'. This allowed her to tolerate and resist the strong pull to rescue her partner. Subsequently, the counsellor saw both Anna and Greg separately on a number of occasions to help them adjust to and process the new reality; they were embarking on separate lives.

Conclusion

The clients I see in therapy are usually faced with choices that they do not like and are not prepared to make. Hence, they are stuck. Counselling can be viewed as a way of getting them unstuck. For Greg, he was not prepared to make the choice between the pleasure he gained from sexual interaction with women other than his partner, and a harmonious relationship with Anna and the continuation of their business. Anna did not want to choose between the hope that she could rescue Greg, and ending an unsatisfactory relationship which was causing her much pain. In the course of therapy, she was able to choose the latter. This meant her maturing: accepting that, like everyone, she could not control the choices, behaviour and destiny of other people in order to make life happy and safe. She could only attempt this for herself.

Practice points from this chapter

- There are pros and cons to providing therapy to partners as a couple and on a one-to-one basis
- It is important to consider whether counselling is adding to or detracting from safety when one partner is at risk of domestic abuse
- There are various ways to treat sexual addiction
- The three transactional ego states - adult, parent and child - can be utilized to advantage in couple counselling
- Learning about 'good' sex through tantric practices can be as important as clients trying to curtail 'bad' sex
- How partners use power, related to their tendencies to fight/flight/freeze, can be an important therapeutic insight
- Most couples eventually hit 'road blocks' in relationships about various issues, including sex. Overcoming these roadblocks is an important aspect of self-development
- Clients are usually faced with choices they do not like and are not prepared to make. Hence, they are stuck. Counselling can be viewed as a way of getting them unstuck

References

Barrett, D. (2010) *Supernormal stimuli: How primal urges overran their evolutionary purpose*. London and New York: W. W. Norton and Company, Inc.

Berne, E. (1961) *Transactional analysis in psychotherapy: A systematic individual and social psychiatry*. New York: Grove Press.

Birchard, T. (2015) *CBT for compulsive sexual behaviour: A guide for professionals*. London and New York: Routledge.

Carnes, P. (1992) *Don't call it love: Recovery from sexual addiction*. New York: Bantam.

Cherlin, A.J. (2009) *The marriage-go-round: The state of marriage and the family in America today*. New York: Alfred Knopf.

Flores, P.J. (2011) *Addiction as an attachment disorder*. New York: Jason Aronson.

Hall, P. (2012) *Understanding and treating sex addiction: A comprehensive guide for people who struggle with sex addiction and those who want to help them*. London and New York: Routledge.

Hall, P. (2019) *Sex addiction: A guide for couples and those who help them*. London and New York: Routledge.

Harris, A.H. (1970) *I'm OK you're OK*. London and Sydney, Pan Books.

Holmes, J. (1996) *Attachment, intimacy, autonomy: Using attachment theory in adult psychotherapy*. Nothdale, NJ: Jason Aronson.

Irvine, J. (1995) 'Reinventing perversion: sex addiction and cultural anxieties', *Journal of the History of Sexuality*, 5 (3): pp. 429-450.

Kohut, H. (1977) *The restoration of the self*. New York: International Universities Press.

Lorius, C. (1999) *Tantric sex: Making love last*. London: Thorsons (HarperCollins).

Schnarch, D. (2009) *Intimacy and desire: Awaken the passion in your relationship*. New York: Beaufort Books.

Smith, A. (2017) *Counselling male sexual offenders: A strengths-focused approach*. London: Routledge.

Thompson, D. (2012) *The fix*. London: Harper-Collins.

Volkow, N. and Li, T.K. (2015) 'The neuroscience of addiction', *Nature Neuroscience*, 8 (11): pp. 1429 – 30.

Walden, C. (2011) *Babysitting George*. London: Bloomsbury.

Ward, T., Mann, R.E. and Gannon, T.A. (2007) 'The good lives model of offender rehabilitation: Clinical implications', *Aggression and Violent Behaviour: A Review Journal*, 12: pp. 87-107.

PART 2

COUNSELLING PARTNERS WHERE THERE ARE CHILD PROTECTION SAFEGUARDING ISSUES

FIVE
EMILY

Introduction

Part two of this book depicts cases where partners of individuals who have sexually offended have to cope with child protection inquiries. In all the chapters in this second part of the text, the individual who has been accused or convicted of sexual offending poses some risk to children in the family home. Consequently, Children's Services expect the non-offending partner to play their part in safeguarding children from this risk. The non-abusing partner in the following case study, Emily, faces the common dilemma of wanting to remain in a relationship with a partner who has committed sexual offending on the internet. Such a choice is commonly perceived by Children's Services as indicative of a lack of ability to protect. Emily has not come to terms with this reality. Like many partners in her position, she is isolated, due to the stigma attached to sexual offending, and needs somebody to talk to. The chapter depicts how the counsellor attempts to enlarge Emily's perspective, both with regard to how she and her situation may be perceived by Children's Services, and what having good ability to protect might look like. What further complicates matters in this case is that the male counsellor finds himself attracted to his client, feeling rivalry with Emily's husband, Richard.

The common experience of a parent wanting to stay with an offending partner when there are child protection concerns

As noted in the introduction, it is a common misconception that all individuals who have sexually offended will inevitably re-offend: that they are like ticking time bombs ready to go off at some point in an uncertain future. Having said this, in my experience, counsellors and psychotherapists who do not have responsibility for child or public protection and who are primarily concerned with the welfare of their clients, have tendencies to underestimate any risk posed by their clients.

Social workers with a prime responsibility for child protection tend to have a more cautious view of risk. However, working as an expert witness in the family court arena, I see a lack of consistency between social workers in different areas. Often a case can take an entirely different trajectory when a new social worker is appointed, who sees the offender as more or less risky than their predecessor. Such differences seem as much to do with the professional's gut feelings about sex offending as any objective measure.

Some professionals take the view that if a person has crossed the boundary of committing a sexual offence, they should never be allowed to live with children again, as risk can never be ruled out. This is an understandable position that many would share. However, it is a moral value judgement rather than a clinical one based on balancing recognized risk and safety factors. If a social worker or other professional holds this view, it is liable to lead to 'confirmation bias' (Nickerson, 1998), where all emerging information about a case is interpreted in the light of the initial subjective view. Parents caught up in the child protection system pick up on this bias, and react negatively to it. Such negativity is then seen as wholly the parents' fault and as evidence of risk and lack of co-operation.

Confirmation bias, of course, occurs the other way around, leading to 'professional dangerousness' (Dale, 1986), with workers taking an overly positive view of a case. Concerning emerging data contradicting the initial sanguine hypothesis is minimized or ignored. Consequently, signs of risk are not adequately explored or responded to.

The ethical or moral position that sex offenders should never live with children does not engage with the reality that offenders are not all the same, having committed very different sexual crimes. In addition, this position does not take into account how the child protection system works in the UK. Research suggests that many convicted sex offenders return to live with their partners and children, or state a wish to do so. Many others move into new family situations.

The above ideological stance also tends to privilege some risks at the expense of others. In many situations there are no 'good' options, just 'less bad' ones, and it is often difficult to decide what the 'less bad' ones are. If somebody commits a sexual crime, risk of sexual offending can never be ruled out. However, the cost to families by removing a low risk but otherwise well-functioning parent - family disruption, loss of stability, fewer resources, the grief involved in children being separated from parents, the vagaries of the care system – is usually significant. The harm caused by family disintegration tends to be less visible, more subterranean, less emotive than that of disclosed sexual offending but may cause, in some cases, as much suffering. Hence there are no easy choices. Working in a child protection context is usually about weighing and managing different sorts of risk, rather than pursuing the fantasy of obviating all risk.

Non-abusing partners face significant challenges when a partner is accused, arrested or convicted for a sexual offence. The situation inevitably has a significant negative impact on the non-abusing partner and other loved ones. Their needs are often ignored or overlooked. They experience overwhelming emotions and conflicts within child protection investigations which they find difficult and intrusive. Child protection investigations are necessarily intrusive. The Court and decision makers need to know what has occurred in the private life of a family and couple, in order to make informed judgements about the future. Professionals should simply acknowledge how tough it is for parents to go through this process and cut them some slack when clients' responses are not always as rational as they might be.

When a father, for instance, has to leave the family home due to concerns about risk, the mother-child relationship is often put under considerable stress. The child picks up on the crisis in the family, misses the absent parent and acts out. The remaining parent's exhaustion, insecurity, loss of confidence and isolation, following a partner's arrest – and simply having to cope on their own - further undermine family resources.

Mothers, rather than fathers, usually have to bear the felt indignity of child protection investigations and interventions, if the father has been removed from the family or is in prison. Social workers usually have far more contact with mothers for the above reasons and sometimes because a non-offending partner is deemed easier to deal with than an offending one, with social work staff not sure how to talk to the offender about his sexual offending. The professional community is also often ambivalent in its approach to mothers and partners. There can be a prejudice against individuals who choose to remain with partners who have sexually offended. The subconscious reasoning can include:

- Once a sex offender always a sex offender
- Why would anybody want to live with someone who poses a sexual risk to children?
- 'Good' mothers don't get involved with 'bad' men
- 'Good' mothers would know what poses a risk to their children
- She must have known he was sexually offending

A sentiment that often appears in child protection reports is 'Can the mother prioritize the needs of the children above her own needs for a relationship with her partner?' Undoubtedly, there are parents who seek to meet their own needs - whether for drugs, alcohol, revenge, excitement, a quiet life, emotional and sexual fulfilment - at the expense of the ongoing welfare of their children. Choosing to live with a risky partner, and burying one's head in the sand about the danger they pose to children, might be an example of this.

However, there are also non-abusing partners who would argue, legitimately in my view, that to break off all contact with a parent who has committed a sexual offence, if he has been assessed as a low risk, might not be in the interests of the children, would profoundly and irrevocably de-stabilize the family unit and deprive the children of what has, in many cases, proved to be a positive relationship with a parent. This is especially the case with internet sex offenders, many of whom, apart from their online offending, have led a pro-social life in the main and have provided good or 'good enough' parenting to their children.

Professionals and others who find the above perspective difficult to come to terms with, remain stuck in a fundamentalist position where it is difficult or impossible to view a person who has sexually offended as having good qualities and being able to straightforwardly love their children. Such positive attributes tend to be perceived as merely manifestations of the grooming process or faking, in order to take people in. Such manipulation definitely occurs with higher risk sex offenders, but by no means with all individuals who have committed a sexual crime.

In addition to the above challenges, the non-abusing partner is frequently concerned about the mental well-being of a spouse who has just been arrested on suspicion of sexual offending. Not all sexual offences are committed by males. Rates of female sexual offending seem to be increasing, but they are still the minority of individuals convicted of sexual crime (Cortoni et al., 2010). There is a high rate of suicide for males accused and convicted of sexual offending because of the extreme social stigma attached to this particular crime. The rate of suicide is particularly high amongst internet sexual offenders (Hoffer and Shelton, 2013). Many internet offenders have had no previous contact with the police and are afraid of going to prison. Men from all social classes commit internet offences, but a significant proportion are from the professional classes, and suffer a particularly painful fall from grace. In extremis, men arrested for sexual offending can think that their family will be better off without them and will be spared the social stigma of a father or a partner being a local, or in some cases a national, media story. Hence, as well as having to cope with their own set of extremely difficult circumstances, the non-offending partner has to cope with the worry that a loved one may harm himself or end his own life.

Often the non-offending partner is conflicted. They feel betrayed, humiliated and angry that, through no fault of their own, they and the family have been placed in such a dire situation. They often feel unable to fully express this anger because, as explained above, they may be worried about the welfare of the loved one. It is a fact of life that people often do not stop loving and caring about somebody because they have behaved badly, no matter how badly. Human bonds tend to be strong. Frequently, the non-offending partner only feels free to express their anger when the crisis has stabilized and they know that the loved one has avoided prison or survived it, is not suicidal and is coping with losses to career and social standing. This is the case with Margaret, featured in Chapter 1.

Parents are often seen as being in denial about their partner's offending. However, denial can be seen as a normative defence mechanism that allows us to protect ourselves from something that is painful and distressing. Denial becomes problematic, in the case of non-offending partners, when they remain in this state. An analogy can be made with the 'grief journey' (Kubler-Ross, 1969). Kubler-Ross posited that five stages can be noted in the grief journey:

- Stage 1: Denial
- Stage 2: Anger
- Stage 3: Bargaining
- Stage 4: Depression
- Stage 5: Acceptance

In her final book (Kubler-Ross and Kessler, 2005) Kubler-Ross states that these five stages were never meant to suggest that grief or emotions can be neatly packaged. Each individual has their own different journey, completed over a different time span, ending up in a different destination. However, the model usefully conceptualizes loss as a process with some commonalities, which takes time to work through. When a person discovers that their partner has been sexually offending, this involves all sorts of profound losses, as hopefully the case studies in this book illustrate. These include loss of trust, innocence, friends, family, finance, social status, privacy, identity ('good' mother), and loss of future dreams. It takes time for people to process these profound changes. This can take the form of a non-offending partner using denial as a coping strategy to deal with the impact and consequences of a loved one having sexually offended. Anger is often displaced onto intervening child protection professionals, with partners allying themselves against a common enemy. This is often easier for the non-offending partner than directing the anger against the offender whom they love and whose mental health may be fragile because of the crisis of being caught. Bargaining occurs as the non-abusing partner battles child protection professionals about the degree to which their loved one is a risk to children. Depression sets in as the consequences of having a relationship with a sex offender unfold. Acceptance of the situation, and sometimes of the risk that a partner poses or is perceived by professionals to pose, is the final stage in this journey of risk acceptance and risk awareness.

Some partners negotiate this journey more easily than others. It is possible that certain individuals will never reach the point where they can genuinely accept that their partner poses a risk to children which they will be expected to play their part in managing. When this is the case, family reunification is not likely to take place. However, some non-offending partners do reach this point, although they will often need the assistance of professionals to raise their awareness of risk.

A repeated pattern is that child protection social workers make an assessment of a partner's ability to protect at the early stages of this journey, when the individual's offending has first been discovered, and when the non-offending partner is apt to be at their most defensive, hoping that if they say loudly enough or often enough that their loved one is no risk to children, then the authorities will believe them. Understanding that risk awareness is a process can prevent premature judgements.

Case study: Emily

Emily (36) is married to Richard (49), a history professor. They met when she was his PhD student. They have been married for 15 years. After completing her PhD, Emily decided to postpone her own academic career, remaining at home to look after their two children: Jake (8) and Chloe (13).

Richard has recently been arrested for downloading sexual images of children, the majority of which (found so far) feature girls, aged between 13 and 18. The police say that it could be anything between 3 and 9 months before all of Richard's computer equipment is investigated and he is charged with an offence - they are inundated with similar cases to process. Meanwhile, Children's Services have said he must leave the family home, or the children will be taken into care. Richard is allowed to see his children at a contact centre for two hours per week, supervised by professional contact workers. Unlike in some such cases, Emily has not been allowed to supervise contact between her husband and children because the case social worker considers neither parent takes risk seriously, both maintaining that Richard poses no risk to his own children. Emily and Richard are shocked and indignant about the power of the state to intervene in family affairs. Richard likens the way he has been treated as akin to 'a medieval witch hunt', a view he has expressed in child protection meetings. He is perceived by the newly qualified social worker as arrogant and dismissive, with the social worker struggling to understand, given the circumstances, why Emily wants to remain married to Richard and why she wants him to return to the family home. Richard is presently living in rented accommodation. He has been suspended by the University, until he is charged and convicted. Like many internet offenders, Richard intends to plead guilty because he knows material evidence of his offending will be found on his computer. He realizes that it is only a matter of time before he is dismissed from the University and understands that he will never be allowed to teach again or to work with young or vulnerable people.

As for Emily, she was part of a small group of three close female friends, all of whom have children similar in ages to her children. Emily had considered these friends closer than family. Her parents died in a car accident when she was a teenager and she has little in common with her two brothers, who live at the opposite end of the country. Two of these friends have cut all contact with her and the third friend, Sally, says that she wants to continue her relationship with Emily but, at the moment, does not want to see Richard.

Before Richard's internet offending came to light, Emily had planned to restart her academic career, now the children are getting older. The couple's sex life had been fine, if routine, although it had tailed off in the last few years. Emily considered this normal and was, on the whole, content with her lot. Or she had been until the Tuesday morning when a bomb exploded in her life, a bomb that had been silently ticking away without her knowledge.

Early dynamics in the counselling process

Emily parked her Toyota Prius in the community centre car park. It was an early summer day, and the prosperous Cotswold town was looking its best. From her window, the counsellor saw a group of well-dressed young mothers pushing pushchairs towards the trendy coffee shops at the top of the hill. Smart German cars glided up and down the tree-lined street, with its Georgian houses. A woman dressed in the latest lycra jogged along the pavement beneath the window.

Emily looked like a bohemian version of the mothers pushing their prams. She had travelled from a prestigious university city nearby, being unable to find a local counsellor specializing in child protection issues of this sort. She sat down in the counselling room and smiled nervously. The counsellor made small talk to relax her, asking how her journey had been and if she had found the place OK.

Emily replied that the journey had been fine, despite being caught up in rush hour traffic. She looked out of the window in a desultory fashion. Head turned away from the counsellor, she said, 'I might end up crying, you know', and on cue she burst into tears. The counsellor remained silent, allowing her to sob for a time, before offering her a tissue from the obligatory box of Kleenex sitting on the table nearby.

Emily blew her nose and laughed, revealing a set of beautiful, uniform teeth: 'This is a good flipping start, isn't it?' The counsellor discerned the remains of a working-class accent - Yorkshire, he guessed. She wore no make-up, had freckles and luxuriant red hair, worn long. The counsellor felt attracted to her. Emily had recounted the history of her relationship when she made the appointment and it was easy to see the bright, unworldly student, bowled over by an older, sophisticated lecturer, and the lecturer being equally bowled over by her.

Emily explained how Richard had always been a gentle husband and father. One of the things she had initially liked about him was his shyness. 'Sort of naive for his age, a refreshing change from the jerks' she had known when she was in her 'crazy stage' as an under-graduate. The counsellor picked up the glass by the side of him. Taking a sip of the water, he reflected on his initial thoughts about his client's past: so much for his hypothesis about a sophisticated academic seducing a naive student. No, it had been the other way round.

The thought that she had seduced an older man aroused him. He was now the older man.

An imaginary future flashed before him. A passionate affair with a younger client. A trip to Paris, or perhaps somewhere less obvious like Trieste. Afternoons spent looking at Modern Art. He would explain Jung. She would be fascinated.

The counsellor felt ashamed, suddenly worried that, by some unex-plained process, his client was able to read his mind. He hoped he was not blushing. A different future flashed before him. His marriage over.

Being disciplined, struck off the register. Having to drive a cab for a living. He told himself not to be stupid and to concentrate on his client.

Sexual attraction between a therapist and client is a well-documented phenomenon (Birchard, 2015). Good practice when this dynamic surfaces includes maintaining the following boundaries. Most are common sense and applicable to all clients:

- The counsellor should always maintain professional boundaries
- The counsellor should not physically comfort a client by touching them or hugging
- The counsellor should not see a client outside of the session
- The counsellor should not informally communicate with a client through phone or email
- The counsellor should not discuss their attraction with the client, as this is usually a come-on, dressed up as therapeutic congruence
- We can all have fleeting feelings of attraction for clients, but any enduring feelings should be taken to supervision and not, as noted above, discussed with the client
- The counsellor should consider with their supervisor whether any attraction towards a client is hindering therapeutic progress, and if and how this can be ameliorated
- If necessary, a change of counsellor may be appropriate
- Clients usually come to counselling in a stage of emotional vulnerability. Any breaching of the above boundaries constitutes an abuse of professional power

In this situation, the counsellor thankfully did not cross any professional boundaries with Emily. However, his attraction to his client remained, resulting in his feeling rivalrous with her husband, Richard. At a later stage in the chapter, part of a supervision session is illustrated, in which the counsellor discusses these issues with his supervisor. But for now, the focus returns to the client, and her grievances against Children's Services.

Common tensions between the non-offending partner's and Children's Services' perception of concerns

> *Emily:* I don't understand what they keep going on about. I know that he's done wrong, but there's never been any indication that Richard has harmed the children. The kids love him, for goodness' sake. They go on about Richard posing a risk, but I know he would never harm his own children.

A full discussion of how to assess the risk of sexual offending is beyond the scope of this book. However, risk of sexual offending is usually conceptualized and expressed as being part of a dynamic continuum. How sexual risk is assessed has been comprehensively expanded upon by Beech and Ward (amongst others) in their seminal article (2004). A more updated discussion of sexual risk is provided by Wills and Wills (2021).

Risk assessors have various ways of talking about risk. Some use the language of 'high', 'medium' and 'low' risk. Others adopt 'highly likely', 'likely', 'unlikely', when considering whether a person will sexually offend. Any competent risk assessor, however, should address the likely level of harm and to whom, if risk were to materialize, as well as factors likely to decrease and increase risk.

Generally, once a person has committed a sexual offence in the UK, a number of criteria have to be satisfied before the person will be allowed to live with or to have unsupervised contact with a child again. The following generally has to be the case:

- The offending parent is assessed as low risk to the child/children in question
- The victim is almost always not a child in the current family
- It is in the interests of the child/children for the offending parent to have contact
- The child (if old enough to express an opinion) wants a relationship with the offending parent

- The non-offending partner accepts there is a risk and is assessed as being able to reasonably protect children from that risk

I usually provide the above information to offenders and non-offending partners. Frequently, parents caught up in the child protection system are unclear about how the system works. Hence, I explain what is expected of them by the system. In my previous book (Smith, 2017: 53-54), I outline what is expected of an offending parent, with regard to safeguarding children and reducing their risk. I will reiterate this information for the sake of clarity:

- The longer there is an absence of sexual re-offending or allegations of sexual abuse, the less child protection professionals will worry about the risk of re-offending
- Whilst you do not have to admit to sexual offending or say you pose a risk, it is necessary to genuinely acknowledge that others have legitimate concerns which need to be addressed
- Rather than being preoccupied with why life is not as you would want it, focusing on everything you can do to change the situation
- Understanding the factors (including your life history) which resulted in your current situation
- Understanding the thoughts, behaviour and situations to avoid in order to make future sexual offending and allegations less likely
- Understanding the impact and consequences of sexual offending on victims and loved ones
- Establishing a satisfying, safe life where you don't have to resort to destructive behaviour to meet needs and desires
- If you remain in a relationship with a partner, developing a relationship in which you are open and transparent and accountable as regards your behaviour
- If Children's Services require your partner to monitor your

risk with regard to children, doing everything you can to make this as easy as possible for them

- Negotiating a *Safety Plan*, consisting of *Signs of Safety* that you are living a constructive and safe life, *Signs of Risk* that you may be going down a pathway which could cause harm to others or yourself, and agreeing *Responses to Emerging Signs of Risk* which could be implemented if things started to go wrong
- Agreeing that this *Safety Plan* can be shared with significant others, in order to freely make yourself accountable, so you can be supported in living an offence-free life

As for the non-offending partner, it is constructive to empathize with the feelings behind the grievance, but not collude with the client. If the counsellor joins the client in bemoaning the powers that be, this is unlikely to help in the long term. Even if Children's Services appear to be heavy-handed and risk averse (and this is usually a matter of perspective), the client still has to deal with 'what is' and it is important for the counsellor to help the client make the best of it.

> *Counsellor:* OK, you say that Children's Services think Richard poses a risk to the children, and you disagree with this.
> *Emily:* Yeah, the social worker is just a kid. She's newly qualified and has never had a child of her own … she knows nothing about my family. She's only talked to Richard once, outside of a formal meeting. She seems scared stiff of putting a foot wrong - she sees risk everywhere.
> *Counsellor:* How do you feel when you meet her?
> *Emily:* As if she thinks I'm an idiot for staying with Richard. She keeps on saying 'he' rather than Richard, as if she can't bear to say his name … and the worst thing is, now I feel afraid to say anything that might come across as bolshie, in case they take the kids off me. I never realized the power of the fucking state in this country.

Counsellor: It must feel as if you're completely disempowered in the situation, and am I right that you've never felt in this position before?

Emily: That's right – fucking Social Services!

Counsellor: You're in a tough spot. What do you think the social worker expects from you?

Emily: To leave Richard.

Counsellor: Anything else? What would she want you to do if you stick to your guns, and remain with him?

Emily: She goes on about being risk aware. But I don't really know what she means.

Counsellor: OK, imagine two mothers sitting in the chairs over there (the counsellor nods in the direction of two chairs placed against the wall). Both mothers have partners who have sexually offended on the internet, much like Richard. Each of them has children whom they love very much. Mother 1 takes up the following position. She says that if she ever thought that her husband posed a risk to the children, she would end the relationship with him. She maintains that he has never harmed the children and that fantasy - viewing indecent images of children on the internet - is different from sexually abusing a child, especially one's own child, in real life. She says that professionals do not know her husband like she does. She thinks that if she says all this often enough and loud enough, the social worker will be convinced by her arguments. She says that she doesn't have to know about how sexual abuse occurs in families because this just wouldn't happen in her home. She is an able mother and knows how to look after her own children, for goodness' sake! Mother 1 looks at all the reasons why her husband is unlikely to pose a risk to their children, but blanks out all the reasons why he may pose a risk.

Emily: Are you saying that's me?

Counsellor: Well, let's hold on to that one, while I describe Mother 2. Mother 2 loves her children and her husband as much as Mother 1. She also says that she doesn't think her

husband would sexually abuse their children and has seen no indication of this. But she adds, 'I would say this wouldn't I, because I'm emotionally involved with him, and we never want to think bad things about people we love'. She takes the view that in order to protect her children to the best of her ability, she needs to take on board that professionals are more likely to be objective. They consider that if a person has viewed sexual images of children online, he must pose some risk to children he meets in 'real' life, including his own children with whom he has regular, intimate contact. Mother 2 says to Children's Services that she wants to know all about why people sexually offend on the internet, the impact this has on victims, and how sexual abuse typically takes place in the family home. She reasons that if she knows all about this, then she would be better able to identify emerging signs of risk and respond to these signs of risk if and when they materialize. (The counsellor pauses and looks at his client). Emily, if you put yourself in the shoes of child protection professionals, who would you be most convinced can protect their children, Mother 1 or Mother 2?
Emily: Mother 2.
Counsellor: (Looking towards the two chairs again). Emily, what chair do you think you are sitting in: the chair occupied by Mother 1, or the chair occupied by Mother 2?
Emily: (Sheepishly) Damn it! I've been sitting in chair 1, haven't I?
Counsellor: Which chair do you want to be sitting in?
Emily: Chair 2.

The above exercise can be undertaken through drawing some chairs on a piece of paper or some other image that illustrates the two above positions. The exercise can also be completed using some other imaginative medium a therapist may come up with. The value of the exercise is that it creates objective space in which the client can view how she may be being perceived by others. The exercise can be highly effective in shifting a client's position.

Counsellor: OK, you want to sit in chair 2. Let's look at what this would mean and the potential cost of this.

Often clients can be persuaded to take a course of action without weighing up the likely costs, whereas good ideas come with an emotional price tag if they are to be adopted. Motivation is more likely to be sustained if the client can be helped to weigh up the pros and cons of any course of action before taking it. From a strengths-focused perspective, the most effective way for a counsellor to do this is to remain fairly relaxed and neutral. If the counsellor is too invested in a particular outcome, no matter how sensible and positive, this can easily tip over into paternalistic prodding to 'do the right thing'. This is usually counterproductive, relying too much on the counsellor's commitment rather than the client's motivation. It can also produce a parent-child dynamic: the client (child) resisting the advice-giving counsellor (parent).

Providing a non-abusing partner (NOP) with choices at the start of the safeguarding counselling process

Counsellor: OK, would it be helpful if I explained what Children's Services might expect from you, if they considered that you had good ability to protect?
Emily: Go ahead.

The counsellor proceeds to provide Emily with the following information about what good ability to protect generally looks like. The forthcoming chapters of the book will go into detail about how counsellors and therapists can help clients achieve these outcomes.

- Evidence of sustained compliance with child protection agreements
- The NOP being able to identify and explain if, how and why she failed to protect in the past

- The NOP being able to describe discrepancies between the victim's account and the perpetrator's account
- The NOP being able to describe any grooming behaviour used by their partner when they committed the offence
- The NOP being able to describe signs of risk
- The NOP being able to identify factors which are likely to increase or decrease risk
- The NOP being able to describe how they are implementing and maintaining safe boundaries and ground rules in the house
- Witnessed evidence that the NOP can openly talk to the partner about convictions, allegations or risk issues, without feeling intimidated, embarrassed or protective of their partner
- The NOP being able to describe what they would do if signs of risk emerge
- Witnessed evidence that the NOP can tell the partner to their face what they would do if signs of risk emerged

Counsellor: How does that sound?

Emily: Heavy, but doable.

Counsellor: OK, have you really thought about this? If Richard is assessed as being a low risk to his children and allowed to return home to you and the children, you will have a responsibility to monitor any emerging signs of risk, and to maintain boundaries. These boundaries will probably include you being responsible for all intimate care tasks with the children. Richard will not be allowed to be alone with the children overnight or alone with any of your children's friends, especially teenage girls as your children get older. You will have to have the passwords of all Richard's online devices and check his history from time to time. This can be a difficult emotional juggling act, trying to maintain respect for someone, while having to monitor his behaviour.

Emily: Doesn't sound easy, but I think we could manage.

Counsellor: OK, would it be helpful to consider the pros and cons of remaining with Richard?
Emily: Well, the cons would be not knowing if I could ever trust him again. And, of course, the kids' friends finding out about his offending, and the children getting bullied … and checking up on him all the time … I wouldn't like that.
Counsellor: Anything else?
Emily: If Richard is allowed to come home; we've decided to move to another town. Richard won't be able to work as a lecturer anymore, so he'll have to find some other job. I'm not really worried about that, as Richard can turn his hand to anything – he's an extremely able and clever man. We'd get quite a bit for our house, and we thought we might move to somewhere in the country where houses are cheaper, and set up a market garden business for ourselves. We would both like that and the children and I would see a lot more of him. But that's getting onto the pros, isn't it?

The counsellor could see that this future was feasible for the couple and recognized in himself a hint of dismay. It was when she said in such admiring tones that her husband was an 'extremely able and clever man' who could 'turn his hand to anything' that the counsellor felt the stab of jealousy.

Counsellor: And the pros of remaining with Richard?

The counsellor congratulated himself on his neutral, slightly upbeat tone.

Emily: Well, we would be together as a family. We have always been happy together, especially before Richard became really successful, with his books and a promotion to Head of Department. As he got more in demand, the children and I saw a lot less of him. He was always attentive, though, when he was around. Both Chloe and Jake adore him. They would be devastated if they lost their father.

The counsellor self-observed feeling rivalrous with his client's husband, particularly as Richard seemed to be more successful than the counsellor, in conventional career terms.

Counsellor: (With disguised irritation) Well, the children wouldn't exactly lose him, would they? He just wouldn't be allowed to live with them.
Emily: (Looking sharply at the counsellor) Great!

The counsellor immediately felt bad about his last cheap shot, and recovered enough to affirm how it sounded as if Emily and her husband had a relationship worth preserving, and seemed to have come up with a viable plan for the future. He added that if Emily remained sitting in chair 2 (see above), and was prepared to work in counselling to become more risk aware (as described above), then there would be a greater possibility that Children's Services might agree for the family to be reunited, although he (the counsellor) could not guarantee this. Emily said that she definitely wanted to become more risk aware, have a more conciliatory attitude towards the case social worker, and work towards these goals in future counselling sessions.

Below is a selection of strengths-focused questions which may be useful when talking to clients about their partner's offending, and related child protection issues. As always, these questions should be adapted to the personal style of the therapist, with the therapist using their clinical judgement about how and when to ask such questions:

- This must have been a really tough time for you; how have you coped so far?
- What is the most difficult thing about this situation?
- What would it help to talk about?
- What do you want from me?

- What has been the impact of this on your partner (use first name)?
- What has been the impact on the children?
- What support could others possibly give to the family?
- What would be the pros and the cons of telling people who could support you at this time, about the child protection concerns?
- People are worried about your partner posing a risk. How do you see the situation?
- What do you think professionals are worried about your partner doing?
- On a scale of 0 to 10, if 0 is no risk and 10 is very high risk, where would you put your partner at the moment?
- Where would your partner put themselves on the scale?
- Where would others/different professionals put them on the scale?
- Why do you think people have different views? Can you say how the different people see it?
- What have you done to help make the children safe, since all this came about?
- Are there any other safeguards that can be put in place?
- When have been the happiest times in the family/with your partner? What was happening at these times?
- What are the good things about your relationship with your partner?
- What are the not-so-good things about your relationship with your partner?
- Have you ever felt intimidated or frightened by your partner?
- How have you coped with your partner or anybody else trying to frighten or control you?
- If professionals were no longer concerned about the risk to your children, what sort of things would have happened to make this the case?
- Can I make some suggestions?

- What do you think would be expected of your partner?
- What would be expected of you?
- If you could have your life as you would ideally want it, what would it be like?
- What would be some steps towards bringing about this new life?
- What would be the signs that the children were safe?
- What would be the signs that the children were at risk?
- How could you respond if signs of risk were starting to emerge?
- How do you feel about the restrictions put on contact with the children?
- Are there times when you think it may be difficult to stick to these contact arrangements?
- Can I share with you some common challenges? (i.e. times of stress and loneliness, times of celebration), when it comes to sticking to child protection agreements?
- What could you do to cope with these difficult times?
- How does the prospect of life without your partner seem to you?
- What are the pros and cons of staying with or leaving your partner?

Supervision Session

The counsellor went on to work with Emily productively, helping her to enhance her safeguarding ability. However, after the above session, he took his feelings of attraction towards his client and jealousy towards her husband to supervision. With the help of his supervisor, the counsellor gained understanding that, as a middle-aged man, he was coming to terms with some of his own life choices. He had always been something of a perfectionist, and anxious about getting things right. He would study hard as a teenager, but then go to pieces in exams. He would try to know everything about a subject, but never developed the knack of focusing on the core pieces of information that really mattered. Consequently, he never got the grades he was expected to get at A Level, and did not go on to university. This had deeply disappointed him and he had turned his back on the world of study, although he always loved learning. Instead, he devoted himself to public service jobs, gravitating to the care sector. He had then studied to be a counsellor, deliberately choosing a course that majored upon experiential learning and submitting course work, rather than sitting exams.

He was married to a bright woman he loved very much, but she was sporty and practical and did not share his love of reading and learning. He had from time to time fantasized about having gone to university and become an English Literature lecturer, and having relationships with bohemian women like Emily.

Supervisor: So, let's look at this. How do you know that you would have liked a bohemian partner, the sort of woman your client appears to be?

Counsellor: I don't know, I've always been attracted to those sorts of women, I suppose.

Supervisor: How would it be if you didn't have that thought?

Counsellor: (Laughs) I'd probably be more content, and not fancy my client.

Supervisor: Well, that's one option, isn't it? You know the score. Replace that thought with a more constructive one as in CBT, or mindfully observe the thought with detached compassion until it dissipates and another thought form takes its place. Right?

Counsellor: Right.

Supervisor: Let's take this from another angle. (The supervisor takes off her glasses, looking thoughtful). How long have we known each other?

Counsellor: Twelve years, about?

Supervisor: In all that time, I've noticed that what seems to make you happy is when things are in order. We've talked enough times about you hanging loose more and accepting a bit

more randomness in your life, and giving yourself and others a break. But you know we can't fundamentally change who we are. Maybe Emily is bohemian and maybe she's not, and you are projecting all this stuff onto her. But how do you think you would enjoy a bohemian lifestyle and the, well, the lack of predictability and order?
Counsellor: (Laughs) I would probably hate it.
Supervisor: Sometimes in the second half of life our shadow demands more attention, saying, 'hey matey, how about this part of our personality that you haven't integrated?' Maybe Emily and the lifestyle she describes, or what she represents to you, is a projected part of yourself calling for more attention.

The counsellor went away and reflected on his supervisor's insight, and decided that a bohemian academic life was largely a fantasy that would not suit him in reality. He liked predictability and getting practical tasks done with his wife, rather than just thinking about things. He also knew that the pressure of writing articles and books would drive him crazy. But there was a glamour in the fantasy that he knew was telling him something. The counsellor was not a religious man, but he asked anything out there - the Universe or his subconscious perhaps - to tell him what he was missing in his life, and then left the matter to percolate. A couple of weeks later, he woke up excited. The idea came into his mind of studying literature through the Open University, but for the pure pleasure of it, putting no pressure on himself to pass any exams, and seeing it as personal growth to take such a relaxed, purely pleasure-loving attitude to it.

Exploring with his supervisor what his feelings and thoughts about his client were telling him and not repressing them as a shame management strategy, had opened up an exciting new venture in his life. The exploration process had also released increased compassion for his client and a genuine commitment to want the best for her, whatever Emily decided this was.

Unlike the previous cases in Part 1 of this book, Emily came to counselling because of child protection issues in the family, following her husband being convicted of sexual offending on the internet. Rather than just allying himself with the client against the state, the counsellor, despite his complicated reaction to the client, was able to provide her with information concerning what the state (in terms of child protection professionals) would likely want from Emily and her husband, if the family had any chance of being reunited. Counsellors and therapists will have different views about undertaking this sort of safeguarding role in a counselling setting. However, in my view, not providing this sort of information to non-offending partners and other loved ones can leave them in a fog, and deprive them of the ability to make informed choices about a possible way forward.

Practice points from this chapter

- Take any continuing sexual transference or counter transference issues with a client to supervision and explore compassionately
- Maintain strict boundaries (as depicted above) if you feel any sexual attraction to a client
- Empathize with clients' feelings but do not collude with them against Social Services or other professionals
- Enable clients to constructively deal with what is
- When there are child protection issues, it can help clients make informed decisions if they understand what is expected of them and a partner or loved one who has sexually offended, by child protection professionals
- Help the client to explore the possible costs of any choice or change of behaviour, as well as the likely benefits

References

Beech, A.R and Ward. T. (2004) 'The integration of etiology and risk in sexual offenders: A theoretical framework', *Journal of Aggression and Violent Behavior*, 10(1): pp. 31-63. Birchard, T. (2015) *CBT for compulsive sexual behaviour: A guide for professionals*. East Sussex and New York: Routledge.

Cortoni, F., Hanson, R.K. and Coache, M. (2010) 'The recidivism rates of female sexual offenders are low: A meta-analysis', *Sexual Abuse*, 22 (4): pp.387-401.

Dale, P. (1986) *Dangerous families: Assessment and treatment of child abuse*. London: Tavistock.

Hoffer. T.A. and Shelton, J.L.E. (2013) *Suicide among child sex offenders*. New York: Springer.

Kubler-Ross, E. (1969) *On death and dying: What the dying have to teach doctors, nurses, clergy & their own families*. New York: Scribner (Simon and Schuster).

Kubler-Ross, E. and Kessler, D. (2005) *On grief and grieving: Finding the meaning of grief through the five stages of loss*. New York: Simon and Schuster.

Nickerson, R.S. (1998) 'Confirmation bias: A ubiquitous phenomenon in many guises', *Review of General Psychology*, 2 (2): pp. 175-220.

Wills, D. and Wills. A. (2021) *A practical guide to working with sex offenders*. London and Philadelphia: Jessica Kingsley Publishers

SIX

SIAN

Introduction

The following case study is written to provide a further insight into the experience of a non-offending partner who, unlike Emily in the previous chapter, is disadvantaged in many ways. Emily attended counselling of her own accord but Sian is pressurized to attend counselling, rather than freely choosing to do so. The very different life experiences of the women in the two case studies will hopefully provide an idea of the diverse range of issues related to this client group. Sian has agreed to attend counselling because her children have been removed into temporary foster care, and she wants them to be returned to her. For this to happen, she must undertake therapeutic safeguarding work in order to become more risk aware and better able to protect. A main theme of this chapter is how a history of abuse can undermine a person's ability to parent protectively. The female therapist working with Sian is a caring, highly responsible person. As such, she initially finds Sian challenging to work with, coming in and out of being judgemental about her client's (from the counsellor's perspective) feckless and irresponsible behaviour.

Assessing a non-offending partner's ability to protect

The ability to protect children from risk posed by a partner and loved one can sometimes seem like a nebulous concept. How can one know if the non-offending partner of a person posing a sexual risk, or any other risk, is protective or not? Below are some questions which can aid decision making about this matter. Most of the questions, or variants of the questions, can also be applied to other loved ones of individuals posing a risk to children:

- Does the partner acknowledge, or are they willing to accept professional opinion, that there is a risk to children from which they need to be protected?
- Is the partner fearful?
- Is the partner dependent?
- Is the partner isolated?
- Can the partner accept that the child's disclosure is/may be true?
- Can the partner remain supportive to the child even if they doubt the truth of the disclosure?
- Can the partner encourage the child to be open?
- Can the partner engender the child's trust?
- Can the partner consistently prioritize the child's wellbeing?
- Are there secure and affectionate bonds between the partner and the children?
- Can the partner offer stable and appropriate boundaries in the home?
- Does the partner have an adequate appreciation of the child's needs?
- Are the children prospering emotionally, socially and educationally?
- Did the partner have a stable upbringing?
- Is the partner's life free from emotional, physical and sexual abuse issues?
- Has the partner been able to attain social capital, education,

occupation, stable family relationships, constructive social relationships?

- Has the partner been able to maintain non-abusive, non-exploitative relationships with partners?
- Has the partner been able to flee abusive relationships?
- Has the partner been able to live independently without a partner?
- Is there a discrepancy between the partner's intellectual appreciation of risk and their emotional capacity to respond to risk?
- Is the partner's inability to protect temporary, due to grooming on the part of the offender?
- Is the partner's inability to protect due to grooming, compounded by historical deficits which are difficult to change?

Being a victim of abuse and ability to protect

There is research to indicate that partners who have suffered attachment and trauma problems are more likely to have difficulty in protecting children from harm (Bentovim et al., 2009). Hence, in order to assess ability to protect, and to enhance protective ability, such dysfunctional issues in a person's background have to be considered. There is a tension in safeguarding work between pathologizing a parent, and not overlooking psychological deficits related to past experiences which may make it difficult to protect children from the risk of harm.

When conducting safeguarding work there is always the danger of shifting responsibility for risk management away from the offender (the source of risk) onto the non-offending parent. Expecting the non-offending partner to monitor, identify and respond to signs of risk can exacerbate an existing co-dependency dynamic in a couple's relationship, as discussed in the first section of the book. However, on a pragmatic level, the consequences of a parent's decision to remain with an offending partner mean that, from a child protection perspective, the non-offending parent will be expected by Children's Services to play an important part in managing risk within the family setting, if there is any chance of family reunification taking place. This said, the main focus and responsibility for family safety should rest on the internal controls of the offender.

If a non-offending partner has suffered abuse or disempowerment, this can distort understanding of what is normative. Often individuals become caught up in cycles of abuse, going from one abusive situation and partner to another. If there is an intergenerational culture of abuse in a person's background this can erode the sense of what is acceptable - the abnormal becomes the normal – with the person having been socialized into tolerance of maltreatment or loose, aggressive and sexual boundaries.

The last thing victims of sexual abuse usually want is for their own children to become victims of sexual crime. Many victims of sexual abuse go on to live constructive lives, parenting children well. Nevertheless, in some cases the traumatic impact of abuse – emotional, physical and sexual - can lead to low self-esteem and self-medication through substance misuse. Whereas some victims of sexual abuse shy away from sex, others respond by developing promiscuous lifestyles. Experiencing the power to choose to have sex when and how they want to, and with whom, can seem like a corrective to having being placed in the disempowered victim position, having little or no choice in sexual decision making. Victims of sexual abuse have been sexually objectified and commodified. The mis-learnt lesson that sex can be exchanged for affirmation and love is then internalized. All the above factors can propel victims of abuse towards risky groups where there is a heightened chance of meeting dysfunctional partners, more likely to mistreat and/or abuse them and children.

When a person has socialized and identified with anti-social, risk-taking groups, and if early experiences with authority have been abusive, this can lead to a mistrust of, and hostility towards, authority figures such as police, social workers, and possibly the therapist. Such transference issues can be worked through to advantage within the therapeutic relationship, but can also problematize the child protection process.

Victims of childhood traumas of all kinds frequently survive by disassociating, compartmentalizing, denying and minimizing the abuse suffered. 'Repetition compulsion' and 'destiny neurosis' are theories of how clients can be compelled to repeat scripts of victimization (Freud, 1920), including forming relationships with abusive partners. Individuals can seek to understand or control sites of historical distress through familiarization (Fenichel, 1946). 'Opponent process theory' (Solomon, 1980) posits how we can seek to survive trauma by focusing on or inventing positive aspects to it, resulting in trauma being domesticated. There can be positive aspects to this sort of reframing. However, reframing also leads to victims rationalizing abuse as being 'not that bad'. The human need to feel there is a 'good' parent there for me (especially when this has not been the case) can result in the abusive caregiver being idealized, leading to a distorted idea of what is acceptable and not acceptable behaviour in the family setting, and to the minimizing of abuse that has taken place within the family system.

Victims can become practised at employing the above coping techniques, making it easier to disassociate, blanking out signs that their own children might be being abused. Individuals who have suffered trauma may also have insecure or chaotic attachment styles (Salter Ainsworth et al., 1978; Main and Solomon, 1990; Bartholomew and Horowitz, 1991; Brennan, Clark and Shaver, 1998). This leads to the erecting of defence mechanisms, described above. In addition, trauma frequently causes hypervigilance (Creeden, 2009), overreaction to perceived threat leading to increased avoidant or aggressive behaviour. One of the main bulwarks protecting children from sexual abuse is parents being sufficiently attuned to notice any changes in the child's inner emotional world which may betray if they are being groomed or abused. The above deficits compromise this capacity.

There is a significant emotional cost to engaging with the likelihood that one's child may have been sexually abused, or is at risk of being so by a loved other. The cost to parents who have been victims of sexual abuse can be higher. They have to come to terms with history repeating itself. Their dream of an abuse-free family life, in contradistinction to their own abusive family background, has been shattered, perhaps as the result of choices to allow a risky person to have contact with their children.

There is significant evidence that neglect and trauma in childhood, especially without significant protective factors, lead to poor outcomes in terms of establishing stable and satisfying adult lifestyles (Bentovim et al., 2009). Such deficits can lead to dependency and lack of assertiveness - 'learnt helplessness' (Seligman, 1975). If a non-abusing partner is dependent on and fearful of a partner, this renders it difficult to protect children from them. When surrounded by poverty, crime, substance misuse, domestic abuse and general chaos, life is often experienced as overwhelming. The risk of children being sexually abused can seem like just one more thing to cope with, in the context of trying to survive a chaotic and distressing life.

Protecting children from risk involves basic problem solving skills such as the ability to be objective, to see the wider picture, to prioritize what is important, to defer gratification, to be assertive. If the non-offending partner has been unable to apply these skills in life generally, they will probably have problems in applying them to the protection of children specifically, especially in the heat of the emotional moment.

Case study: Sian

Sian was brought up on a deprived social housing estate. There had been a culture of inter-generational sexual abuse in the extended family, and Sian was sexually abused by her maternal grandfather. An only child, she was raised by her mother. This was a stormy relationship, with Sian being violent and generally out of control, and she was put into care when she was 14. Sian ran away when she was 15, misusing alcohol and drugs and becoming involved in promiscuous, risk-taking and anti-social behaviour, including being convicted of assaulting police officers on two occasions, when she was drunk.

In her early twenties, Sian went through a substance detoxification programme and received counselling. She seems to have managed to give up hard drugs, but still occasionally smokes cannabis and sometimes binge drinks. When she was 24 years old, she met Steve (then 45) who organized raves. Sian became pregnant by him. They subsequently married, and had two daughters: Taylor (now 8) and Lucy (7). The poor state of tidiness and hygiene in the family home caused concerns. The neighbours made complaints about late night parties, and the police were called to domestic disputes between the couple. The father has previous offences for dealing cannabis and violence, and there were a number of allegations of sexual abuse made against him that came to nothing. The children were unruly at school and displayed sexualized behaviour. At the age of 6, Taylor told a teacher that her father plays with her 'minnie' when he showers her. Taylor was medically examined, but the doctor concluded that there were no injuries suggestive of sexual abuse. Her sister Lucy, a year younger, told the investigating social worker that her father locks the door when he showers her, but would say no more than this. The father, Steve, was not charged with sexual offending, as Taylor did not repeat her allegation and there was no medical evidence supportive of sexual abuse. Nevertheless, Children's Services required Steve to leave the family home, with contact being professionally supervised. Sian and her husband denied that there was any risk of sexual abuse, and Sian allowed the father to see the children, against the contact agreement with Children's Services. Sian has occasionally been verbally abusive to the case social worker.

When Sian allowed the children to see their father for a second time, against the stipulations of the child protection agreement, her children were taken into temporary foster care. Children's Services are considering whether the children should be adopted permanently, and the case has been referred to the Family Court. Having her children put into care has been a wake-up call to Sian, and she says that she has now ended her relationship with Steve, and will never allow him to have unauthorized contact with her children again. Children's Services are sceptical that Sian really means this, and view her change of heart as disguised compliance. They are also concerned that, even if she has ended the relationship with Steve, she will bring other risky men into the lives of her children.

Sian's solicitor, however, won the argument in Court that everything possible should be done to improve Sian's capacity to keep her children safe, before a decision is made to remove the children permanently from her care. As the result of this, Children's Services has agreed to pay for Sian to undergo safeguarding counselling, in order to achieve the following:

- To explore how her past impacts on her present choices and behaviour
- To improve her ability to protect her children
- To build up her resilience against becoming involved in the future with abusive men, including Steve, who might put her children at risk
- To raise her awareness of how to identify and appropriately respond to signs of risk
- To empower her to increase her confidence, choices, independence and resilience, to offset any potential dependency and/or disempowerment issues she may experience in future relationships

Sian walked into the counselling room, and flopped down sullenly in the chair. The counsellor was reminded of some of the girls she had encountered in school, when she used to teach Maths, before becoming a psychotherapist.

Sian: I don't know why I'm here, really.

The counsellor considered this unlikely to be true.

Counsellor: Right, what has your social worker said about why they wanted you to come to see me?

Sian: Nothing really, just you need to go and see this counsellor lady.

The counsellor handed over to Sian the referral letter from Children's Services to read. The letter described the above instructions for the work, instructions fairly typical for this type of safeguarding counselling intervention. As the counsellor recalled the instructions, she felt uncomfortable, thinking of how the formal, clinical language might seem to Sian. The counsellor felt compassion for her client. Having snatched the Letter of Instruction out of the counsellor's hand, Sian scan read it. She pursed her lips, defiantly.

Sian: Yeah, yeah, yeah! I know all that stuff. I know how to protect my kids.

A kaleidoscope of images whirled around the counsellor head: Sian's children in care; wild parties at Sian's house; the children's thug of a father in the shower with them with the door locked - *know how to protect her children!* In an instant, compassion turned into anger. The counsellor swallowed. She managed to bracket her judgementalism, and was able to respond in a strengths-focused manner.

Counsellor: Maybe, Sian, you can tell me all the ways in which you feel you've protected your children in the past.
Sian: (Hostile). Not 'feel' I've protected them, I have protected them.

The counsellor felt embarrassed about underestimating her client's intelligence; Sian had picked up on the ambivalent use of the word 'feel'. The counsellor's discomfort was compensated for by the realization that Sian was bright. This was a strength. The counsellor decided to employ the solution-focused technique of 'exception seeking' (de Shazer, 1985), purposely ignoring the obvious (in this case Sian's children being taken into care because she has not protected them) in order to focus upon a potential area of competence (ways in which Sian may have cared for and protected her children in the past), so that any such resources could be utilized further.

> *Counsellor:* OK, sorry, how have you protected them in the past?
> *Sian:* I've fed them. Gone without sometimes to put clothes on their backs. Chucked Steve out when he's come back to the house pissed, shooting his mouth off about something or other and frightening the kids.
> *Counsellor:* That sounds brave. How did you manage that? From the file, I gather that Steve is a heavy character.
> *Sian:* (Sian laughs) He is a heavy character, as you say, but never with me and the kids. He would never lay a hand on us. Besides, I don't back down to nobody.
> *Counsellor:* What has made you so fearless?
> *Sian:* It's what's happened to me, isn't it? You've probably read it all in the file. After a while you get used to trouble. You learn that you've got to stick up for yourself.

The counsellor reflected on how scared of physical violence she was, although she had never actually experienced any. She felt admiration and a certain awe for this secret knowledge of not being afraid, or getting over the fear of being hurt, that her client had acquired through life. The counsellor had indeed read the file. It was clear that Sian had survived and coped with the sort of threatening and adverse situations that the counsellor suspected she, herself, would be unable to tolerate. Perhaps this was part of the problem. Sian had learned to accept situations and behaviour which should not be accepted and tolerated.

For the first half of the session, Sian was unco-operative, bordering on hostile. Her narrative was full of anger and grievance over the way Children's Services had removed her children, and how Social Services had always tried to 'ruin my life ever since I've been little'. Sian took little responsibility for her children being removed from her care. The counsellor 'rolled with the resistance' (Miller and Rollnick, 1991), attempting to empathize with the feelings of the client, without colluding with the blame shifting.

When mandated clients first come to counselling, or when clients in general have come to discuss threatening and shameful issues, they are usually at their most defensive early on, displaying avoidance, evasion, blame shifting and hostility (Jenkins, 1990; Turnell and Edwards, 1999; Turnell and Essex, 2006). Before a degree of trust is established, the client is often threatened by the therapist - and vice versa.

The counsellor in this case successfully negotiated this early stage, eventually developing a degree of rapport with the client. Rapport established, the counsellor proceeded to motivate Sian to take part in safeguarding work in similar ways to how the therapist achieved this with Emily in the previous chapter. With Sian, this proved more challenging. The first part of the safeguarding work was to explore how Sian's past had impacted on her ability to protect her children.

Sian's life background

A strengths-focused way to explore a client's past is to first focus on positives. If there are no positives, a client will soon tell you and, at least, you have given the client the opportunity to speak about better times and resources. It is relatively rare in any person's life to have the experience of sitting down with a skilled listener and having the listener concentrate solely on you for an hour. This can be a special, nurturing experience. However, it can also be a disconcerting and humiliating one. When the client starts to become more objective, their hitherto unexamined life story - what has been normal for them - can start to seem dysfunctional. Initially inquiring about strengths can offset and soften this awareness-raising process, which is often necessary in order for the client to reset their antennae for what constitutes 'good enough' and 'not good enough' parenting.

With regard to Sian, she quickly told the counsellor that she could remember little about her life, and what she could remember was 'bad'.

Counsellor: All that sounds pretty difficult.

Sian: It was fucking grim.

Counsellor: What was the biggest challenge that you had to cope with?

Sian: My grandfather sexually abusing me, and my mother doing nothing about it. I almost hate her more than I hate him.

Counsellor: Who have you talked to about this, before now?

Sian: No one, well not in detail. I've probably gone on about it when I've been off my head on drink or drugs in care, or when I was in the homeless hostel. But I can't remember really. Have I got to talk about it now? What's the point? It's all in the past.

Counsellor: Well, I guess from a child protection point of view, there's a number of reasons. The majority of people who are sexually abused go on to make fine parents …

Sian: … but I haven't, have I?

Counsellor: Is that how you see it?

Sian: Yeah, I love my kids, but I've been a shit parent really.

Counsellor: If you hadn't been a shit parent, what would you have done differently?

Sian: Fewer parties. Less drinking. Not letting so many losers come around the house. Not letting the house getting into such a fucking tip.

Counsellor: It takes courage to admit all that.

Sian: Courage? I'm just telling the truth.

Counsellor: You seem to find it hard to take a compliment.

Sian: (In tears) Well, it's hard to take a compliment, when you feel like a piece of shit.

Counsellor: When don't you feel like a piece of shit?

Sian: When I'm off my head and when I had Steve. (Bursts into tears) I know Steve wouldn't do anything to his own kids. He's not like that. He hates nonces.

The counsellor left space for Sian to cry.

Counsellor: One of the reasons for talking about abuse is

because victims can feel like shit about themselves, as you say, and can go on to self-medicate with alcohol, drugs, sex. This risk-taking lifestyle can then put children at risk, when they come into the picture.

Sian remained quiet. Red-eyed, slumped in the chair, she looked like a lost child.

Counsellor: If you are prepared to tell me about the abuse, can I suggest some ground rules that might make you feel safer?
Sian: (Blowing her nose into a tissue) If you like.
Counsellor: Well, how about a word or a signal when you want to stop talking about something?
Sian: I'll just say stop or put my hand up.
Counsellor: Fine, we'll go for that. Also, talking about being abused can be upsetting. If it does prove upsetting, what support have you got after the session?
Sian: I'm seeing my friend, Steph. She knows some of it, she's great. I'll be OK.
Counsellor: Just one other thing. Sian, do you remember when we first met, and I said that if you told me anything that made me think that somebody might be at risk or a new crime had been committed, I might have to report it?
Sian: Yeah.
Counsellor: (In a gentle voice) Well, this still stands.
Sian: Oh, that's OK, he's dead anyway.

Here, the counsellor was putting some boundaries around the forth-coming disclosure session, in terms of support for the client and limits of confidentiality. When a client discloses sexual abuse to a therapist this should, ideally, be a corrective experience to the abuse suffered. This can be partially achieved by allowing the client to retain power over the flow of information, proceeding at the client's pace, and providing clear information about confidentiality boundaries, so the client can make informed choices about what to reveal.

Counsellor: Where do you want to start?

Sian: Well, it was my grandfather. He's dead now. But when I was young, I used to be sent round to look after my grandmother on a Saturday, and stay overnight, because she was losing it a bit. It was also an excuse for my mother to go out on the piss with her mates and bring men back home. Not that she needed an excuse. She would sometimes bring them home when I was there, and I could hear her at it with them in the next room.

Counsellor: How old were you when this used to happen?

Sian: 8 probably, up to when I got put in care. You get used to it. I think Mum would feel guilty about having a one night stand afterwards and would be nicer the next day, so it was alright really.

The counsellor was not sure how to respond. The disclosure had taken the form of Sian discussing her mother bringing men home. It was clear that, from an early age, Sian had experienced a lack of sexual boundaries in the family home. Her comment - 'it was alright really'- suggested that the lack of boundaries had been normalized. This was consistent with Sian's subsequent parenting of her own children, with reports of parties at Sian's home, where the children had witnessed adults having sex with each other. History was repeating itself. The counsellor wanted to know if Sian had been sexually abused in any way by the many men frequenting her childhood home. At the same time, she also did not want the session to go off at a tangent, distracting Sian from talking about her grandfather's abuse.

During a session, counsellors are faced with choices about where to take the conversation. Even client-centred counsellors influence the course of the session through micro choices about whether or not to remain quiet, encourage or discourage a narrative through body language, facial expression, clarifying questions, or an empathic summary etc. One can never be sure about the best option. However, it is important for the practitioner to be able to quickly reflect in the here-

and-now of the therapeutic moment, the possible pros and cons of any intervention.

In this case, the counsellor decided that it would be beneficial to follow the conversational flow of the client, and to obtain clarification about the mother's boyfriends. As well as potentially providing some valuable safeguarding information, talking about non-family members first might prove less threatening, perhaps making it easier for Sian to talk about a family member – her grandfather.

Counsellor: Did any of your mother's boyfriends ever mistreat you?
Sian: When I was older, a couple tried it on, but nothing serious.
Counsellor: What do you mean, tried it on?
Sian: One of them tried to kiss me in the kitchen once, but I told him to fuck off. Another one (Sian begins to laugh), I don't want to shock you – you might disapprove.
Counsellor: (Feeling somewhat attacked) Try me.
Sian: When I was around 15 one of my Mum's boyfriends asked me out.
Counsellor: How old was he?
Sian: Early thirties - fit though – I said yes, and ended up fucking him. Quite enjoyed it actually.

The counsellor felt angry. She had been trying her best to be as sensitive and empowering as possible with Sian. In return, she was being brazen about having underage sex and it felt as if Sian was talking about the experience brazenly, to taunt her. After the session, the counsellor took her feelings to supervision.

Supervisor: How did you expect Sian to react to being sexually abused by her mother's boyfriend?
Counsellor: Well, that was just it. She didn't seem to see it as sexual abuse. She insisted she enjoyed it, the experience.
Supervisor: … and why did this bother you?

Counsellor: Well, she was normalizing abuse. She was having underage sex. This is part and parcel of the way she's been corrupted - seeing underage sex as normal, because of the lack of boundaries growing up. It's why there's no proper boundaries in her own home now, as an adult. She sees it as all right to have wild parties, and for her kids to see adults having sex. It's this very sexualized environment which allowed her ex-partner to shower her daughters and lock the door - if he is her ex. I wouldn't be surprised if she's still seeing him. It's just a flaming cycle, isn't it?

Supervisor: You're right, of course. You are correctly identifying an intergenerational cycle of abuse - this is how it works. Even though she might have given consent to have sex with an older man, she was legally too young to make an informed choice, and the older man was entirely responsible for committing an offence of underage sex with an impressionable and obviously disturbed teenager. But why the anger with the client? I'm picking up anger in the way you are talking about her.

Counsellor: I guess I thought she was making fun of me, seeing me as a middle aged, staid do-gooder, who would be shocked at her sexual lifestyle.

Supervisor: Anything else?

Counsellor: Well, she seemed ungrateful somehow. I was being so careful to empower her and then she takes the piss.

Supervisor: Anything else?

Counsellor: No.

Supervisor: Sure?

Counsellor: (Blushing, as a silence descends on the room) Maybe a part of me, a small part of me, perhaps felt – feels - jealous of Sian's liberated lifestyle, even though I know it's abuse.

Supervisor: (Leaving a gap) Well done - you're in touch with your contradictory feelings. She didn't act like a sexual abuse victim ought to act: obviously traumatized, ashamed and so on?

Counsellor: (Laughs) I guess.

Supervisor: I'm impressed by your willingness to be honest with yourself.

Counsellor: Well, you need to be, don't you? I don't want my own stuff to get in the way of maintaining a good therapeutic relationship with the client, and I just thought she was talking in such a blasé way about her sexual experience. But I'm thinking, this is why your children are in the bloody care system and why they've probably been sexually abused!

Clients can challenge a therapist's expectations, not coming up with the desired response. Mandated clients who have to attend therapy, or clients who feel in the one-down position, can attempt to claw power back by boasting about extreme events outside of the therapist's personal life experience. If this pushes the therapist's buttons – e.g. feeling insecure about having led a sheltered or unadventurous life - the therapist can react punitively, if such insecurities remain repressed rather than being owned and compassionately examined.

Anybody with a professional background in child protection, working with victims of sexual abuse, is likely to understand the harmful impact of sexual offending and the baleful consequence for a child of a non-offending parent not believing a child's disclosure, or colluding with the abuse through denial, minimizing, and/or not being able to maintain appropriate sexual boundaries within the home. When the above occurs, the child remains unprotected from continued abuse, feels the loss of parental protection, and often internalizes the message that *I must not be worthy of protection, so the abuse must be my fault.* Hence, the child internalizes dysfunctional models of authority and care.

Most professionals are all too aware that the ability of the non-offending parent to provide support following disclosure is a crucial factor influencing the child's post-abuse wellbeing. Child protection workers, including counsellors and therapists practising in the field, have to develop good working alliances with non-offending partners, whose attitudes and behaviour have harmed or are harming children.

This requires practitioners to acknowledge negative feelings and be able to set them to one side, when they observe values and behaviour harmful to children. This is a complex emotional juggling act, requiring maturity and self-knowledge. What can help prevent judgementalism contaminating a relationship with a client is for practitioners to reflect from time to time on the following:

- Why do I work in child protection?
- Am I optimistic or pessimistic about sex offenders changing?
- What are my *gut* feelings about partners having relationships with sex offenders?
- What, if any, are my main anxieties about working in the area of sexual offending?
- As a person, do I naturally tend to think that everything will be OK or that the worst will happen?
- Can my standards, in relation to the behaviour of other people, be too high, or too low?
- Does my experience with children (highly involved or not involved in child care) affect my work in child protection?
- Do I tend to get too involved in people's pain or do I tend to remain too distant?

We will now return to the therapy session with Sian.

Counsellor: Sian, can we go back to your grandfather? Tell me about your relationship with him before the abuse began?
Sian: Well, he wasn't frightening or anything. I used to feel sorry for him. He used to get nagged by my grandmother all the time. I suppose me and Mum sided against her. She was an old witch.
Counsellor: So, it was you and him against her. Can you say how the abuse started?
Sian: He used to come into my room to kiss me good night. Then he started tickling me, and it went from there.

Often it is more important to understand the emotional dynamics of an abusive relationship, rather than concentrating on the physical details. However, it is usually helpful to gain some understanding of the extent and the duration of the abuse. Each victim experiences sexual abuse differently. However, below are some factors which tend to make the abuse particularly damaging:

- If the abuse was prolonged
- If the victim was very frightened by the abuse
- If the victim felt/feels unprotected from further abuse, and lives in a state of fear
- If the abuse was carried out by a trusted family member the victim relied on for security (e.g. a parent figure)
- If the abuse was particularly invasive i.e. oral sex, intercourse
- If the victim was not believed by family members and blamed for causing trouble
- If the victim was made to feel responsible for the abuse
- If the victim was particularly vulnerable, with existing emotional and welfare problems

In the case of Sian, she disclosed that the abuse occurred between the ages of 9 and 14, when she finally told her grandfather to 'fuck off', and the abuse stopped. She said that it gravitated from touching to him making her masturbate him, and him performing oral sex on her.

Counsellor: How come you never told anybody?
Sian: I knew my mother wouldn't do anything. He used to pay
for lots of stuff. I got some vague memory of going into the
kitchen once, and catching my mother sucking him off. I don't
know if it happened or if I'm making it up. But in the memory,
it's like I know she is doing it to get money off him.

In a therapeutic setting, where the client is not sure whether memories related to abuse are real or not, a way forward is to focus on the feelings of the client about the past memory, avoiding expressing an opinion on whether or not the memory is true or false. This is up to the client to decide, without being influenced by the therapist.

When clients have been traumatized by sexual abuse, their accounts can be vague, having a dreamlike quality, lacking narrative structure in terms of time, place and detail. This is partly due to the passage of time and also because, as explained above, victims of abuse disassociate from traumatic memories. This is one of the reasons why the conviction rate for sexual abuse is far lower than the actual prevalence of sexual offending. Sexual abuse is termed a dark figure crime and likened to an iceberg, with the majority of sexual abuse out of sight, as it were, remaining undisclosed by victims. Where it is disclosed there is not, in many cases, sufficient coherent evidence to obtain a conviction.

In one of the largest ever surveys into child sexual abuse in England, Children's Commissioner's Inquiry Report (2015) notes that it is estimated that 1.3 million children living in England today will have been sexually abused by the time they reach 18. Child abuse in and around the family is likely to account for two thirds of all child sexual abuse, with 75% of victims of child sexual abuse in the family environment being female, although boys and young men are likely to be under-represented because of additional barriers to male reporting. Many female victims report that their sexual abuse in the family environment began when they were around 9 years old. Most of those who do disclose abuse, do not disclose until they are adults. Much sexual abuse occurs when children are younger, but they do not have the words to report it. Abuse of children from some Black and Minority Ethnic groups, and those with physical or learning disabilities, is less likely to come to the attention of the authorities. Below are some other reasons why most sexual abuse never results in a conviction. The list is not exhaustive:

- The victim didn't think it was serious or wrong
- The victim didn't want their parents to find out
- The victim didn't want friends to find out

- The victim didn't want authorities to find out
- The victim was frightened
- The victim didn't think they would be believed
- The victim had been threatened by the abuser
- There is often no physical evidence
- Child and traumatized witnesses can be unreliable
- Details of historical abuse can be difficult to remember
- The adversarial legal system can tend to undermine victims
- Victims can love their abusers (not just trauma ties)

The counsellor continued to explore with Sian her memories.

Counsellor: Can you tell me about any feelings attached to your memories of your mother and grandfather?
Sian: It's as if me and Mum were in it together, somehow. Both taking him for a ride.
Counsellor: … and this feels like?
Sian: As if we were ganging up on him.
Counsellor: Can you say more?
Sian: I feel guilty, I suppose.

At this point, the counsellor might have said to Sian something like the following: *You have nothing to feel guilty about. It was your grandfather and your mother who were the adults in the situation.* Of course, this is perfectly true and it goes without saying that the adult is always responsible for sexual abuse of a child. However, just saying this might not alter the way the client perceives past experiences. Clients have to come to this place for themselves. For instance, a child victim may have an essentially stronger force of character than the adult abuser. Whilst hating the abuse, the victim may have valid memories of feeling stronger than the perpetrator. To dismiss this simply as the effects of grooming is, in my view, to prioritize ideology over the client's authentic life experience. This will likely harm the therapeutic relationship, produce resistance and hinder the client from fully exploring the many possibly contradictory elements of their relationship with the abuser. The first step in facilitating a genuine and permanent shift in a client's thinking is to be open to, and accepting of, the client's current view of the past, before encouraging the client to undertake further emotional expression and critical reflection.

> *Counsellor:* OK, so you feel that you and your mother were ganging up on your grandfather, taking him for a ride, and you feel guilty about this, right?
> *Sian:* Yeah.
> *Counsellor:* If you had a magic wand and you could wave it and have the childhood you really wanted, what would that childhood have been like?
> *Sian:* (Cynically laughs) We would have been rich and lived in a big house.

This magic wand question is a variant of the solution-focused miracle question (de Shazer, 1985), or the 'problem gone' question. The technique can be traced back to the work of hypnotherapist and psychotherapist, Milton Erickson, working in America in the 1950s. When a client used to arrive for the first session, Erickson would ignore the client's present problem and ask the client to imagine sometime in the future when the problem did not exist, and to describe what life would be life without it. The rest of the therapy would be concerned with earthing the, often idealistic, answer into concrete, achievable reality. At the time, this way of undertaking therapy was fairly original as psychotherapy was, and still is to a large extent, taken up with past problems.

The magic wand question used with Sian borrows this technique, but applies it to the past rather than the future, albeit in a solution-focused way, as Sian is asked to imagine a different past without the problems which have, in large part, brought her into therapy. This sort of question often produces an idealistic or cynical answer from the client. However, there are more often than not hidden clues as to what a client really wants out of life.

Clients can also respond to the magic wand question through

different sorts of illustrative media such as paint, plasticine, stones, or arranging chairs in the room, to help express the ideal childhood they would like to have had. In my experience, this can be a very emotional exercise for clients as it bypasses the intellect and gets to the primal emotional, relational and social needs which were not met. The intervention can also encourage cognitive shifts, light- bulb moments which can burst through cognitive distortions, resulting in the client developing a more realistic, mature view of the past, resulting in increased ability to respond constructively to the present. This occurred with Sian, as the therapist unpicked her response.

Counsellor: OK, tell me what's so good about being rich and living in a big house.

Sian: Well, you get respect. You get what you want.

Counsellor: So, you feel that people value you and that there are enough resources around to keep you well and happy, and safe maybe.

Sian: All those things.

Counsellor: OK, so how would your mother and grandfather be in this big house? What would they be doing and what would they be saying?

Sian: (Tears in her eyes) They would be happy. Mum wouldn't be so thin. She would be calm and ladylike and wouldn't always be getting drunk, and there would be no nasty men around.

Counsellor: And how would your mother be behaving towards you?

Sian: She would be behaving like a proper mum, not needy, not always talking about herself but concerned about me. Making sure I do my homework, but having fun together - playing games and going on holidays.

Counsellor: Take me through a day. How would it be when you all got up in the morning?

Sian: Mum would be up before me. She would be up before me to fix my breakfast.

Counsellor: OK, so that's what your mother would do. How would she be in the mornings?
Sian: What do you mean?
Counsellor: How would she look? How would she sound?
Sian: Well, there would be a smile on her face. She'd be happy.
Counsellor: Anything else?
Sian: She would be dressed, not slobbing around in her dressing gown, smoking a fag.
Counsellor: Anything else?
Sian: Yeah, she would be going to work. Have a proper job, and she would drive a car to work. Come to think of it, my mother has never had a proper job. Just running catalogues and stuff. And she's also done Ann Summers' parties, (laughing), selling dildos and stuff.

The counsellor proceeded to ask what life would be like throughout the day and at weekends. The name of this strengths-focused therapeutic game is detail, detail and more detail. What the counsellor was doing here is facilitating the client to think about how a caring, responsible mother would act. This can both help the client to realize what she has missed out on as a child, and also provide concrete inspiration for how the client can provide nurturing parenting to her own children. The counsellor repeated the process with respect to Sian's grandfather.

Counsellor: And how would your grandfather be in the house?
Sian: (Laughing through the tears) He would be clean. He wouldn't smoke and drink so much. He would be wearing a waistcoat and be funny, like the grandfather in 'Only Fools and Horses'.
Counsellor: And how would your grandfather behave towards you?
Sian: He would take me out for ice-creams, to the seaside, and even to museums.
Counsellor: What else?

Sian: He and my mother wouldn't argue all the time. They would respect each other.
Counsellor: How would they show their respect?
Sian: They wouldn't shout and scream at each other, and wouldn't swear at each other. He would be someone my mother could rely on for support and good advice rather than the usual crap that came out of his mouth.
Counsellor: And how would he show respect to you?
Sian: (In tears) He'd buy me things and take me places with no strings attached. He would keep his hands to himself.

The counsellor left time to honour the moment and allowed Sian to cry for a while, before offering a summary and empathic perspective taking.

Counsellor: So, it sounds as if you would like your grandfather to have been a grandfather: treating you, taking you to nice places, buying you things, thinking you're special. Sian, these are things that most children want from grandparents, and I wonder if you can forgive yourself for wanting all this from your grandfather, but not wanting the abuse that went with it.
Sian: (In tears) I was just being a kid.
Counsellor: That's right. If that kid was sitting in the chair opposite us now, what would you say to her?
Sian: I would want to put my arms around her and give her a hug, and say that it wasn't your fault. You wanted the stuff because you were just a kid.
Counsellor: So, if that's the case, who was responsible for the abuse?
Sian: He was.
Counsellor: Can you say again who was responsible for the abuse, but louder.
Sian: (In an assertive voice) He was! He was!

The counsellor decided to end the session at the above point, making sure that the client was all right to go home, inquiring how she would look after herself that evening. In the next session the counsellor explored, in similar ways to those above, the lack of a consistent father figure in Sian's life, by asking Sian to think about what her ideal father figure would have been like. Sian was then able to realize that she had been looking for this father figure and craving security from Steve, the father of her two children. Having made this link, she was now in a place to begin more structured, psycho-educational safeguarding work, although this safeguarding work would not be straightforward. The content of this safeguarding intervention is the subject of the next chapter.

Conclusion

Providing counselling safeguarding interventions to partners of sex offenders who have minimized risk can be tough work. Often clients who are mandated or have no choice about attending counselling if they want to have restrictions lifted with regard to their children, can present as resistant and even hostile. If the safeguarding work is to prove effective, it is important that the Rogerian core relational conditions - empathy, congruence and unconditional regard - are established. Having to establish such a good working alliance can be challenging for child-centred practitioners, when clients' irresponsible attitudes to parenting have led to children being harmed. In order to enhance Sian's ability to protect her children from sexual offending, it was necessary for the counsellor to access Sian's own experiences of sexual abuse. This allowed Sian to place responsibility for the abuse with the abuser and consequently her thinking about what constitutes neglectful, unsafe parenting became less distorted. Her concept of what constitutes a safe, nurturing environment for a child and her concept of a 'good enough' parent were starting to be realigned. Having established a good working alliance with Sian, and addressed her victim issues through the free-flowing counselling method, the counsellor could now provide more structured, psycho-educational safeguarding work, which is the subject of the next chapter.

Practice points from this chapter

- It is important for the counsellor and client to have a shared, clear picture of what ability to protect looks like, and what emotional resources, knowledge and skills it takes for a parent to protect a child from the risk of sexual abuse
- The counsellor may have to constructively respond to resistance and hostility if the client has been pressurized to attend safeguarding work by child protection professionals
- Rapport can be built by initially focusing on exceptions to the problem: excavating examples of good parenting, and bringing to the surface the client's best hope for the children involved
- The counsellor might have to deal with their own judgementalism when faced with a parent who has neglected or not protected their children
- It is important to explore the roots of such judgementalism, or any other punitive feelings towards the client, in clinical supervision
- If a non-offending partner has been sexually abused or mistreated in other ways, it may be necessary to attend to such issues, before moving on to psycho-educational safeguarding work
- Any therapeutic exploration of a person's abuse experiences should hand as much power and control over to the client as possible, to act as a corrective to the disempowerment they have suffered (see above for details)
- It can be effective to use the magic wand or miracle question to explore with the client how they would have ideally wanted their childhood to be. This can throw into relief what constitutes abusive and inadequate parenting and 'good enough' parenting
- When using the magic wand or miracle question, it is

important for the therapist to keep on focusing on practical detail in order to avoid idealistic platitudes about child care

References

Bartholomew, K. and Horowitz, L.M. (1991) 'Attachment styles amongst young adults: A test of a four-category model', *Journal of Personality and Social Psychology*, 61(2): pp. 226-244.

Bentovim, A., Cox, A., Bingley Miller, L. and Pizzey S. (2009) *Safeguarding children living with trauma and family violence: Evidence-based assessment, analysis and planning interventions.* London: Jessica Kingsley Publishers.

Brennan, K.A., Clark, C.L. and Shaver, P.R. (1998) 'Self-report measurement of adult attachment: An integrative overview', in J.A. Simpson and W.S. Rholes (eds.) *Attachment theory and close relationships.* New York: Guilford Press, pp. 46-76.

Children's Commissioner's Inquiry Report (2015), *Protecting children from harm: A critical assessment of child sexual abuse in the family network in England and priorities for action.* Available from: https://www.childrenscommissioner.gov.uk/wp-content/uploads/2017/06/Protecting-children-from-harm-full-report.pdf [January 2022]

Creeden, K. (2009) 'How trauma and attachment can impact neurodevelopment: Informing our understanding and treatment of sexual behaviour problems', *Journal of Sexual Aggression*, 15 (3): pp. 261-273.

de Shazer, S. (1985) *Keys to solutions in brief therapy.* New York: W.W. Norton.

Fenichel, O. (1946) *The psychoanalytic theory of neurosis.* London: Routledge and Kegan Paul. (Reprinted in 1990 by Routledge).

Freud, S. (1920) *Beyond the pleasure principle.* Available in Dover, Thrift Addition (2015) Dover Publications.

Jenkins, A. (1990) *Invitations to responsibility: The therapeutic engagement of men who are violent and abusive,* Adelaide: Dulwich Centre Publications.

Main, M. and Solomon, J. (1990) 'Procedures for identifying

infants as disorganized/disoriented during the Ainsworth Strange Situation', in M.T. Greenberg, D. Cicchetti, and E.M. Cummings (eds.) *Attachment in the preschool years: Theory, research and intervention.* Chicago: University of Chicago (pp. 121-160).

Miller, W.R. and Rollnick, S. (1991) *Motivational interviewing: Helping people change.* New York: Guilford Press.

Salter Ainsworth, M.D., Blehar, M.C., Waters, E. and Wall, S.N. (1978) *Patterns of attachment: A psychological study of the strange situation.* Hillsdale NJ: Lawrence Earlbaum Associates.

Seligman, M.E.P. (1975) *Helplessness: On depression, development and death.* San Francisco, CA: W.H. Freeman.

Solomon, R.L. (1980) 'The opponent-process theory of acquired motivation: The costs of pleasure and the benefits of pain', *American Psychologist*, 35 (8): pp. 691-712.

Turnell, A. and Edwards, S. (1999) *Signs of safety: A solution and safety oriented approach to child protection casework.* New York: W.W. Norton.

Turnell, A. and Essex, S. (2006) *Working with 'denied' child abuse: The resolutions approach.* Maidenhead: Open University Press.

SEVEN

SIAN (CONTINUED)

Introduction

The Sian case study from Chapter 6 is continued here. The chapter takes the reader through a course of safeguarding work with a client. Having explored Sian's victim issues, the counsellor persuaded the client that, in order to have any chance of having the children returned to her care, she needed to demonstrate to Children's Services that she was more risk aware in relation to her partner, specifically; how sexual abuse occurs in families, generally; and how to protect her children from this risk. In order to make such progress, Sian agreed to undertake a 16-hour programme of psycho-educational safeguarding work over the course of eight two-hour sessions. Some of the educational safeguarding content that follows can also be found in my previous book about counselling male sexual offenders (Smith, 2017). However, in this book, the content is applied differently and specifically to working with non-offending partners. This chapter has two separate aims. The first aim is to provide practitioners with an idea of how to conduct psycho-educational safeguarding work with clients within a counselling setting. The second aim is to provide the outline of a discrete course of one-to-one safeguarding intervention that can be undertaken by generic child protection workers.

Some general comments about psycho-educational work

As already noted in the previous chapter, Sian was sent to counselling with these aims:

- To explore how her past impacts on her present choices and behaviour
- To improve her ability to protect her children
- To build up her resilience against becoming involved in the future with abusive men, including Steve, who might put her children at risk
- To raise her awareness of how to identify and appropriately respond to signs of risk
- To empower her to increase her confidence, choices, independence and resilience; to offset any potential dependency and/or disempowerment issues she may experience in future relationships

The above goals are fairly typical of many safeguarding courses offered in England and Wales, for use with non-offending partners protecting children from sexual abuse (Still, 2016), although many such courses tend to be manualized, risk-focused and do not address the individual psychodynamics of the client. It is my view that learning does not take place in a neat, linear fashion, as is sometimes suggested by manualized programmes. Such programmes provide a focus and a framework, and can prevent safeguarding work veering off into irrelevant areas or being delivered at the level of a cosy chat. Nevertheless, learning, especially when it involves personal change, is a complex, multi-layered process.

The counsellor had already completed valuable work in facilitating Sian to explore her abusive past, and how past experiences might be linked to how she has functioned as an adult parent. In itself, this raised awareness is likely to promote insightful and, hopefully, safer, more child-centred parenting. Now, the counsellor focuses on providing Sian with some basic information about sexual abuse. The following safeguarding information which appears in this chapter is by no means exhaustive, but it serves the purpose of encouraging the client to have a more enlightened perspective concerning sexual offending.

When conveying safeguarding information, I provide the client with a folder in which to keep information sheets. At the start of each session, the client is asked to recall the information sheets already discussed. This rote learning can be seen as more pedagogic than therapeutic but I find it, nevertheless, to be effective. My experience is that as the work progresses, an increasing amount of information is remembered and internalized by the client, with each revision session consolidating and deepening learning.

When conducting this more structured work, I extend sessions from one hour to two hours. I find this extra time is needed if I am to attend to the client's ongoing life issues as they arise, complete the revision work and then go through that session's particular safeguarding material. Other therapists will want to stick to the usual 60 or 50 minutes for pragmatic or ideological reasons. If this is the case, elements of the safeguarding material which appear below can be woven into the 'therapeutic hour', as the therapist deems fit.

Once again, I would point out that any delivery of psycho-educational material is only likely to be effective if it is delivered within the motivational framework of the client, at the client's pace and with sensitivity to the client's learning style (Andrews and Bonta, 2003). If the therapist's main concern is getting through the programme of work at the expense of the process issues and the therapeutic alliance, this is likely to compromise effectiveness.

Some practitioners can have a hidden agenda, either conscious or subconscious, when conducting safeguarding work with non-offending partners. As sometimes happens when working with victims of domestic abuse, this agenda can be to persuade the participant to leave the offending partner. In some cases, adopting such a stance can be tempting, if the relationship seems obviously dysfunctional or abusive. However, when such an attitude exists, there is a high likelihood that a spirit of judgementalism towards the participant's loved one will contaminate the therapeutic relationship with the client, producing resentment and resistance in the client or their offending partner. Moreover, the paternalistic misuse of power by the practitioner - 'I know best' – can echo the disempowerment the client has experienced in previous abusive or coercive relationships. If a more neutral position is taken, the safeguarding work is more likely to raise clients' awareness of risk issues, enabling them to make more informed choices where their children are concerned, including regarding the future of the relationship with the person posing the risk.

The programme of safeguarding work with Sian took the form of the following eight sessions:

- Session 1: What is sexual abuse?
- Session 2: Who commits sexual abuse and where does it typically occur?
- Session 3: Grooming the victim in order to make them give in and not tell
- Session 4: Grooming others to get them out of the way in order to create the opportunity to sexually offend
- Session 5: Three profiles of sexual offenders
- Session 6: The impact of sexual abuse at the time of the offending and later in life
- Session 7: Case study work
- Session 8: The Safety Plan

Session 1: What is sexual abuse?

- Unwanted sexual contact between one adult and another
- Unwanted sexual contact with an older or more powerful person
- Sexual contact between an adult and a child under the age of 16 (18 via the internet)

- Inappropriate sexual talk, sexual jokes, sexual innuendo
- Showing a child pornography
- Adults performing sexual acts in front of children
- Inappropriate intimate contact with children in an unobserved setting
- Looking at sexualized images of children online
- Talking to children sexually online
- Sending to and receiving from children sexual images online
- General touching of a child with sexual intent
- Touching sexual parts of a child's body
- Oral sex, vaginal sex or anal sex with a child

One of the findings from my PhD research (Smith, 2009) was that offenders valued being treated as persons and not just as a collection of risk factors by the probation officers who supervised them. The same principle, I believe, is relevant to all client groups. Hence, in this spirit, at the start of each safeguarding session the counsellor checked in with Sian to see how her week had been, before moving on to the psycho-educational work itself.

It is important for practitioners to use their clinical nous to determine how much time to give to fire-fighting the ongoing ups and downs in a client's life. When it comes to the time for the session, a client can be unmotivated or anxious about focusing on the agreed safeguarding work, and can sometimes employ talking about what is happening in their lives as a psychological smoke screen, in order to cope with perceived threat. A constructive way to respond to this is for the therapist to gently bring what they think could be occurring into the room. An adult-to-adult frank discussion can then be had about whether or not the client is truly motivated to take part in the work. If the client says that they are prepared to take part in the work, a useful response can be:

Counsellor: OK, I get that you want to do the work. If, in the future, I think that you're avoiding engaging in the work, what should I say to you?

Sometimes, however, the hold-up can be that the counsellor is being too reactive. This can be especially the case with counsellors heavily influenced by the client-centred approach. What is sometimes needed is simply for the counsellor to refocus the client onto the task at hand.

A general strengths-focused principle I employ with safeguarding work is to ask the client what they know, before providing them with information. This allows clients to experience the mastery of 'knowing stuff': avoiding the, sometimes felt, ignominy of 'being told stuff'. The counsellor employed this principle.

Counsellor: OK, Sian, are you ready to start the more structured part of the counselling, where I give you information about how sexual abuse occurs and how a parent can play her part in protecting children from such abuse?
Sian: That's what we agreed.
Counsellor: I've brought this folder in for you, Sian, for you to keep information handouts I'll be giving you over the next weeks. If you bring the folder to each session, we can begin by going over each time what you have learnt. Don't worry about forgetting stuff, this always happens. But as we go over it each time, more information will stick.
Sian: (Uncertain) Alright.
Counsellor: OK, let's begin by you telling me what makes sex, or sexual contact, abusive or illegal.
Sian: When it's forced.
Counsellor: Yep, good. Anything else?
Sian: I don't know. That's it really.
Counselling: Just relax, no rush. Take time to think. What else makes sex abusive or illegal?
Sian: I'm being thick. I don't know.
Counsellor: Just think for a minute. We can sit here in compan-

ionable silence, no pressure, no big deal. If you don't come up with anything else, I'll tell you at the end of the silence and, in the meantime, we can enjoy a bit of peace and quiet.
Sian: (After a while) Oh, underage. If you have sex with anybody who is underage.

Above, the counsellor had two aims. Firstly, she was trying to create space for the client to think for herself. Secondly, she was attempting to create a relaxed, supportive learning environment in which the client could experience being comfortable with not knowing, which can then, paradoxically, facilitate knowing.

Counsellor: Yep, you've got it. Two things which makes sex abusive are when it's not wanted and when there is sexual contact with somebody below the age of consent. Do you know the age of consent?
Sian: Yeah, it's 16, isn't it?
Counsellor: That's right, the age for sexual contact between two persons is 16. Do you know the age of consent for looking at sexual imagery on the internet?
Sian: The same, I suppose.
Counsellor: Well, it's 18 actually.
Sian: But that's mad. Why is it 16 in real life and 18 on the internet?
Counsellor: The main reason is that almost all children and young people access the internet. They're vulnerable to abuse – people can contact them at any time, in the privacy of their homes and elsewhere, without parents knowing, and lie about their age and who they are. This is why the age of consent threshold is higher for contacting somebody sexually on the internet than in 'real life'.

When talking to clients about age of consent issues, the following additional questions often come up:

- What about the age of consent being different in other countries and at other times throughout history?
- What about two young people who are both underage having sex? This happens all the time

The practitioner will probably have some sense of the spirit in which these sorts of questions are asked. Is the client asking in a combative manner, trying to dumbfound the therapist in an effort to claw some power back? Are these questions indicative of the client having distorted thinking, believing that children having sex with each other or with adults is legitimate? Is the client simply curious about moral complexities? The attitude behind such questions can provide insight into the risk posed by the client (if the person is an offender) or ability to protect (if the person is a non-offending partner).

Whatever the attitude and motive in raising the issue, such questions present learning opportunities. With regard to the age of consent being different in different countries and at different points in history, this is what I term 'the relativity fallacy'. Just because a different morality existed in the past and may exist now in other cultures, this does not legitimize a particular behaviour. For instance: slavery, women not having the vote, child labour, and homosexuality being deemed illegal are just a few examples of human conduct considered respectable and morally acceptable at one time, but no longer.

It is counterproductive to become embroiled in long, drawn-out arguments with clients about these matters as this can clog up sessions and prevent any constructive progress being made. My response is to say something like the following, in a detached, non-argumentative way:

- I guess each person has their own private morality about sex, but the law of the land says that underage sex is illegal and if a person does not want to risk all the consequences of prosecution, then it's best if they, or their loved one, develops the capacity not to offend or reoffend sexually (I then ask the client if this is a goal they want to work towards).

If the client still wants to argue about culturally relativistic moral positions with regard to what constitutes sexual abuse, I will interject by saying something like:

- It sounds really difficult for you to be so at odds with the prevailing view. Would you like to learn how to accept this difference more amicably, or continue to use the counselling sessions to rail against the law as it stands and the dominant moral view?

If the client still wants to argue in sessions, each time they start on this tack, I might ask one, two, or all of the following:

- How long would you like to rail against the prevailing view, in this session?
- How would you like me to respond each time you start to rail?
- What are the pros and cons of arguing against the status quo?

If, after a while, it becomes impossible to refocus the client, then I would discuss with the client whether the counselling is serving any purpose.

A second argument frequently raised in terms of the age of consent, is that many teenagers below the age of consent have sex without getting into trouble with the law. When this query is raised, I use it as an opportunity to discuss power in relationships. I tend to say something like:

- In my experience, when the police investigate a case where two underage people are having sex, what they are most concerned about is whether or not there has been an abuse of power, in terms of one underage partner being older, or significantly more mature, or taking advantage of the other underage partner's vulnerability. In the case of younger children, if the sexual contact is significant, then the authorities would be concerned about why the children are behaving outside of the norm, and the harm this could cause long term. What do you think of what I've just said?

In the case of Sian, she queried this very point with her counsellor.

Sian: But loads of teenagers have sex before their 16th birthday - I did.

Counsellor: OK, if we take teenagers having sex, I guess one of the main issues is if one of the teenagers has more power than the other. What sorts of power do you think I might be thinking of?

Sian: Being older, bigger maybe.

Counsellor: Yes, great, you're getting the point. How else could one person have power over another?

Sian: If somebody is a bit slow - has learning difficulties, or just kind of naive. Or maybe somebody is afraid, or somebody is blackmailing them. An older boy once told me that if I didn't have full sex with him, he'd spread it around that I sucked him off. I told him where to get off.

Counsellor: How old were you and how old was he?

*Sian:*I was around 15, he was about 23 or something.

Counsellor: What made you able to tell him where to get off?

Sian: Well, he was good looking but he was a bighead, nobody liked him.

Counsellor: So, it sounds that you weren't afraid of what he would say?

Sian: Too damn right.

Counsellor: OK, let's look at who had the power.

The counsellor proceeded to suggest the different forms of power individuals bring to relationships (see Chapter 2, and the relationship between and Anthony and Harry). She then asked Sian to apply these sources of power to the relationship with the older male, above, who attempted to blackmail her.

> *Sian:* OK. He was older than me, bigger than me, he had more life experience, more money, he even drove his parents' car. He was an adult, I suppose, and I was just a kid really.
> *Counsellor:* So, why do you think it is morally wrong for an adult to have sex with an underage teenager, a kid as you say?
> *Sian:* Well, an underage kid isn't mature enough to make that decision.

The counsellor had been trying to raise the client's awareness of the moral reasons for the age of consent, underpinning the illegality if it. Having explored the power differentials with Sian in relation to herself as a 15-year-old and the older male, the counsellor asked Sian to go through the same process with regard to her children's father, Steve. Sian was able to see that in relation to Steve, she also had less power. When this power differential became glaringly apparent, Sian remained silent. At this stage the counsellor did not push the issue, as she considered that it would be more effective to leave a silence, and allow Sian to internalize this new way of conceptualizing her relationship with Steve.

Having spent time discussing with Sian what constitutes sexual abuse, the counsellor provided her with a handout, consisting of the information which appears at the beginning of this section. The counsellor then asked Sian if any of the information was consistent with the disclosures made by her daughters. Whilst maintaining she did not think that her daughters' disclosures were true, Sian was able to point to how her elder daughter's account was consistent with the following points in the information sheet:

- Unwanted sexual contact with an older or more powerful person

- Sexual contact between an adult and a child under the age of 16 (18 via the internet)
- Inappropriate intimate contact with children in an unobserved setting
- Touching sexual parts of a child's body

The counsellor was content not to challenge the client about not believing her daughters' disclosures at this stage. The counsellor had trust that the process of risk awareness work would render it increasingly difficult for the client to be so certain that no sexual abuse had occurred.

The counsellor affirmed Sian for taking part fully in the session. Sian said she had 'learnt stuff', but still did not think that Steve had 'done it' (i.e. abused his daughters). Sian also agreed that she would read the information in the folder once a day throughout the week, and bring the folder with her to the next session.

Session 2. Who commits sexual abuse and where does it typically occur?

- Most sexual abuse is committed by men, often fathers, stepfathers or men who are known to the children
- Children and adults suffer much sexual abuse that is never reported
- Adolescents also commit high levels of sexual abuse
- Anyone can suffer sexual abuse, regardless of age, sex or background, although teenage girls under the age of 16 from troubled backgrounds are common victims of sexual abuse
- Contrary to popular fear, children being abused by people in the street whom they don't know, is relatively rare
- Most sexual abuse occurs in the home and commonly occurs around the following activities and situations: applying medicinal creams, physical play with children,

> bath time, bed time, lack of sexual boundaries in the home,
> baby-sitting, being alone in a car with an adult, adults being
> drunk and/or on drugs

The counsellor began the session by asking Sian how her week had been. She said that she had been depressed, thinking about Christmas and not having the children with her, and being on her own. The counsellor empathized with Sian, and did some basic strengths-focused work about what behavioural distraction techniques might help her manage negative thoughts and feelings.

Having attended to what the client brought to the session, the counsellor asked Sian if they could go over the information sheet they had worked on the previous week. Sian took her folder out of her bag, saying she had not had time to look at the information in the folder. This was clearly untrue, although the counsellor decided not to challenge Sian on this matter, as it would risk her losing face. Moreover, Sian had few positive memories of education to call on to buffer her against any perceived criticism or fear of failure. Hence, the counsellor complimented Sian for bringing her folder into the session, before facilitating the revision session.

When conducting a revision session of the psycho-educational work, I major on the 'no-big-deal' nature of the exercise. As noted above, I emphasize that I don't expect the client to remember everything, but that recall will probably improve over the course of coming sessions. I tell clients that after they say what they can remember, I will read out all the information on the handouts as this, in itself, will help the information and ideas find a home in the long-term memory. Once clients relax and get used to this procedure every time we meet, it usually turns into a sort of game, as clients gain satisfaction from remembering an increasing number of points. With some clients who have never achieved academically, this rote learning provides a sense of mastery and more confidence in their ability to learn, increasing self-esteem. The counsellor demonstrated this process with Sian.

Counsellor: OK Sian, if you pass over the folder, then I'll ask what you can remember. As I say, don't worry if it's a bit hazy. Let's start with what makes sex illegal or abusive.

Sian: If it's underage or forced. If a person doesn't give consent.

Counsellor: Excellent. And the age of consent?

Sian: 16

Counsellor: … and?

Sian: Oh yeah! 18 on the internet.

Counsellor: … and different forms of abuse?

Sian: Umm, touching, intercourse, showing kids pornography, telling them sexual jokes.

Counsellor: Anything else?

Sian: Looking at sexual stuff with children online. I can't think of anything else.

Counsellor: Just take some time (counsellor leaves a silence).

Sian: Nope, can't think of anything.

Counsellor: Don't worry. You've done well. You've got the basics. I'll go through the list of different sexual behaviours on the information sheet, and you tell me how many you've got. As I said last week, every time I read out the examples, more will stick in your mind.

Sian: Go on then.

Counsellor: The age of consent is 16 and 18 on the internet. What makes sex abusive is sexual contact between one adult and another and unwanted sexual contact with an older or more powerful person.

Sian: Got three of those. Didn't get the age of consent is 18 on the internet straight away, but got there in the end.

Counsellor: Sexual abuse can take the form of showing pornography, adults performing sexual acts in front of children, looking at sexualized images of children online, talking to children sexually online, sending to and receiving from children sexual images online, general touching with sexual intent, touching sexual parts of the body, oral sex, vaginal sex, and anal sex.

Sian: Got some, but not in the right order.

Counsellor: Don't worry about the order, as long as the information gets to stick. I think you've done really well. Now I know you said that you still think that Steve has not abused the kids, but can you say what behaviours on the list are similar to the disclosures made by your daughters?

Sian: I still don't think he's done it, but (in a sarcastic sing-song voice) unwanted sexual contact with an older person, sexual contact between an adult and a child under the age of 16, inappropriate intimate contact with children when nobody's around, touching sexual parts.

Counsellor: I get the sarcasm there, but well done. Are you ready to get on with today's stuff?

Sian: (Yawns) I guess so.

Above, Sian is displaying ambivalence in terms of the work. In the space of a short time, she goes from wanting to engage and remember the safeguarding information, to communicating disdain for the work, especially when the topic becomes more personal, in terms of her daughters' allegations against their father. The yawn is designed to communicate her indifference. Such ambivalence and zig-zagging of motivation to engage in the work is to be expected in most cases, especially when working with clients who are effectively mandated to undertake safeguarding interventions. However, with humour and good grace, the practitioner can flow with the resistance, maintain the therapeutic bond and progress with the work.

Counsellor: OK, Sian, where do you think that most sexual abuse occurs?

Sian: Kids getting snatched in the street and sexually abused. That's one thing I've always been careful of, not letting my kids out of my sight when we're out and about.

When working with partners or relatives of sexual offenders, risky and deviant behaviour is frequently displaced onto other groups, as a way of bolstering ego identity i.e. *at least I'm, or he's, not as bad as this; at least I don't, or he doesn't, do that.* This can test unconditional positive regard, with the judgemental part of the practitioner itching to say something like: *after how your partner has offended and how you have failed to protect your children, you're talking about the shortcomings of others?* However, in this case, the counsellor resisted venting her spleen, handling the situation in a skilful, strengths-focused way, using selective inattention (deliberately not challenging defences) in order to focus on the positive.

> *Counsellor:* It sounds as if you want to keep your children safe, but can I share some research with you?
> *Sian:* If you want.
> *Counsellor:* Well, study after study shows that the vast majority of sexual abuse occurs in the family home or in groups of friends. Children and adults do get sexually abused by strangers in the street but this is fairly rare, as victims usually know their abusers.
> *Sian:* Is that true?
> *Counsellor:* Yes… I guess you, yourself, were typical: sexually abused by somebody in the family.
> *Sian:* (Nods her head)
> *Counsellor:* I wonder, can you say what kind of people commit most abuse?
> *Sian:* (Defensively) Anybody can do it, even women, and social workers.

Some people whose lives have been adversely affected by sexual crime i.e. victims, perpetrators, non-offending partners, can consciously or subconsciously seek to manage distress by distancing themselves from the abuse, citing sexual abuse within groups with which they have few connections, groups who are dissimilar to themselves or to loved ones accused or convicted of abuse. Clients can also seek redress by suggesting that people like the person interviewing them (police officers, social workers or therapists) also commit sexual abuse. Rather than being defensive about this, it is usually more constructive for the practitioner to acknowledge this, before going on to provide a balanced picture.

> *Counsellor:* That's right, anybody can commit sexual abuse, but studies show that most abuse is committed by male family members or friends of the family, who know the children, and males in a position of power or authority over children. Let me pass you this information sheet you can keep in your folder. If you read it, we can then discuss each point. We've already started to discuss some of the points.

The counsellor proceeded to discuss the rest of the points on the information sheet, listed at the beginning of this section. The purpose of providing this sort of information is to give clients accurate information about sexual abuse, so they will be more aware of high-risk situations. Another purpose is to encourage the client to make links between the details of an allegation or an offence and commonly observed patterns of abuse, challenging denial and minimization.

Session 3: Grooming the victim in order to make them give in and not tell

- Picking on a child in need of attention
- Saying nice things and giving treats
- Cuddling and play-fighting in order to touch the child sexually
- Sharing problems and secrets so the child will feel close and feel good about being treated like an adult
- Asking the child to keep secrets
- Bribing and corrupting the child by giving cigarettes, alcohol or drugs
- Making sexual jokes and talking about sex to gradually sexualize the relationship

- Showing pornography
- Getting naked with a child and/or getting the child naked
- Using guilt to keep the child quiet after the abuse, e.g. saying *I'll go to prison; I'll harm myself or commit suicide; you led me on*
- Using fear to keep the child quiet: using threats of violence, e.g. saying *nobody will believe you; if you tell, it will break up the family; I'll harm you or your family*
- Letting somebody else make abusive videos of children, so the abuser can watch online
- Lying about age on the internet to talk to children and young people online for a sexual purpose

An important part of making non-offending partners more risk aware is to help them understand how the grooming process works. There are two main parts to the grooming process: 1. Grooming the victim's protectors: 2. Grooming the victim. This section deals with grooming the victims, in ways listed above. Although the above list is not exhaustive, it provides sufficient examples to raise awareness of the grooming process and to stimulate relevant awareness-raising discussion.

As usual, Session 3 began with the therapist checking in with Sian about how the week had been, and then proceeding to revise the safeguarding information already given to her. The revision process is depicted above, so will not be repeated from this point onward. Sian's week had been uneventful, and she showed increasing recall and deepening understanding of the information previously given and discussed with her.

Counsellor: OK Sian, what does the word grooming mean to you?
Sian: It's like on East Enders and Coronation Street (British TV soap operas), when someone bribes or frightens somebody to have sex with them.

Sexual abuse narratives are frequently depicted on popular TV programmes. Rather than being sniffy about popular entertainment programmes, it can be useful to utilize these sources of information by inquiring about the storyline and the relationship between the characters.

Counsellor: OK, if I give you this piece of paper and pen, can you write down all the ways an adult can groom a child, thinking about what you've seen on TV programmes, and what you know from your own experience?

Sian completed the above task, coming up with half a dozen ways an adult can groom a child. The therapist then provided Sian with a third information sheet, consisting of the points depicted at the beginning of this section. The examples Sian came up with matched ones on the information sheet, allowing the therapist to compliment Sian about this. The therapist then discussed with Sian the other examples of grooming on the information sheet.

Counsellor: Sian, you're working well this week. I'm going to ask you now to do something you might find difficult. Tell me if you do, and we can talk about it. But do you think you are able to say whether any points on the information sheet can be applied to your grandfather's sexual abuse of you?
Sian: (Looking at the sheet) Maybe I needed attention; I don't know. He often used to talk about normal things, but everybody does that. He would be nice and give me treats. But then I used to ask him for stuff, because I knew I would get it after he abused me. He wasn't a joker – he would never play-fight. He was never naked, but I can remember him staring at me in the bath. He definitely used to talk to me about how my grandmother gave him a hard time, and he always used to say that we must keep it secret, or 'Gramps will be sent to prison'. He didn't exactly tell me that nobody would believe me, but I knew my mother probably wouldn't, or she would be too

wrapped up in herself to do anything. I used to cadge fags off him when I was older, but he never gave me any alcohol, even though he used to drink like a fish. He wouldn't ever take drugs or show me pornography. There was nothing with the internet.

Sian goes silent, and tears begin to well up in her eyes.

Counsellor: (Leaving a silence to acknowledge Sian's obvious pain) What are you feeling now Sian, at this moment?
Sian: I don't know, I hate him, but I also feel sorry for him. He was a pathetic little man. I used to manipulate him really, getting him to buy me stuff all the time, but, like we said last time, he was the adult and I was the child, so it was his fault.
Counsellor: It sounds as if you still have a lot of mixed feelings about him and yourself. At times you might hear that voice that's been there a long time, saying you are to blame. Can you think of anything to shut that voice up?
Sian: Yeah, to say it was his fucking fault.
Counsellor: Sian, if that works for you, great.

The counsellor drew a large circle on a piece of paper.

Counsellor: If this is your grandfather, how much of this circle is the good bit of your grandfather and how much is the abusive bit?

Sian drew a smaller circle inside the larger one, taking up roughly a quarter of the total area of the circle. She coloured this circle in with a black pen. She left all the rest of the circle white.

Sian: This bit was the bad part of him. All the white space is the good bit of him. I felt he loved me more than my mother loved me, and I was closer to him than anybody really, when I was a kid (Sian cries some more, and then recovers). He was right about my grandmother - she was a hard cow (laughing ironically). I think I might be like her.

Part of the psychological damage of being sexually abused, especially by a close family member, is the conflicted feelings produced. In my experience, all the victims I have ever worked with have wanted the abuse to stop, but some also love the family member who has abused them. In my view, this love cannot always be put down to trauma ties, but can also be explained by the natural bond between family members and the, sometimes, healthy part of the relationship between victim and abuser. Victims can feel guilty for having such tender, positive or even protective feelings, and can be further damaged by having such feelings pathologized by professionals.

As explained in the previous chapter, the dynamics between a child victim and an adult perpetrator can be further complicated when the child has, or feels they have, an essentially stronger personality than the abusing adult. This is not to suggest that the adult is not totally responsible for the abuse and has not used coercion, but such a dynamic can lead to the victim feeling overprotective towards the abuser and towards potential abusers in later life. The counsellor repeated the empty chair exercises depicted in the previous chapter, in order to consolidate attempts to facilitate Sian to view her grandfather from a more objective, adult standpoint.

Counsellor: I want you to imagine again, like you did in the last session, that you're sitting in that chair there, as the little girl who was being abused by her grandfather, like you did in the last session. What would you say to that little girl now?
Sian: That it's not your fault; you're just a kid. You didn't think there was anybody there for you, and you were just a kid making the most of the situation. You didn't have a mother there to believe you. Your grandfather used that and manipulated you.

Sian began to cry. The counsellor again honoured the moment to allow for catharsis. At such watershed moments in therapy, the force of emotions can lead to a cognitive shift in the client's perception.

> *Sian:* This is what I've been doing to my babies, isn't it? I've been like my mother, not believing them because I've been too fucking selfish.
> *Counsellor:* It's a brave thing for you to say that.

The counsellor was now satisfied that Sian did place the responsibility for her sexual abuse onto her grandfather. Moreover, as Sian got in touch with compassion for her inner child, this softened her, freeing her to realize that she had not shown compassion to her own children, repeating the pattern of her mother not engaging with her, as a victim of abuse.

Therapeutic or safeguarding progress is rarely straightforward. It is often two steps forward and one step back in a sort of zigzag pattern, as already noted. Despite this breakthrough, as will become apparent below, Sian could not entirely maintain the distressing perspective that Steve had abused their daughters. To do so would be to face the prospect of history having definitely repeated itself. However, she had moved forward from dismissing out of hand the prospect of her daughters having been abused to accepting that this might be a possibility, and that she had to keep an open mind with regard to her daughters being sexually abused by their father.

Session 4: Grooming others to get them out of the way in order to create the opportunity to sexually offend

- Making the mother think she can't cope or live independently, fostering general dependency
- Making sure that the sex with her is good, so she'll never think that her partner is sexually interested in children
- Talking about how disgusting sex offenders are
- Being helpful with the children

- Taking the child out on their own
- Helping the child with homework in isolated places like the child's bedroom
- Making the mother feel too guilty or embarrassed to challenge them
- Making everyone too afraid to challenge them by looks, tone of voice, body language, threats, shouting, smashing things, hitting

Another aspect of grooming is gaining the child's protector's (often the mother's) trust in order to be alone with the child, providing an opportunity to abuse. After checking in with Sian and revising all the previous safeguarding information in her folder, the counsellor addressed this issue.

The counsellor began this part of the safeguarding work by asking Sian to repeat the exercise format she had completed in the previous session, writing down on a piece of paper all the ways a partner can groom the parent, in order to gain access to the child. Sian found this exercise more difficult than when she was asked to brainstorm how a perpetrator grooms a child. She could only come up with 'gaining somebody's trust'. The counsellor hypothesized that there were three possible explanations for this seeming block.

The first explanation was that Sian simply could not think of any examples. This was unlikely, as Sian had no learning disabilities and was perspicacious. Alternatively, Sian might have felt exposed in the previous session and thus was more defensive in this one – a common waxing and waning of the motivational dynamic. Thirdly, Sian prided herself on being strong; taking no 'bullshit' was part of her ego ideal. To begin to entertain that she might have been groomed, was perhaps dependent on Steve and vulnerable to grooming, was perhaps too threatening.

Sian declared that she had been thinking about the previous week's session and had decided that she still could not believe that Steve would sexually abuse his own daughters. However, she was now prepared to have an open mind about this. She then broke down in tears, saying she could not face Christmas (now a month away) without Steve and the children.

> *Sian:* I'm all on my own and I can't bear all the stupid Christmas music in the shops. The kids want to buy presents for us and their friends and the social worker has arranged for me to go Christmas shopping with them, with the contact supervisor. I don't think I can go through with it. I'm afraid I'll lose it and just break down in front of them. It's so fucking sad. And the contact worker is so sweet and everything. She used to be in the class behind me at school. She went to Uni and married a teacher. Now she's one of those yummy mummies who do lunch. I hate her (Sian laughs). But she's so nice.

The counsellor decided to stay with Sian's concerns. Sian's self-esteem had taken a battering, and she needed building up before undertaking the safeguarding work planned. For interventions to be effective, practitioners must have sensitivity and flexibility, not allowing clients' fluctuating moods to dominate but responding to significant need. The counsellor was able to employ this nuanced approach.

> *Counsellor:* When you feel at your lowest, what are the thoughts that go through your head?

The counsellor and Sian conducted a self-talk exercise, identifying the repeated negative thoughts which plagued Sian, and positive behavioural and cognitive responses which could help manage the negative thinking and associated painful feelings. This self-management work is only likely to be effective if the therapist invests time teasing out with the client what has worked in the past and what is likely to work in the future, based on the client's own lived experience and expressed in the client's own language. Sian and the counsellor came up with the following:

<u>Negative thoughts</u>

Losing the kids made me feel like a criminal

How do I know that Steve didn't abuse the children?

I'm a failure as a mother

I'm a failure as a person

I'm a failure as a person nobody to turn to

I want to take the kids on holiday and I can't

I feel worthless

I hate crying and feeling the way I do

I burden my friends and inconvenience others

<u>Positive thoughts</u>

I love my kids and I'm trying to do everything I can to get them back

I'm mature enough to know that nobody will ever know for certain.

Being a protective mother is keeping an open mind

I love my daughters. I learn from my mistakes

I'm getting to be a better person all the time

I have control of my own happiness

It is what it is

Get a hold of yourself

I cry to get it out of my system which allows me to get a grip and take control

I'm only human. I can only do what I can. I'm not a miracle worker

The above self-talk exercise is not a panacea for maintaining good mental health, but it can provide an additional tool in the client's toolbox for dealing with distressing negative mood states. The success of this sort of self-talk exercise, or any plan to manage risk or distress, does not depend on the final words on the page, but on the quality of the negotiating process between practitioner and client that has produced the strategy.

Ensuring that a genuinely collaborative process occurs can be challenging for a practitioner, as the values, sensibilities and priorities of the client can be very different from those of the worker. In the above instance, the counsellor felt that Sian's focus on wanting to take the children on holiday was shallow and misplaced, within the context of the inadequate care and protection which led to the children being taken into care. The counsellor was able to bracket these considerations, being sufficiently aware that, for Sian, taking the children on holiday had a metaphorical significance associated with providing for her children. There can be a class element to such clashes of values: middle-class professionals judging working-class clients on relatively low incomes for spending the little they have on expensive toys for children at Christmas is a prime example. Overall, therapeutic safeguarding work is about challenging clients' values and behaviour with regard to parenting, as should be evident throughout the book. In order for self-talk strategies to be effective, they must be embedded in the genuine concerns of the client, as long as the process does not encourage unsafe parenting practices.

Within the above self-talk exercise, there appeared to be a cognitive shift in the way Sian was perceiving Steve. Her positive self-talk to counter the distressing thought that she could not know for sure whether or not Steve had abused the children was a definite acknowledgement that he might have sexually abused the children, and that a way to counter this was to be open-minded: i.e. to hold on to the possibility that sexual abuse could have happened. From a safeguarding point of view, this was progress.

Another important related point to be made is that there can be a difference between a non-offending partner's public statements about risk and their private thoughts. Non-offending partners have told me that they have often argued forcefully (in public) against a social worker's opinion that their partner poses a risk to children, only to be plagued by that very fear in private. This is why it is so important for practitioners to avoid getting into the 'confrontation/denial trap' (Miller and Rollnick, 1991), but rather to tease out and explore the private side of a client's ambivalence. This technique, albeit employed with sexual and violent offenders, is ably demonstrated by Jenkins (1990).

The counsellor explained to Sian that there are two main ways of coping with negative thinking and distressing mood states: self-talk (a cognitive-behavioural strategy) employed above, and mindfulness - observing thoughts and feelings in a detached way until they dissipate and lose their power. The counsellor went through with Sian a selection of mindfulness techniques, found in many popular books on the subject such as that of Verni (2015), to help her practise mentally surfing negativity by breathing deeply and observing a negative thought or feeling until it passes and another feeling or thought form emerges. In subsequent sessions both counsellor and client referenced these emotional management techniques at times, when talking about challenges occurring in Sian's day-to-day life.

The counsellor moved on to asking Sian to think of names she could give herself when she was not functioning well and when she was functioning well, as a parent and a person. She decided upon the following:

- Crap Sian
- Determined Sian

The counsellor commented that 'Crap Sian' sounded a bit of a harsh description. Sian insisted that this was the term she wanted to use, as this summed her up. The counsellor accepted the term because it is important for clients to use the language that has meaning for them. The counsellor then asked Sian to draw two circles: a 'Crap Sian' circle and a 'Determined Sian Circle'. The client then put the negative aspects of 'Crap Sian' in one circle, and the positive aspects of 'Determined Sian' in the other circle. The counsellor suggested that it was important for Sian to focus on the positive circle, and to look at it when she was besieged by negative impulses.

The above self-management work can have a holistic, knock-on safeguarding effect and, indeed, contribute to positive parenting. Parents who have good safeguarding ability tend to have the capacity to acknowledge their thoughts and feelings with self-acceptance and have the ability to then compassionately self-soothe. The ability to regulate emotions leads to more considered decision making.

Having attended to Sian's immediate concerns, the counsellor reverted to the safeguarding programme, with regard to how sex offenders can groom carers of children. The counsellor provided Sian with a handout, with the information on it outlined at the beginning of this section. To recap:

- Making the mother think she can't cope or live independently, fostering general dependency
- Making sure that the sex with her is good, so she'll never think that her partner is sexually interested in children
- Talking about how disgusting sex offenders are
- Being helpful with the children
- Taking the child out on their own
- Helping the child with homework in isolated places like the child's bedroom
- Making the mother feel too guilty or embarrassed to challenge them
- Making everyone too afraid to challenge them by looks, tone of voice, body language, threats, shouting, smashing things, hitting

The counsellor then engaged Sian in discussing this material, enabling Sian to relate the information to relationships and events in her own life and the lives of others.

Session 5: Three profiles of offenders

The inoffensive seeming offender

- Views the world as a hostile place, so seeks solace in the world of children
- Emotional congruence with children
- Emotional loneliness
- Problems with forming intimate adult relationships
- Anxious personality type

- Views the world as a scary place, so seeks solace in the world of children
- Idealizes relationships with children

The king of the castle offender

- Views the world as a hostile place, so seeks to dominate others, including sexually
- Enjoys power and control
- Intimidates people
- Problems controlling anger
- Believes that they are entitled to put their needs and desires before those of others

The chaotic offender

- Views the world as a hostile place, so exploits others to meet pleasure needs, including sexually
- Behaves generally irresponsibly
- Behaves in generally anti-social ways
- Poor emotional management
- Indulges in pleasure without thinking too much of the consequences

When explaining the above profiles to clients, I explain that human beings cannot be put neatly into boxes, as each person is a complex and unique individual. However, if not held onto rigidly, models can help us make sense of people's behaviour. I also point out that we all display some of the above traits illustrated in the three profiles, and that the models overlap to some extent.

Depending on the sophistication and interest of the client, I go into more or less detail about the theoretical assumptions underlying the above three profiles. However, as this book is primarily aimed at practitioners, I will provide some more in-depth theory.

The psychological schema (i.e. deep-seated way of looking at the world) described as a 'dangerous world' schema by Ward and Keenan (1999) can be found in the way some individuals who sexually offend talk about their crimes. Of course, we all know that the world can be dangerous, but this theory is related to individuals who are overly preoccupied with the world being a hostile place.

A likely explanation for the development of the 'dangerous world' schema is related to the 'fight' or 'flight' response to early attachment deficits or trauma. If an individual has not experienced secure parenting and attuned nurture from main caregivers, this can result in the person having a deep sense that life is a Hobbesian jungle where you need to do one of the following:

- Dominate and subdue others in order to meet needs and obtain desires (the 'fight' response of the 'king of the castle offender')
- Avoid experiences in order to meet needs and obtain desires (the 'flight' response of the 'inoffensive seeming offender')
- Use both dominance ('fight') and avoidance of consequential thinking and 'responsibility ('flight') in order to meet needs and obtain desires, as is the case with the 'chaotic offender'

A note of caution with regard to all theories and models concerning people who have sexually offended is that many evolve out of research with sexual offenders who are in prison. It is often easier to conduct research on prison populations as they are a captive audience, may want to curry favour with prison authority figures, and might agree to take part in research projects to break the tedium of prison life. Apart from the methodological biases in many research studies, prison populations tend to consist of higher risk, more deviant offenders. Research findings amongst this high-risk group are then unhelpfully generalized to lower-risk sex offenders and to those individuals not convicted of a sexual offence, who have had allegations made against them.

Whereas the above theoretical discussion may prove interesting to some, in the context of this book the most important point of the above profiles is how they can be used with clients to good safeguarding effect. The counsellor demonstrates how this can be achieved with Sian.

Counsellor: Sian, can I run past you three different sorts of sex offenders? You can then tell me what you think, and if they ring any bells.

Sian: Go ahead.

Counsellor: The first one is called the 'inoffensive offender', not because what they do is inoffensive, but because they appear inoffensive. In fact, their sexual offending may be very serious. This person seems a bit like a child themselves. They may have problems getting close to adults and can be frightened of the adult world. They have not developed the social or relationship skills to make deep emotional connections to adults, or even sometimes to make friends with adults. This sort of person often feels more comfortable around children than around adults, and may relate well to children. They may think that childhood is the best it gets, and that the adult world is a bit disappointing. They may also idealize their relationships with children and can view any abuse of them as being part of a special friendship they think they have with a child.

Sian: Yeah, I get the picture.

Counsellor: OK, if somebody was in a relationship with a person like this, what would be the challenges in trying to protect a child from them?

Sian: I dunno.

Counsellor: Have a think.

Sian: Maybe the person would feel sorry for them, and wouldn't want to hurt their feelings by asking them any awkward questions.

Counsellor: Excellent, good; anything else?

Sian: Well, they wouldn't seem to be risky, would they?

Counsellor: That's right; they might not. With this sort of offender, the protective instinct of the person who is in a relationship with them - a partner, mother, other family member - can shift from making sure children are safe to trying to ensure that the offender is not upset in any way.

Sian: (Nods)

Counsellor: The 'king of the castle offender' can look like the opposite of the 'inoffensive offender'. This person is more like many who commit domestic violence. They frighten people to get what they want by the threatening way they look, speak or behave. People walk on eggshells to please them, and can end up dependent on them. The 'king of the castle offender' can be an important person in an organization, or a family man, a successful professional or a criminal. The thing people like this have in common is that they use their power and influence to abuse others and to get away with it.

Sian: A bit like Jimmy Savile?

Counsellor: Yes, he would probably fit this profile. Sian, same question as before, if somebody was in a relationship with a person like this, what would be the challenges in trying to protect a child from them?

Sian: Well, that's obvious. People would be shit scared of them, so would be too afraid to do anything or blow the whistle.

Counsellor: You've got it. Ready for the third one?

Sian: (With humour) You're gonna tell me, aren't you?

Counsellor: (Returning the humour) Afraid so. The 'chaotic offender' takes pleasure where he finds it, without thinking too much about the consequences or the impact their behaviour will have on themselves or others. Often, this sort of person may have problems controlling themselves in other areas of life. They may have substance misuse problems, may get into debt, be a risk-taker and have a criminal record for general offending. They may be promiscuous, sleeping around. They might present as charming, good looking, a laugh. They might seem like a catch. Often, they will have younger partners because young people will be too immature to see through them. A typical way in which this person might offend is, for instance, going to an all-day barbecue with a partner on their arm. They might get gradually drunk or stoned throughout the day. By the evening, they eye a 14-year-old they take a fancy to. If they have the opportunity, they might sexually assault the 14-year-old and think nothing of it, going home with their partner as if nothing has happened.

Sian: Well, the problem with this person is that the offending is opportunistic, is that the word?

Counsellor: That's the word. Anything else?

Sian: Can't think.

Counsellor: Well, if this person is a man, they will come across as a normal, blokey guy, and the people around him might not make the link between how he looks and generally behaves, because he doesn't look like the stereotype of sex offenders.

Sian: A weirdo in a dirty mac, you mean?

Counsellor: Something like that.

Sian: How can you tell, then?

Counsellor: Well, you can't always. Most sex offenders look like anyone else, and may have perfectly good sex lives with their partners, with their partner noticing nothing out of the ordinary. But this doesn't mean someone is incapable of committing a sexual offence, including against a child. It just means that if an allegation of sexual abuse is made, it must be taken seriously

Sian: But people make false allegations.

Counsellor: This can happen, but it shouldn't stop people taking all allegations seriously, even if they turn out to be false, or probably false, as sometimes nobody will ever be sure, only the two people involved. Anyway, I'm telling you what I think, but what do you think?

Sian: (Shrugs her shoulders) I guess.

Counsellor: With regard to the three profiles, do you know anybody in your life who is a bit like this?

Sian: My mother had lots of men like the 'king of the castle' and the 'chaotic' type. My grandfather ... he was definitely the 'inoffensive type' … Steve … he's a bit like the chaotic one, I suppose. I'm starting to feel a bit sick now.

The above exercise can evoke uncomfortable emotions for non-offending partners, as it facilitates them to view partners in their lives from an objective distance. In the process, they begin to recognize abusive patterns in their loved one's behaviour which have, hitherto, been normalized.

Session 6: Impact of sexual abuse on victims at the time of the offence and later in life

Each individual's experience of sexual abuse is different. However, the following factors tend to be aggravating features:

- The more frightened the victim was by the abuse
- If the victim felt/feels unprotected from further abuse, and is living in a state of fear
- If the abuse was carried out by a trusted family member the victim relied on for security (e.g. a parent figure)
- If the abuse was particularly invasive e.g. oral sex, intercourse
- If the victim was not believed by family members, and was blamed for causing trouble
- If the victim was made to feel responsible for the abuse
- If the victim was particularly vulnerable, with existing emotional and welfare problems

Just as offenders can insulate themselves from the distress caused to victims by sexual abuse, offenders' partners can undergo a parallel process. In order to maintain a relationship with a person who has harmed another, the non-offending partner has to disassociate from the suffering caused to victims. Victims or persons alleging abuse are often vilified by offenders or alleged offenders as unreliable, promiscuous, trouble makers or simply 'bad'. This 'othering' serves the purpose of undermining the credibility of the victim's statements, or making any abuse seem less 'real' and minimizing harm. Raising the non-offending partner's awareness of the harm caused by sexual abuse and the long-term consequences of it, can serve as a corrective to such collusion, and act as a motivator for the non-offending partner to play their part in helping to keep children safe.

With regard to safeguarding work, the counsellor suggests to Sian that each victim experiences abuse in a unique way, and that many victims overcome abusive experiences to lead fulfilling and constructive lives, not letting the abuse define them. It is important to make this point. If the client has been abused themselves, the message that a person's future is not determined by the abuse they have suffered can be liberating. Having made this point, the counsellor asked Sian if she had any ideas about what can aggravate the harm caused by sexual abuse.

Sian: Well, it's all bad isn't it?
Counsellor: That's right, but what do you think can make sexual abuse worse?
Sian: Violence, rape?
Counsellor: Yes, the more extreme the abuse, the more damage it can cause. Anything else?
Sian: I'm not sure, really.
*Counsellor:*All right, if I pass over to you the information sheet (containing the points which appear at the beginning of this section), could you read it, and make any comments you want?
Sian: (After reading the points in the information sheet) What do you want me to say?
Counsellor: Well, does any of this apply to your experiences of abuse?

The counsellor, above, was being very challenging, having made the decision that her client was sufficiently robust to cope with talking about her victim experiences in this way. With another client, the counsellor might have made a different choice, sensing that the client would be too emotionally fragile to engage at this level. As with all choices about what to say or not say in the therapeutic moment, efficacy depends upon the clinical sensitivity of the therapist.

Sian was able to identify that, in relation to being sexually abused by her grandfather, it involved a close family member over a long period of time. The abuse did not involve penile penetration, but did involve oral sex. Sian maintained that she was not living in a state of fear at the time, that her grandfather was not responsible for her day-to-day care. Sian generally seemed to have now come to terms with having been sexually abused by her grandfather, placing the responsibility on his shoulders.

An interesting question is how a therapist can know if a client has come to terms with, or processed, abuse suffered: if there is no 'unfinished business', as it were. Perhaps, to make an obvious point, only the client can ever know this. Nevertheless, there are indications, including the following:

- When the client is no longer in denial or minimizing the abuse
- When the client has normative insight into the harm that abuse causes
- When the client consistently places the responsibility where it belongs – with the perpetrator
- When the client can speak about the abuse without it being overly painful to do so
- When the client no longer defines themselves in terms of being an abuse victim
- When the client is relatively free from abuse symptomology such as: nightmares, flashbacks, hypervigilance, self-harming behaviours, including being caught up in abusive relationships

I remember conducting a training day with counsellors. One of the counsellors came up to me and said that he had been a victim of sexual abuse and that he was not ready to 'forgive' the abuser yet. In my view, if a person still holds hostile feelings against their abuser, then the person should not be offering counselling to offenders, as it will be very difficult to prevent hostility towards one's own abuser adversely affecting the relationship with a client who has also committed sexual offending.

The above said, is it necessary to forgive an abuser in order to recover from abuse? I would suggest that forgiveness means different things to different people and is a complex construct. However, forgiveness would seem to me to rarely be a one-off event but an ongoing process, perhaps characterized by the bullet-point list above.

Therapeutic practitioners of all kinds are usually very good at defining problems, but less practised in asking ourselves what successful therapeutic outcomes would look like. Hence, to reiterate the point made elsewhere in the book, it is always worth asking ourselves, and more importantly the client, how their life would be changed if they no longer had the problem – in this case continued suffering because of being sexually abused.

In my experience, clients are rarely 'cured' by therapy. It is also difficult to always know whether depression or anxiety, or any other life problem, is related to abuse suffered or some other factor such as temperament or circumstances. Depending on your perspective, life is a series of problems to be solved or managed, offering the opportunity for growth. In this sense, the business of therapy is never done. However, a time comes in the therapeutic process when the 'juice' seems to just run out of it. I feel this, and the client usually feels it too. When this occurs (and it is often constructive for a therapist to congruently call this feeling out into the room) the client may have come to the end of a growth spurt with the particular therapist that they have been seeing, at least for the time being.

With regard to Sian, the counsellor asked her how the disclosure of abuse made by her children against their father stacked up against the aggravating factors outlined at the beginning of this section.

Sian: Well, he is their father. They talked about touching, not intercourse. I don't think they were frightened of him, but he could speak harshly sometimes.

Counsellor: He is also a big man physically, so could he seem intimidating to children perhaps?

Sian: Perhaps.

Counsellor: Anything else?

Sian: I can't think of anything.

Counsellor: How about you not believing them?

Sian: (In tears) I suppose so. I didn't, did I?

Counsellor: If you could play the DVD back, how would you now want to respond?

Sian: Give them a hug, not shout at them, and say to them they could tell me anything they wanted. I wouldn't have automatically believed them, I still don't, but I would have sort of kept an open mind.

Counsellor: And why do you think they disclosed to a teacher, and not you?

Sian: They didn't think I would believe them, and they were right, weren't they?

The counsellor left a long silence, for Sian to reflect on what had been said. She then complimented Sian on being able to look at some painful issues. In the second half of the session, the counsellor went through with Sian the long-term impact of sexual abuse on victims. This can be helpful in safeguarding terms as it again counteracts any minimizing of sexual abuse, and can increase the motivation for non-offending partners to prevent such harm occurring to their children. In the case of Sian and other non-offending partners, who have been victims of abuse themselves, it can also throw light on their own feelings, thoughts and behaviour.

I am always mindful, however, of the dangers of consolidating life stories of failure and misery, so I make a particular effort to remind clients that the common effects of abuse, which appear below, do not happen to all people who have been sexually abused, and that many victims demonstrate great resilience and resource in managing and overcoming the consequences of being abused. The following information can be presented to clients in similar ways to those demonstrated above, with an emphasis on weaving the information into the client's own experiences:

- Not being believed and being labelled as a trouble maker
- Rejected, scapegoated by the family because of reporting abuse
- Guilt about reporting the abuse
- Falsely believing there must be something wrong with them for attracting the abuse
- Low self-esteem
- Trust issues
- Fear about or aversion to sex
- Feeling different from others
- Mental health/psychological problems
- Drugs/alcohol problems
- Self-harm
- Eating disorders
- Low educational and occupational achievement
- Relationship problems
- Promiscuity (sleeping around)
- Difficulty in forming sexual and emotional relationships
- Caught in cycle of abusive relationships
- Social isolation
- Problems with authority figures

Impact on children and young people, who appear in images uploaded onto the internet:

- Many of these children/young people are being abused in order to appear in the images
- Many of these children/young people lack adequate parenting

- Many of these children/young people are from developing countries and living in desperate circumstances
- Images are notoriously difficult to erase from the internet. Hence, many of these children/young people grow up knowing that individuals (mostly men) around the world are masturbating about them. This can have a devastating impact on self-esteem and sense of self
- Engaging with sexual abuse material on the internet, even if this material is not paid for, sustains a market for the continued sexual abuse of children and young people via the internet

Session 7: Case study work

I find that using case studies in safeguarding work with clients is one of the most effective ways of raising awareness of how to identify and appropriately respond to signs of risk. Many people relate to stories more readily than ideas divorced from narrative. Case study work can also help clients reflect on their life experiences through the lives of others, albeit the fictionalized lives of others. In my previous book (Smith, 2017), I write about conducting safeguarding work, including some good practice tips. I will repeat this information here, as it is as relevant to working with non-offending partners as it is to working with offenders.

- The therapist should always use clinical judgement as to whether or not the client is sufficiently robust to engage with the material in any case study
- Use a case study which includes pertinent themes to the client's offending, but is not obviously the same as the abuse in question
- Do not use a case study that includes far more serious sexual offending than the client has been convicted or accused of, as this is likely to be experienced as stigmatizing, provoking resistance

- Use case studies at the appropriate level of sophistication
  for the client
- Explain to the client that there might be material in the case
  study that they might find upsetting
- Ask permission to use a case study, explaining that it is a
  way of helping to understand how sex offending happens,
  and can be avoided

Once agreement to using a case study has been negotiated, the client can be provided with a copy, with the practitioner retaining a copy for themselves. Below is an example of a typical case study that was used in my previous book on counselling offenders. It can also be used with non-offending partners, with the counsellor demonstrating this to good safeguarding effect, with Sian.

Michael (40) met Janet on an internet dating site. He seemed a bit shy but very nice, and gentler than her previous partner, who had been intimidating and emotionally abusive to her. After they had seen each other for 3 weeks, he moved in with her and her three children: two boys (8 and 10) and a girl (6). Janet thought he was great with the children. He would often take them to the park and play football with the two boys, and he always brought sweets home for them on the day he received his benefits. Janet worked part time and it was nice having someone she could trust to look after the children, apart from her elderly mother. It was also useful when she was exhausted after work that Michael offered to help with the children's homework and bath-times. Sometimes Janet would ask Michael to babysit if she was going out and he would offer to take Suzie, her daughter, swimming while she took the boys to football practice. He seemed to spoil Suzie, buying her more things than the boys. When Janet spoke to him about this, he just said it was because she was the only girl, the boys had each other. Janet thought no more about it. She did sometimes wonder what they got up to as they seemed to spend so much time together, but Janet put it down to the fact that little girls need a father figure and Suzie did not see her Dad any more. It wasn't until Suzie mentioned to Janet that she had touched Michael's 'willy' that Janet realized that Michael had been abusing Suzie. Janet talked to Suzie some more to try to find out exactly what had been happening and then immediately contacted the police and Social Services. Michael was arrested and held in custody. Eventually Suzie told her mum and the social workers that Michael had begun playing 'tickling' games that she did not mind at first. But then he started putting his hand under her clothes to tickle her. She said she told him she didn't like it and he stopped for a while. Sometimes when he was putting her to bed (to help her Mum out) he would watch her while she went to the loo and got undressed and then would start trying to tickle her under the bedclothes. She woke up one night and he was lying in bed beside her and he was touching her vagina. He told her not to tell anyone or she would be in big trouble and he would have to go away. The next day he took her out to McDonalds and treated her to her favourite meal. Suzie also explained that Michael often came into the bathroom when she was in the bath and would help her to wash and dry herself. When charges were put to him, he denied that he had done anything wrong. He said that he had never touched Suzie, but that she often came into the bathroom when he was in there and liked to watch him having a wee. He also said that Suzie would get into bed with him and tickle him. He told police that ever since he moved into the home, Suzie had 'fancied' him and followed him around.

Counsellor: Sian, is it OK with you if we look at a story of how sexual abuse tends to typically occur in families? The story is not real. It's been made up to help people have a better idea of how to manage risk issues.

Sian: Is it about me?

Counsellor: No, the situation is different, but you may see some overlap. I have two copies. Would you like to read it yourself, or I can read it out loud and you can follow the text on the page?

Sian: I don't mind.

Counsellor: You choose.

Sian: You read it then, and I'll follow it on the page.

The counsellor handed a copy of the case study to Sian, and read her copy out loud.

Counsellor: How do you feel at the end of that?

Sian: It's a bit heavy, but I'm OK.

Counsellor: Right. So I'm going to read it again, a little piece at a time, and then ask you what's going on in that bit? Is that OK?

Sian: Go ahead.

The counsellor reads out the case study again but in short segments, asking Sian to comment, using the following sorts of questions and prompts:

- What do you think is happening at this point?
- What do you think are the feelings, thoughts and motivations of the characters?
- What were the main triggers to the offending?
- How did Michael gain Janet's trust to be alone with the child?
- How did Michael kid himself it was OK to offend?
- How did Michael groom Suzie?
- What could Janet have done differently?
- How could Janet have been more protective?
- What prevented Janet from being more protective?
- What skills and abilities would she need to have been more protective?

- What would Janet have to lose if she had recognized risk sooner?

Below is an extract from the conversation that the counsellor had with Sian about the text.

Counsellor: OK, what is the first choice that Janet could have made to protect her children better?

Sian: Well, she shouldn't have let him move into the house in the first place.

Counsellor: OK, what do you think was behind Janet's decision to move Michael in?

Sian: She's lonely. He seemed like a nice guy, somebody to help out with the kids.

Counsellor: Right, so she made the choice to allow him to move in. What is the next point where Janet could have acted differently?

Sian: Not let him get so close to the kids.

Counsellor: But remember, at the time, Janet did not know that Michael was going to sexually abuse one of her children. This possibility might have not entered her head.

Sian: Yeah, I suppose.

Counsellor: At the beginning he seems like a nice guy, helping out with the kids, being helpful …

Sian: … And she probably thought that he was a lot nicer than her last partner.

Counsellor: Exactly, so how could Janet have known the difference between Michael being a nice guy - helpful with the children - and him grooming them?

Sian: I don't know, it's difficult isn't it? How do you know what's going on in a person's mind?

Counsellor: Well, I guess you don't. It really depends on the circumstances, the age and sex of the child, and the relationship between the adult and the child. Can I suggest some questions to consider in your own mind which may help you tell the difference and to spot emerging signs of risk?

The counsellor suggested the following questions for Sian to consider, in specific relation to an adult having emotional, social or physical contact with a child:

- How long has the person known the child?
- What is the person's relationship to the child: parent, step-parent, grandparent, non-parental relative, family friend?
- Is the contact appropriate to the relationship between the adult and the child?
- Is the contact appropriate to the age and sex of the child?
- Is the contact occurring when there are people present or when the adult is on their own with the child?

Counsellor: OK, Sian, in the light of the general safety considerations I've just given you, can you identify any of Michael's behaviour with the children that seemed inappropriate, leading up to him abusing Suzie?

Sian: Well, he got to know them too quickly, didn't he? She should have asked herself why he was so interested in her kids.

Counsellor: Anything else?

Sian: It seems a bit odd that he wanted to take the girl swimming, and not go playing football with the boys.

Counsellor: Why odd?

Sian: When you go swimming, people haven't got many clothes on, and he would have to have helped Suzie get undressed.

Counsellor: Anything else?

Sian: He's favouring Suzie over the boys. Grooming her, making her feel special.

Counsellor: Yes, that seems to be the case. Janet does challenge him over this, doesn't she?

Sian: I think at this point, she feels that something isn't right.

Counsellor: What happened when she challenges him?

Sian: He makes excuses, and she backs off.

Counsellor: Why do you think she backs off?

Sian: Doesn't want to upset him. Afraid of losing the relationship.

Counsellor: Anything else?

Sian: Maybe she doesn't want to look at the fact that he might be abusing her kid. Easier to bury her head in the sand

Counsellor: OK, what did she do right?

Sian: Call the police, when her daughter said about the abuse.

Counsellor: What could she have done differently?

Sian: Not allow him into the home, when she didn't know him very well.

Counsellor: OK, she didn't make that decision. What would have been the next point, where she could have made a more protective choice?

Sian: Not let him have so much contact with the children, and treat one child differently from another.

Counsellor: And the next point of choice?

Sian: When he didn't listen to her, when she said she was unhappy about him treating the children differently.

Counselling: What could she have done, when he didn't listen?

Sian: Insist more!

Counsellor: What else could Janet have done?

Sian: Tell him to pack his bags and leave.

Counsellor: You made loads of excellent safeguarding points; you're good at this. You said that Janet shouldn't have let Michael into the house in the first place because she didn't know him that well. You talked about Janet not allowing Michael to have so much contact with the kids, and insisting on him not treating the children differently. You said that she should have told him to pack his bags when he wouldn't listen to her. What would have she needed to be like to do all these things?

Sian: How do you mean?

Counsellor: What qualities, knowledge or strengths would she have needed to act in the protective ways you describe?

Sian: Well, she would have to stand up to him, and not let him make excuses and take her in.

Counsellor: How would she have done this?

Sian: Be firm, look him in the eye, give him the message that she's not going to roll over.

To reiterate a point made elsewhere, a feature of the strengths-focused approach is asking for detail, detail, detail: breaking down big ideas and concepts into recognizable, manageable and achievable small steps or chunks of behaviour. Below are some questions which can achieve this, in terms of facilitating the client to think about body language, facial expression and tone of voice.

- How would you be standing or sitting if you did that?
- How would you be using your arms and hands?
- What would your breathing be like?
- What would the expression on your face be?
- What would your voice sound like: low, high, soft, hard?
- Would you be speaking slowly or quickly?

If I have developed a trusting relationship with a client, and I assess that the client is sufficiently comfortable and confident, I will set up various role-play exercises. This can take the form of role-playing characters from a case study, in order to act out how they could have responded more protectively, or role-playing possible future scenarios, where the non-offending partner will have to challenge somebody about an emerging sign of risk, or to re-assert boundaries.

In the case of Sian, the counsellor was confident that she would have the strength of character and assertiveness to challenge a partner about risk issues. With Sian, it was more the case of what she would have to lose if she made such a challenge. Hence, the counsellor focused on this issue, using the case study to do so.

Counsellor: So, if Janet did challenge Michael about his behaviour, what would she be at risk of losing?
Sian: Well, she would lose him and the support he provides. She would also lose the dream of a possible happy future with him, even though he's a loser.
Counsellor: Sounds about right.
Sian: It's what I've done with Steve, isn't it?

The counsellor leaves a silence for Sian to reflect on this last point.

Session 8: The New Life Safety Plan

Safety plans work best, in my experience, when they incorporate the gains in knowledge and self-awareness that the client has made throughout the counselling process or safeguarding course. A safety plan is ultimately words on a page. If clients want to, they can ignore what is written and even when safety plans such as child protection agreements are monitored, the monitoring ends at some point. When this happens, behaving in a protective way is an inside job; it relies on the internal motivations and controls of the parents and carers involved. Hence, safety plans have more likelihood of being effective and avoiding disguised compliance, if the negotiating of the safety plan is a genuinely collaborative effort. There is then more chance that the client is fully signed up to and invested in the words on the page.

Sian came into the safety planning session, saying that Steve had 'shacked-up' with another woman 'half his age' and that now their relationship 'is definitely off'. She added she now realizes that he could have abused their children after all and that she 'now, definitely' does not want anything more to do with him.

The counsellor noticed that she was disappointed in Sian. Sian had been maintaining that she had given up hope of continuing her relationship with Steve for some time, although it seems that she had only truly reached this decision after discovering that Steve had moved in with a much younger partner. Sian appeared more exercised over Steve finding another partner, than over the prospect that he had sexually abused their children. The counsellor tossed around in her head the idea of confronting Sian, saying something like, *but I thought you had already decided to end the relationship with Steve.* The counsellor was sufficiently mature to realize that if she said this, she would have the momentary satisfaction of venting her frustration, but she doubted if this would improve Sian's safeguarding ability, as it would probably just make her defensive. The counsellor accepted 'what is' and attempted to utilize Sian's hurt and resultant jealousy, in order to enhance safety for the children in the future.

> *Counsellor:* Sian, you sound hurt that Steve has set up home with a younger partner.
> *Sian:* Bastard, I always knew he had a roving eye, especially for younger women.
> *Counsellor:* How could you ensure that you don't make a relationship with a guy that may hurt you and your children again?
> *Sian:* (Angrily) I don't know. It's the luck of the draw. You don't know them properly until they live with you, do you?
> *Counsellor:* Perhaps not, but there may be signs. What signs would there be that a prospective partner might hurt you or your children?
> *Sian:* You tell me.
> *Counsellor:* Well, if I make some suggestion, you tell me if you agree and would put these on your 'No Way' list.
> *Sian:* Go ahead.

The counsellor came up with the following suggestions:

- If somebody has a criminal record
- Any convictions or allegations with regard to domestic or sexual abuse
- Previous involvement with child protection services

Sian: But everybody I know has that stuff in their lives.

Counsellor: OK, so what would your bottom line be about forming a relationship with somebody in the future?

Sian: Well maybe he can have a criminal record, but no crimes or allegations to do with violence or sexual abuse.

Counsellor: And being involved with child protection issues, if he has been thought to pose a risk to children.

Sian: Yeah, I agree with that. Also, with drugs - I probably would go out with a guy who used a bit of cannabis and speed, but not a complete dope-head, and nobody who's involved with harder drugs such as heroin or is using cocaine all the time.

It would have been the counsellor's wish that Sian would change her lifestyle, so that most of the people she knows, and the men she is likely to meet, do not have criminal convictions, and do not use drugs, although this would probably be unrealistic. In the longer-term future, Sian might use her undoubted intelligence and force of character to escape the structural limitations of her present life conditions - poverty and crime - to the point where she could live a predominantly pro-social lifestyle. However, she was not at this place yet. Hence, it was a case of realistic damage limitation and potential harm reduction. The counsellor also felt conflicted because she knew many people in her own circle who smoked cannabis, and a few who had probably taken cocaine recreationally from time to time, although none of these friends had allowed their children to be at risk, as Sian had done.

The final part of the work with Sian was the counsellor agreeing a New Life Safety Plan with Sian. The following plan is related to Sian's specific background and circumstances, although much of the content is generic to most households where safeguarding work needs to be completed with a non-offending partner or carer, to help manage potential risk to children.

New Life Safety Plan

<u>Signs of Safety</u>

- Sian complying with all future child protection agreements
- Future partners will not undertake any intimate care tasks with the children
- Future partners will not be left overnight with the children
- Children not being afraid of either parent: no hitting or sustained shouting, children being disciplined through distraction techniques, naughty step and removing privileges
- Future partners not undermining Sian, especially with the children

<u>Signs of Risk</u>

- If the above boundaries are broken
- Sian forming a relationship with a partner who has convictions or allegations of violence or sexual abuse in his background
- The above type of partner having contact with the children or moving into the family home
- Sian and any other adults being drunk or stoned in the presence of the children
- Sian having adult parties in the home when the children are present

In addition, below are some generic, common signs of risk with regard to sexual abuse:

- Children being afraid of or intimidated by adults
- Children desperately wanting to please
- Children not wanting to be left alone with a person

- Sudden, unexplained change in children's behaviour: becoming withdrawn or aggressive, self-harming
- Children having gifts or money and being unable to explain where they came from
- Children being overly embarrassed or unusually ashamed of their bodies for their stage of development
- Children continuing bedwetting beyond the usual developmental stage
- Children displaying age-inappropriate sexualized behaviour/language, and not stopping when told to do so
- Children behaving sexually abusively toward younger/weaker children
- Injuries/soreness/unusual marks/discharges around sexual areas of children's bodies, loss of appetite, nightmares

<u>Responses to Signs of Risk</u>

- Sian talking to the children about any concerns
- Sian talking to any future partner about any concern
- Sian talking to teachers or the GP about any concerns
- Sian contacting the Lucy Faithfull Foundation Stop It Now helpline: 0808 1000 900, www.stopitnow.org.uk
- Sian calling Children's Services (the duty social worker)
- Sian calling the police

Conclusion

This chapter has hopefully demonstrated how safeguarding work can be woven into the talking method of counselling, but can also be delivered as a structured programme. It is unlikely to be effective in enhancing a parent's or carer's protective ability, if previous abuse or trauma in a client's life remain unaddressed. However safeguarding work is delivered, it is likely to be most effective if the practitioner remains client-centred, and maintains a balance between addressing the client's issues as they arise, without losing focus on raising the client's awareness and capacity, with regard to playing their part in protecting children from sexual abuse and other mistreatment.

Practice points from this chapter

- Learning, especially when about personal change, is a complex, multi-layered process
- If the practitioner has a hidden agenda involving persuading a non-offending partner to leave a relationship, this is likely to provoke counterproductive resistance
- When conducting safeguarding work, it is important not to neglect process issues and the immediate concerning issues for the client, but without losing focus on the overall child protection agenda
- The counsellor may have to be proactive at points (a possible challenge for client-centred counsellors), in refocusing the client onto the safeguarding learning tasks at hand
- Avoid getting into drawn-out discussions about the relative responses to sex with children and young people at different times and in different cultures
- Attempt to link theoretical ideas about sexual abuse, risk management and safeguarding generally to the life experience and existing knowledge base of the client
- The aim of safeguarding counselling is to enable the client to make more informed, safer choices about relationships
- Revising material already discussed at the beginning of each new safeguarding session can significantly consolidate learning
- Base any self-talk strategies on the lived life of the client and the client's own language
- The practitioner should use clinical sensitivity when delivering information about sexual abuse generally, including when using case studies

- The risk management gains of safety plans are related to the quality of the negotiation between practitioner and client, which has gone into agreeing the contents

References

Andrews, D.A. and Bonta, J. (2003) *The psychology of criminal conduct,* 3rd edition. Cincinnati, Ohio: Anderson.

Jenkins, A. (1990) *Invitations to responsibility: The therapeutic engagement of men who are violent and abusive.* Adelaide: Dulwich Centre Publications.

Miller, W.R. and Rollnick, S. (1991) *Motivational interviewing: Preparing people to change addictive behaviour.* New York: The Guilford Press.

Smith, A. (2009) *Sex offenders and the probation officers who supervise them: How relevant are strengths-based approaches?* Doctoral thesis for Cardiff University School of Social Sciences. Available from: http://orca.cf.ac.uk/55909/1/U584448.pdf [Jan 2022].

Smith, A. (2017) *Counselling male sexual offenders: A strengths-focused approach.* London: Routledge.

Still J. (2016) *Assessment and intervention with mothers and partners following child sexual abuse.* London and Philadelphia: Jessica Kingsley Publishers.

Verni, K.A. (2015) *Practical mindfulness: A step-by-step guide.* London: Dorling Kindersley Limited.

Ward, T. and Keenan, T. (1999) 'Child molesters' implicit theories', *Journal of Interpersonal Violence,* 14 (8): pp. 821-838.

PART 3

COUNSELLING PARTNERS AND OTHER FAMILY MEMBERS IN A SYSTEMIC WAY TO CONSOLIDATE AND ENHANCE FAMILY SAFETY

EIGHT

YASMIN, ZARA AND GRANDPARENTS

Introduction

The first section of this book examined counselling partners of individuals who have sexually offended, but where there are no current child protection concerns. The second section explored situations where there are current worries about children being at sexual risk, necessitating partners to undertake safeguarding work. This third section deals, not only with working with the person who has offended and the partner of that person, but also with the system of the family itself. The case study in this chapter features Zara and Yasmin. Children's Services have concerns that Yasmin might pose a risk to Zara's two children, because she has a history of mental health problems and a conviction for underage sex. The couple receive support from Zara's parents, who live nearby, so the grandparents of the children are also participants in the safeguarding work. As well as addressing systemic, safeguarding practice issues, the chapter explores the relationship between mental health problems and sexual crime, and also female sexual offending. In addition, the counsellor's insecurities about working with a client who is politically aware and assertive are explored. Most of the suggestions for good strengths-focused practice in working with individuals and couples, which appear in the previous chapters, also pertain to work with families. Hence, to avoid repetition, the remaining two chapters will focus on the main themes of the work completed with the respective families, rather than forms of practice which have already been elucidated.

Working with families in a systemic way

The risk posed by an individual who has sexually offended is the most crucial factor in the calculation of risk within a family setting. It is very rare for Children's Services or the Courts to allow a person who has committed a sexual offence to return to the family where their victim still resides, given the likely negative psychological impact this would have on the victim. However, some individuals who have committed sexual offences are allowed to live within families again, depending on the seriousness of the offence, and the risk posed to potential victims in the family setting. It is rare for a person to be allowed to live in a family or to have unsupervised contact with children, if the risk posed is deemed to be any higher than low. No matter how robust the safeguards are, it is unrealistic to manage anything other than a low risk within the intimate and private context of a family. The conditions below usually have to be in place before a person who has sexually offended is allowed to have unsupervised contact with children, or to live again in a family home, where children reside:

- The offender (potential offender) is assessed as low risk
- The previous victim/s is not a child in the family
- It is in the overall best interests of the child or family unit for the offender to have contact
- The child genuinely wants a relationship with the offending parent, is mature enough to make this decision and the decision is not the result of grooming or trauma ties
- The non-offending partner accepts there is a risk and is assessed as being able to reasonably protect children

Some therapists such as myself, who practise within the child protection system, work with a number of family members simultaneously, in order to build more safety into family situations. Working with different family members can seem like a cross between being a therapist and a mediator. It requires the practitioner to be active, creative, even-handed and to be able to keep the different perspectives of each family member in mind, whilst not being sucked into the often, competing agendas of the individuals in question. This work is not for everyone. However, I personally find helping families to work through conflict and difficulties in order to co-create workable safeguarding solutions, particularly rewarding.

Working therapeutically with families can be traced back to systems theory and family therapy where sexual abuse is seen, in part, as the product of systemic family dysfunction (Bentovim, 1996). The approach is also influenced by child development theories (Winnicott, 1957, 1958). Woods (2003: 22) posits how within this child development paradigm sexual abuse can be viewed, in somewhat Freudian terms, as regression to infantile states in which 'eroticism, desire, instant gratification and violence becomes a dysfunctional response to forms of distress'. This view of working with the problem of sexual abuse has been questioned, however. Jenkins (1990) makes the point that professionals can be in danger of shifting responsibility for sexual offending onto perceived difficulties within the family system, rather than focusing on the individual responsible for the offending.

Within the child protection field, various authors describe working with the family system to build in more safeguarding resources, using strengths-focused approaches (Milner and Bateman, 2011; Selekman, 1997; Turnell and Edwards, 1999; Turnell and Essex, 2006). These authors would generally take a social constructionist approach to solving problems in families, including that of sexual abuse. Parton et al. (1997: 67) argue that definitions and explanations of sexual abuse are often more a matter of 'moral reasoning and judgement' rather than 'medico-scientific reality'. Taking a similar ideological approach, Milner and O'Byrne (2002) illustrate how the strengths-based approach seeks to build on existing competencies and strengths, including within the family system, rather than narrowly focusing on diagnostic categories and deficits. A cautionary note is stuck by Davies (2016: 28), however, pointing out that practitioners should always be alert to becoming enmeshed in a chaotic family system, and having 'their attention diverted away from the welfare and safety of the child by needy parents'. This dynamic can certainly occur, although often the needs of the parents and the needs of the children are not mutually exclusive.

Sexual offenders with mental health problems

As noted above, Yasmin has had previous mental health problems, having been admitted into psychiatric hospital after taking an overdose of tablets, and being diagnosed with an anxious personality disorder. A comprehensive exploration of the relationship between mental health problems and sexual offending is outside the purview of this book. Nevertheless, I will make some comments about this phenomenon.

Sexual offending is not a mental illness, and people with psychotic mental health conditions constitute a small proportion of convicted sex offenders. The same criminogenic risk factors seen in the lives of sexual offenders without any mental illness (Beech and Ward, 2004) can also be observed in the lives of mentally disordered sexual offenders (Garrett and Thomas, 2009). Hence, mental disorder plays a relatively small role in sex offending (Valença et al., 2013). However, command hallucinations with regards to schizophrenia-related jealousy, revenge, obsession and inhibition can be a factor in sexual crime, and this may require a pharmaceutical response to stabilize the individual, before any treatment begins. Also, sexual murders predictably score higher on Hare's psychopathic checklist (Zaranes, 2009).

Some sex offenders are diagnosed with personality disorders although, from a social constructionist perspective, the relevance of such diagnostic categories is contested (Milner and O'Byrne, 2002). Narcissistic, anti-social and histrionic personality disorders are more prevalent amongst individuals who sexually offend against adults, whilst schizotypal, avoidant, dependent personality disorders can be found amongst individuals who offend against children, and who commit non-contact sexual offences (Jones, 2009). With regard to Yasmin, the main protagonist of the case study in this chapter, she has been diagnosed in the past as having an avoidant personality disorder. For further information about working with sex offenders and their families in a mental health context, see Hilarski and Wodarski (2006).

Female sexual offenders

Yasmin has committed a sexual offence against a teenage boy. As with the relationship between mental health problems and sexual offending, a comprehensive discussion of female sexual offending is outside of the remit of this book. However, I will summarize some main points. With regard to the prevalence of female sexual offending, in a meta-analysis based on 17 samples from 12 countries, Cortoni et al. (2016) found that females were responsible for 2.2% of all sexual offences reported to the police. As with male sexual offending, the conviction rate is likely to be significantly lower than the actual prevalence of sexual abuse. Consistent with this pattern, when all reports of female sexual offending are considered in the above study (i.e. including reports not reaching the police), female offending accounted for 11.6% of all reported sexual offending. Other studies estimate that 14%-29% of male child victims and 6%-14% of female child victims were sexually abused by a female perpetrator (Dube et al., 2005; Green, 1999). In an analysis of 800,000 sexual crimes in the USA between 1992 and 2011, Williams and Bierie (2015) found that females were more likely to sexually offend against the same sex: 44% as opposed to 12% of females who offend against the opposite sex. They also found that females were significantly more likely to offend with a co-offender of the opposite sex (33% versus 2%). In an overview of sexual offending in England and Wales in 2011, 103 women were in custody for sex offences versus 10,832 men. Only 2% of the female prison population were there for sex offences. Between 2005 and 2011, 99% of offenders supervised by the Probation Service for sex offences were male (MoJ, HO, ONS Statistics Bulletin, 2013). Reconviction rates are very low for female sex offenders, so identifying the level of risk is very difficult. In a five-year follow-up from first sexual conviction, Sandler and Freeman (2009) identified that 1.8% of a sample of 1,466 had been re-arrested. Cortoni et al. (2010) suggested less than a 3% reconviction rate.

The likely under-reporting of female sexual offending may be influenced by how women and their sexuality are stereotypically viewed as non-threatening. In contrast, males, including adolescent males, are stereotypically viewed as being sufficiently robust not to be harmed by female sexually predatory behaviour. These stereotypical ways of constructing maleness and femaleness can underestimate the harm caused by females who sexually offend.

If the understanding of sexual offending by men is in its adolescence, the understanding of female sexual offending is in its infancy. Measures designed to assess risk of sexual recidivism for males are not appropriate for females, was the conclusion reached by Sandler and Freeman (2009), as risk assessments validated for males would probably over-evaluate the risk of recidivism in females. However, with regard to background risk factors, studies frequently show high levels of emotional, physical and sexual abuse in the lives of female sexual offenders (Matthews et al.,1989; Saradjian, 1997; Eldridge et al., 2009; Cortoni and Gannon, 2013).

With regard to female sexual offenders, two particular gender traps can be observed. Firstly, stereotypical social constructions of femaleness (the archetypes of the idealized mother and passive victim) can lead to societal denial that women can offend. Children thus perceive abuse by females as particularly stigmatizing. The above difficulties can be exacerbated when the perpetrator is the child's mother, leading to an enmeshed relationship with the mother that can lead to psychosis (Saradjian, 1997). A significant contribution of radical feminism has been to explore the impact of sexual abuse on female victims by males, and the concomitant abuse of power. However, the occurrence of sexual offending by women has challenged some aspects of the radical feminist view that sexual abuse is always connected to patriarchy (Harris, 2010). The second gender trap is to simplistically apply theories of male sexual offending to female offenders. This neglects the structural power differences around sex, gender and sexual identity, and how such differences may impact on how and why females sexually offend.

All typologies offer a simplified description of human behaviour and personality. This said, typologies can offer an insight into why and how humans behave as they do. Below are summarized descriptions of the common types of female sexual offenders which appear in the literature on female abusers:

- **Coerced female offenders** (coerced by men to commit sexual offending, with the motivation being fear of or dependence on men, rather than sexual attraction to children)
- **Accompanied female offenders** (sexually offending with another, often a man: create the opportunity or allow the abuse to happen: tend to be less submissive than the coerced female offender)
- **Predisposed female offenders** (offend against pre-pubescent male and female children, including their own children: tend to suffer from a range of comorbid symptomology)
- **Females who sexually abuse adults** (tend to sexually offend against adult females: motivation might include revenge or financial gain in addition to meeting power and sexual arousal needs and desires)
- **Adolescent female offenders** (many have been abused themselves and brutalized in gangs: can be sexually preoccupied and offend against both genders)
- **Female internet offenders** (rare in criminal justice system: motivation can include financial gain, sexual motivation, being part of an online community, assuming a preferred identity: often sexualized early and displaying distorted sexual preoccupation)
- **Teacher/Lover female offenders** (offend from a position of power and tend not to see their behaviour as criminal:

often offend against adolescents, elevating the male or female adolescent to adult status; in addition to being motivated by sexual arousal, can seek emotional closeness and power lacking in adult relationships)

The subject of the following case study in this chapter, Yasmin, had sexually offended in such a way as to conform to the above 'Teacher/Lover' profile.

Case study: Yasmin

Yasmin (36) was raised by her mother, with her younger half-sister, Reeta, on a council estate in the Midlands. Her mother became pregnant with Yasmin when she was 16. Yasmin was bright and always felt that her mother 'never got me', as she put it. Her mother was a no-nonsense, hard-working woman, employed in a canteen in the day and as a cleaner in the evening. She was more closely bonded with Reeta than Yasmin, despite Reeta being the more rebellious sister. Yasmin had no contact with her father since he left the family home, soon after she was born. Reeta was the result of a short-term relationship and, therefore, the family consisted of just the three of them. Her mother had lost links with her religious extended family, and followed no faith. Yasmin was a quiet child, 'a bit of a mouse', as her mother used to describe her. She would spend hours on her own, reading in her bedroom, while her mother was out working, whilst her younger sister was looked after by a child minder. Yasmin had few friends at school and tended to be invisible to her teachers. She and her half-sister were never close. Their mother was never physically abusive to either daughter, but Yasmin felt that she wanted to disappear when her mother told her that she needed to 'get a grip' as life was 'hard' and she had better 'come back down to earth' if she was ever going to make anything of herself.

At the age of 17, Yasmin met Adrian in a local pub. At the time, she was undertaking an office skills course at the local technical college, having achieved low-grade GCSEs as she couldn't be bothered to revise. Adrian was a salesman for an insurance firm. He was 25 and had his own flat and a nice car. They married soon after meeting, with Yasmin relieved to move out of her family home. By this time, her half-sister was into drugs and living a promiscuous lifestyle and Yasmin had found living in the same home as her sister a strain.

Yasmin was a virgin before she met Adrian. At the beginning of their relationship the couple would have regular sex, although Yasmin felt she was going through the motions. She was flattered that Adrian found her sexually attractive, but felt smothered by him. Adrian continued to advance in his career. He was never physically abusive but started to put Yasmin down, saying she was a dreamer and a waste of space, and didn't make the most of her potential. She continued to retreat into reading, became depressed and finally gave up work. She took an overdose of tablets at the age of 22, and was admitted to a psychiatric ward. She was assessed by a psychiatrist as having an avoidant personality disorder. After she came out of hospital, Adrian suggested she learn to drive, so that she had something to focus on. She passed her driving test the first time, and Adrian bought her a second-hand Mini.

When she was really down, she would drive for hours, playing loud music, picking up a few speeding fines. After ten years of marriage, Adrian said he was leaving her for somebody else, and moved to Australia with his new partner. When Adrian left, Yasmin felt numb. Her mother said that there was something about the women in their family; they couldn't keep their men. One night, when out in her Mini, Yasmin stopped at an amusement arcade, got out of her car and started to watch some youths playing on the slot machines. One of them, a handsome, cheeky 14-year-old boy, came over and asked her if she had a cigarette. He was a forward lad and asked if she could give him a lift home. On the journey, the boy, whose name was Billy, put his hand on Yasmin's knee. She stopped the car in a layby and had sex with the boy. His parents found out and she was convicted of having underage sex, and sent to prison for 6 months.

Whilst in prison, Yasmin began studying for a university access course. When she came out of custody, she continued her access course and went on to university to study for a history degree. At university, she met a fellow female mature student, Zara (38), who was coming to the end of her PhD. They became best friends and then sexual partners.

After a few years, they decided that they would like to live together, with Zara's two daughters: Shona (7) and India (8). Children's Services would not allow this, as they consider that Yasmin may pose a sexual risk to the girls. Zara is angry. She argues that Yasmin is a totally different person now compared with when she committed the offence, and Zara is certain that she poses no risk to her daughters, with whom Yasmin gets on very well. Children's Services have said that they will remove the children from Zara's care if Yasmin moves in with her, and have stopped all contact between Yasmin and Zara's daughters. Zara and Yasmin have engaged a solicitor, and the case is now going through the Family Court. They have both agreed to see a counsellor, who specializes in safeguarding work. The counsellor has recommended that Zara's adoptive parents, the daughters' maternal grandparents (Linda and Patrick), also take part in the safeguarding intervention as they live nearby, have a close relationship with their granddaughters and are supportive to Zara and Yasmin. Children's Services agree that the safeguarding work should take place.

The female counsellor has insecurities about working with a client, Zara, who is politically aware and assertive. She had previously undertaken an MA counselling course where all the students, apart from one, were female and younger than her. The counsellor considered that she had been perceived as a reactionary do-gooder. Unlike the others on the course, she did not need to work, as she was supported by a husband, in a well-paid job. She knew that the other members of the group would meet met up outside of the course for boozy nights out, to which she was not invited.

The counsellor suggested the following schedule of safeguarding work, which was agreed by all parties:

- Eight two-hour sessions with Yasmin
- Four two-hour sessions with Zara
- Four two-hour sessions with the couple
- Four two-hour sessions with Linda and Patrick
- Two four-hour sessions with Yasmin, Zara and the grandparents
- Keep Safe work with Shona and India

The purpose of this work was as follows:

- To address with Yasmin how her previous sexual conviction may impact on any risk she may pose to Zara's children
- To raise Zara's awareness of how sexual abuse occurs in family settings and how to identify and appropriately respond to such risk
- To raise Linda's and Patrick's (maternal grandparents') awareness of how sexual abuse generally occurs in family settings, what risk Yasmin specifically might pose to their granddaughters and how to respond to such risk
- To agree with Yasmin, Zara and the grandparents a New Life Safety Plan consisting of Signs of Safety, Signs of Risk and Responses to Signs of Risk

Keep Safe work with Shona and India

Working with children and young people when a parent or close relative has committed sexual abuse within or outside of the family, is a specialist area. I have undertaken such work with adolescent children over the age of 13, but not with younger children. Hence, a comprehensive account of how to conduct therapeutic safeguarding work with younger children is outside the purview of this book. However, the following authors and practitioners offer valuable insights into working with children in a child protection context (Berg, 1991; Milner and Bateman, 2011; Selekman, 1997; Turnell and Edwards, 1999; Turnell and Essex, 2006).

Children who have not been sexually abused but may be at risk of sexual abuse in the future often undertake Keep Safe work (Hackett, 2001; Ironside, 2004; Moore-Malinos, 2005; Sanders, 2016). Children's Services will commonly conduct or source Keep Safe work with children and young people to add to safety in family situations. A child should never be made to feel that they have to rely on themselves to keep safe from an adult who is in contact with them, but Keep Safe work can contribute to overall safety. This work with children and young people typically consists of the following:

- Exploration of feelings in general and specifically the child's/young person's feelings
- Exploration of when the child/young person feels safe
- Exploration of what happens in the child/young person's head and body when they feel safe and unsafe
- Exploration of early warning signs of feeling unsafe
- If feeling unsafe, what would the child/young person do and who would the child/young person tell?
- Who are safe adults?
- What are private parts of the body?
- Exploration of boundaries around private parts i.e. invisible body bubble
- What are good secrets and bad secrets?
- What to do and who to tell if somebody asks you to keep a bad secret?
- Exploration of OK touching and not OK touching
- What to do when not OK touching happens:

1. Say 'stop' in a loud, strong voice, with hand held out
2. Tell a safe adult

Sanders and Hancock (2016: 36) suggest five body safety rules for a child/young person to remember:

1. My body is my body and it belongs to me. I can say 'No!' if I don't want to kiss or hug someone. I can give them a high five or shake their hand
2. I can tell people who are safe if I feel worried, scared or uncomfortable
3. If I feel frightened or unsafe, I might feel sick in my tummy or my heart might beat really fast. If I feel this way, I must tell a safe adult
4. No-one can touch my private parts, or ask me to touch their private parts, or show me pictures of private parts. If any of these things happen, I should tell a safe adult (the identity of safe adults in the child's life should be agreed by all relevant parties)
5. I don't keep secrets, only happy surprises. If somebody tells me a secret or makes me feel uncomfortable, I must tell a safe adult

The counsellor in this fictitious case study did not undertake the above type of Keep Safe work for Shona and India. However, Children's Services provided this for the children.

Safeguarding counselling with Yasmin

Before any work is attempted with a family, the boundaries of confidentiality should be understood by the worker and by all the family members. If the practitioner is working for an organization, the agency should have clear policies and procedures with regard to confidentiality, which the worker should always follow. If the practitioner is a private counsellor or therapist, they should negotiate and provide the family members with a written contract.

An early task is to work out what the different family members make of the situation. Some families are welcoming of outside help. Others are ambivalent, suspicious or even hostile, not wanting outside interference. Each family member will differ in their desires and needs. Below is a list of different goals a family member may want to work towards. The list is not exhaustive:

- To understand why a loved-one has sexually offended
- To be helped to cope with the distress, stigma and grief of the situation
- For the family to be resettled without the offender being in their lives
- For the family to be resettled with the offender at home
- For the family to be resettled, with a family member allowed to supervise contact between the offender and children
- For the family to be resettled, with the parents having to renegotiate or rebuild the relationship, following the disclosure of an offence or allegation
- For family members (parents and carers) to be helped to manage risk

At the start of the work with Yasmin, the counsellor showed her the schedule of safeguarding work, outlined above. Yasmin nodded her head, saying she understood the goals of the work. From the way Yasmin presented, the counsellor guessed that she had learnt to be hyper-sensitive to people's feelings and reactions and had a tendency to avoid conflict, as a way of managing threat. This had likely resulted in Yasmin feeling disempowered and swamped by other people's agendas. Hence, it was important to spend time ascertaining what Yasmin's personal goals were for the work, in order to begin to provide a therapeutic experience of empowerment. Yasmin stated the following personal priorities for the work:

- To be able to live with her partner, Zara, and Zara's two daughters, Shona and India
- Yasmin was worried that Zara's two daughters would not feel safe with her after they had undertaken the Keep Safe work with Children's Services and wanted reassurance that the girls would not think she was some sort of monster
- To understand why she had offended against the teenage boy, something of which she now felt very ashamed

The counsellor said she was encouraged that in many ways Yasmin's personal goals seemed to be in harmony with the official goal of the safeguarding work, as one of her priorities was the well-being of Shona and India, in that she did not want the girls to feel afraid of her. An obvious point here was that if Yasmin chose not to live with Zara and her daughters, then the issue of the girls being frightened of her would be largely removed. Yasmin did not acknowledge this, and it could be argued that she was putting her own interests (moving in with her partner) above the children's best interests. However, there was no indication to date that the girls were afraid of Yasmin. The indications were that they liked her, and the risk she posed to them was probably low. Hence, the counsellor decided to focus on points of agreement between the client and professionals – both parties wanting the girls to feel secure and comfortable.

With regard to Keep Safe work, the counsellor was able to say that, in her experience, Keep Safe work with children is generally carried out in such a way as not to alienate children from the parent figure or adult deemed to pose a risk. The counsellor stated, however, that she could not give any watertight guarantees as to the way the Keep Safe work would be delivered in this instance to Shona and India, as this was out of her (the counsellor's) control. The counsellor suggested that this was also out of Yasmin's control, but empathized with Yasmin's concerns and felt powerlessness about this issue.

Frequently, matters are beyond the control of clients and counsellors are also relatively powerless to affect circumstances. Such constraint is part of the human condition. Counsellors and therapists are not just problem solvers, or even facilitators of problem solving. Part of what we do is help clients process painful feelings about being stuck, acting as midwives to new ways of being which emerge, often imperceptibly, when clients come to accept 'what is', not with resignation but with equanimity.

With regard to Yasmin's third goal - *To understand why she had offended against the teenage boy, something of which she now felt very ashamed* - the counsellor suggested that if, through the safeguarding counselling, she came to understand more about the reasons for her offending, then this would probably help her achieve her long-term goal - *To be able to live with her partner, Zara, and Zara's two daughters, Shona and India.* However, this decision would be largely dependent on the view taken by Children's Services of the safeguarding progress and, finally, by the Judge in the Family Court.

With regard to the sexual offence against the teenage boy, Yasmin gradually gained insight into why she committed the offence through life story work and the counsellor inquiring about the circumstances: her thoughts, her feelings and her behaviour before, during and after her sexual offending. A co-constructed narrative emerged in which Yasmin had never felt recognized and valued for who she was by her mother, who herself had lived a rather bleak life. Sensing that Yasmin's sister, Reeta, was essentially more like her in terms of temperament, values and world view, her mother had favoured her younger daughter, even though she was the more rebellious sibling. Her mother had been threatened by, and excluded from, Yasmin's interest in learning, considering that Yasmin was more intelligent than she was and resenting her for this. Yasmin's mother was a teenager when she gave birth to her, without the emotional maturity to form a strong parental bond with her firstborn, and struggling to come to terms with the disappointment of being left alone to raise a child. When Reeta was born, their mother had matured, had more resources and consequently formed a closer bond with her younger child. All these factors contributed to Yasmin feeling excluded in the familial triad.

Yasmin was able to find compassion for both her mother and herself, reflecting that she had formed a serious relationship with the first boyfriend who had come along, Adrian, in order to escape home. At the time of meeting Adrian, she was desperate for any kind of affection but could never reach an orgasm with him, instead faking pleasure. Living with Adrian, she repeated the pattern that she had developed as a child with her mother, retreating into her books and her own thoughts from a half-lived life, just as she had done in her childhood home. Yasmin reflected that while she was with Adrian, she felt totally unable to change the situation, believing the family script that life was about accepting your lot.

When Adrian left her, she felt no great emotion, considering with the counsellor that such disassociation might have been her usual emotional state at the time, even before Adrian had packed his bags for Australia. However, after he left, she had then lived on her own for the first time and began experiencing a nascent 'tingly' feeling of excitement, especially when driving around in her Mini late at night with the music turned up. She and her counsellor named the car 'the possibility capsule', which Yasmin found funny, likening it to the DeLorean car in the film Back to the Future.

The counsellor asked her about the night she met Billy. It was a drizzly winter's evening. She had been in the habit of parking up alongside the amusement arcades at a nearby seaside resort, for a smoke, drawn by the lights, which held a similar attraction for her to the green lights on the dashboard of her car. She recalled always being attracted to lights, having a night scene of New York on her bedroom wall at home, which she would stare at for hours. Yasmin came to recognize that, for her, the lights of the city, like the lights on the car dashboard and those of the amusement arcades, represented escape into a more fulfilling and exciting life.

In response to the counsellor's query, Yasmin denied that she had deliberately chosen to park by the amusement arcades to ogle the lads, a proposition suggested by the police at the time. After further reflection, Yasmin said that she had been drawn to the youthful energy of the place, sometimes the shouting and swearing later at night, the disinhibition, while she watched from the safety of the car.

On the night of the offence, she had summoned up the courage to go into one of the arcades, sitting on a stool to drink a free plastic cup of coffee, provided to entice customers. Billy had walked over to the change machines and smiled and winked at her as he passed. She smiled back. Ten minutes later, he returned, when all his money was gone, asking for a lift home, saying he had no money for the bus fare. In the car, Billy said that he had noticed her there before, parked in her car, and had clocked that she looked fit. He then placed his hand on her knee. The sexual offence followed.

After further exploration, Yasmin recognized a similar pattern to when she first met Adrian; she was flattered by a male's attention. She reflected, however, that with Billy there was a different dynamic. It was she who was in control, given his young age. It was she who called the shots. She recalled that the sex with Billy had an unreal quality, that it belonged to the world of the night, to half-realized dreams; she described it as an almost out of body experience. She could not remember any physical pleasure, but definitely the thrill of doing something forbidden. When the abusive sex was happening, she had stared into the green lights in the dashboard, certain that something significant would now happen.

Some clients commit sexual offending after many years of conformity. They may want, but feel unable, to change their life in a pro-social way. They then, perhaps subconsciously, decide to let off a hand grenade that will shatter their current existence. Yasmin realized that this was what had happened to her. She wanted change, but did not possess the vision or proactivity to make change happen.

In the sessions, she was able to develop a deeper understanding that, although Billy might have enjoyed the sex, and might even have boasted about it to his friends, she could not be sure of the psychological impact the event would have had on him in the long term. The illegal act might possibly have contributed to him developing cynical ideas about sex and older, authority figures, setting a moral template that legitimized exploitative sex.

Yasmin explained that going to prison was very scary, but it opened up the opportunity for her to lead a different sort of life. It led to her studying for a degree in History, meeting compatible friends at university and meeting a partner in Zara who really 'got' her, as well as helping Yasmin to discover her preferred sexual orientation. Prison is rarely such a positive experience for most people, but it was the starting point of Yasmin in discovering who she truly was in relation to others, and being empowered to meet needs and desires in pro-social ways.

Yasmin probably posed little sexual risk to Zara's daughters. However, she had committed a sexual offence and this meant that she and Zara had to agree on possible Signs of Risk, Signs of Safety and Responses to Signs of Risk, in the context of a New Life Safety Plan, if the couple were going to be allowed to live as a family with Zara's daughters (see New Life Safety Plan, below). In addition, the counsellor provided similar safeguarding psycho-educational information to that delivered to Sian in the previous chapter.

Therapeutic issues discussed in supervision

One of the first challenges for the counsellor was constructively managing her feelings of insecurity in relation to Yasmin's partner, Zara. Zara was an academic, an assertive, strident woman, politically aware, and suspicious of the Establishment. The counsellor took these insecurities to supervision. The supervisor empathized with the difficulty of the challenge and both traced the counsellor's feelings of threat to left-over business the counsellor had with her two brothers, who were both high flying lawyers in the City of London, and her experience of feeling left out on the MA counselling course (see above). Her husband had also been very successful in his career. The counsellor had always felt unable to compete with her brothers and suspected that they were dismissive of what one of them had once called her 'do-gooding', a perception she had had of herself on the counselling course. The supervisor inquired how the counsellor would ideally like to be with Zara. The counsellor came up with the following:

- Focusing on the client's agenda, rather than her own

- Being sufficiently detached as to be non-judgemental about what her client esteemed most in terms of values and behaviour
- Helping the client to come up with unique solutions that could be realistically applied within the inevitable constraints of the client's life circumstances and those of her partner and her children

The dialogue between the supervisor and counsellor continued as follows:

Supervisor: What would be the signs that your insecurities were taking over, preventing you from being your best counselling self?
Counsellor: Retreating into my shell. Being over careful about what I said.
Supervisor: What's the anxiety behind this, what are you trying to prevent happening?
Counsellor: I don't know. It's silly, really.
Supervisor: Give it some thought.
Counsellor: I suppose it's her responding to something I said in a dismissive or superior way.
Supervisor: And if she did this?
Counsellor: I would feel stupid, diminished, naive, I guess.
Supervisor: It's a lot of power you are giving away there.
Counsellor: Yes.
Supervisor: Stay with that thought for just a minute; it's only a thought. Try making friends with the thought that your client might feel superior to you, more sophisticated and worldly, better educated maybe.
Counsellor: But that's terrible. How can I counsel her, if she's better than me in all those ways?
Supervisor: Do counsellors need to be as sophisticated as their clients?
Counsellor: Yes – no. I don't know.

Supervisor: Perhaps counsellors need to be developed in terms of empathy and self-acceptance; able to acknowledge and tolerate insecurities, so that they can model compassion for self and others to their clients.

Counsellor: It's no big deal, is it, if she is more politically aware, as she would probably put it, or if she thinks she is? My challenge is to hold this possibility lightly and continue to be compassionate to myself and others. That's where my professional competence really lies, not in trying to be as smart and 'right on' as my client.

Supervisor: Sounds good to me.

The above exploration of the counsellor's insecurities mirrored the New Life Safety Plans used in this book. The supervisor explored how the counsellor could be her best counselling self (analogous to Signs of Safety), unpacked the counsellor's insecurities (analogous to Signs of Risk) and enabled the counsellor to respond constructively (analogous to Responses to Signs of Risk).

Safeguarding counselling with Zara

Zara was angry that she had to attend the safeguarding work, saying that it was 'ridiculous' for anybody to think that Yasmin would pose a sexual risk to her daughters, and it was all about Social Services covering their backs. The counsellor employed similar strengths-focused techniques demonstrated in previous chapters and my previous book (Smith, 2017), in order to empathize with Zara's feelings and agree goals which Zara would be personally motivated to achieve. Zara said her main goal was to be able to live as a family with Yasmin, and to obtain this she was prepared to 'play the game'.

The counsellor became more relaxed after the supervision session, described above. She felt empowered by adopting a light-hearted, curious stance to the prospect that her client might feel superior, even entertaining the thought that this might be so. Freed in this way, the counsellor felt able to work intuitively, now that her own preoccupations were not getting in the way.

The counsellor commented to Zara that Yasmin might never sexually offend again but that Children's Services would want to know if she (Zara) could play her part in keeping her children safe from any potential risks. To do this, she needed to have a greater understanding than a member of the general public about how sexual abuse happens in families and to have thought, beforehand, about how she would respond to signs of risk emerging, and about the emotional factors involved in this. Zara said, impatiently, that she wasn't 'stupid', and she did not need the State to tell her how to take care of her own children. The counsellor was pleased with herself that she was able to surf the wave of anxiety that swept over her, welcome the thought that she was being dismissed, and to observe these feelings and thoughts with detached interest. This process occurred simultaneously with the counsellor attending to what the client was saying. By the end of the second session, the waves of anxiety were losing their power.

An emotional management technique practitioners and clients can use to help with any anxiety-provoking situation, or with anything that is likely to cause emotional or even physical pain, is to practise mental wave surfing. This exercise takes the form of simply relaxing and taking some deep breaths. On the in breath, the person imagines a big wave (representing problems and the nexus of negative feelings and thoughts attached to it) building out at sea. On the out breath, the person imagines the wave breaking and moving towards the shore, gradually losing its power until it trickles gently onto a beach. Some people might find it helpful, and perhaps even empowering, to imagine themselves surfing the wave. This sort of mentalization can also be used with what neurolinguistic therapists would call anchors, with the individual thinking of an image, a word, a symbol, - blue sky, God, a mandala - to help manage and move beyond painful states. These techniques can also be used with individuals who want to manage anger or problematic sexual feelings and fantasies.

The counsellor provided Zara, as she did Yasmin, with the safeguarding information detailed in Chapter 7. Rather than trying to avoid

Zara's critical appraisal of this information, the counsellor pre-empted and welcomed this, asking some of the following questions:

- What would be your qualms about this information?
- Do you think any of this information applies to you?
- How could this information be better suited to your situation?
- I'm hearing that you don't think much of this. Is there anything here that could be useful to you?
- OK, let's ditch what I'm suggesting. What do you think you need to know?
- Tell me how you would go about things
- OK. Even if you don't value this information or think that you know it already, how could you demonstrate to Children's Services that you know what risks to look out for and you have a worked-out strategy for how you would respond to any emerging signs of risk?

By repeatedly avoiding defensive behaviour and thus being open, curious and empathetic about Zara's point of view, and employing strengths-focused techniques, the counsellor was able to deliver the safeguarding material and negotiate a draft New Life Safety Plan with Zara. She went on to construct an amended version of the New Life Safety Plan, first with Zara and Yasmin, then with the maternal grandparents, Linda and Patrick, and finally in the joint family counselling sessions (see below).

Safeguarding counselling with Yasmin and Zara

Previously in the book, I have illustrated how safeguarding counselling work can be conducted with couples, using the strengths-focused approach. Hence, I will not repeat this information here, but briefly focus on matters particularly relevant to Yasmin and Zara.

The counsellor began her work with the couple by asking how they had felt, coming to the first session. She then moved on by asking each, in turn, if they could explain to the other what had occurred in their individual sessions. The counsellor assisted this process by asking Yasmin and Zara about particular points of safeguarding information which were provided in the individual sessions with each of them. This turned into a sort of good natured, tongue-in-cheek competitive game, with each partner trying to outdo the other, with regard to what they had learnt.

The counsellor asked Yasmin and Zara to say to each other what they most appreciated about the other, and then if there were any issues they would like to work on. At first, the couple said that they felt they had a strong relationship and everything was fine. The counsellor congratulated the couple on having a strong relationship and said that she had noticed the way in which they related together with respect and humour. However, in her experience, most couples have some conflict with each other and she was wondering if this also applied to them and, if so, how they handled such conflict.

True to form, Zara, being the more initiating partner of the couple, said that she got frustrated sometimes and felt 'shut out', alternating between anger and guilt when Yasmin did not express her opinion, or withheld her feelings or thoughts. Zara explained that this felt as though Yasmin was punishing her sometimes, being passive-aggressive.

Having facilitated Zara to express her feelings about conflict with Yasmin, the counsellor asked Yasmin to explain to Zara how it felt to her, when they argued. Yasmin said that it felt sometimes like she was a fly stuck to sandpaper when Zara 'kept on' at her, pressuring her to have opinions about issues she did not have any strong feelings or thoughts about. The more Zara pressurized Yasmin for an answer, the more Yasmin became stuck in the 'freeze' and 'flight' response modes. She described feeling like 'a rabbit caught in headlights' when Zara 'went on' at her. The counsellor asked Yasmin how she would like Zara to raise issues. Yasmin said that she would like Zara to raise issues calmly, and give her time to think. Zara said that she was prepared to do this, as long as Yasmin would promise to come back with a response within a time-limited period, so that matters wouldn't get swept under the carpet. Yasmin agreed to this.

The counsellor pointed out that Yasmin's tendency to feel disempowered was, in her opinion, a safeguarding issue, as feeling disempowered and frustrated had been pro-offending factors when she had committed the sexual crime. Both Yasmin and Zara said that Yasmin would never offend again, but they took the counsellor's point.

The counsellor handed them both a copy of an example New Life Safety Plan (see Appendix). She explained that the example Safety Plan contained everything but the kitchen sink, as it was meant to provide an example of the many things which could be put into such a plan. She then provided the couple with a blank New Life Safety Plan, consisting of the three headings: Signs of Safety, Signs of Risk, Responses to Signs of Risk. Following this, the counsellor asked the couple to complete the plan for themselves, incorporating a discussion of the draft Safety Plans they had each completed earlier, in their respective sessions. In addition, she asked Yasmin and Zara to keep in mind all the issues and ideas discussed in the preceding safeguarding work they had completed with the counsellor on their own. The counsellor told them she would leave the room for 30 minutes, and then come back to check if they had completed the task. She would then go through the Plan with them, trouble-shooting the emotional cost and practicality of putting any of the ideas they came up with into action.

The couple completed this task well, coming up with a draft plan. The results of the draft plan can be seen below, in the section where a final version of the New Life Safety Plan is agreed with Linda and Patrick, Zara's parents.

Safeguarding counselling with Linda and Patrick

Grandparents and other relatives, and even close friends of parents, often play an important part in the lives of children. In terms of child protection, those close to the family can not only be valuable with regard to monitoring if signs of risk are emerging in a family, but can also be identified as safe people whom the children can go to if they have any concerns which they do not feel able to raise with their parents.

My experience of working with grandparents in child protection situations is that they are often placed in an invidious position. They are often in a high state of worry about both their grandchildren and their adult children, and sometimes pulled between the different generations. Grandparents can sometimes see, or suspect, that risky circumstances are pertaining in the family home: adult children forming relationships with risky partners, domestic violence, substance misuse, neglect, the grandchildren displaying concerning behaviour or not wanting to return to the family home after visits. However, grandparents are often on the outside looking in, not in the parental home to offer care and protection, and parents can prevent contact between the children and the grandparents if they feel aggrieved about grandparents interfering or criticizing them. Adult children have a healthy natural urge to individuate from parents and to become the competent generation. However, when they do not have the personal resources to achieve this, a parent challenging their adult offspring about parenting abilities can be inflammatory, especially if adult children are resentful about the way in which they, themselves, were parented by the now critical parent.

Frequently, grandparents will rhetorically pronounce that they will prioritize the interests of grandchildren above those of the parents: 'after all it is children we are talking about, here'. However, the reality beneath the rhetoric is that for a grandparent to report their own adult child to the authorities for actual or suspected child abuse, with all the consequences this will likely mean for the parent, proves a tall order.

What can help in such circumstances is for the adult child to give prior permission to the children's grandparents to report any serious signs of risk to the authorities. This is a similar harm-reduction approach to an individual, with current stable mental health, giving prior permission to family members to inform mental health professionals, if they stop taking their anti-psychotic medication and become dangerously unstable. The unstable person is unlikely to have positive feelings about being reported at the time, but at least they have made a prior choice for this to happen. This can render it both more likely that family members will report risk, and that family rapprochement can occur after the reporting. When working with relatives, I prompt them to consider the challenges of reporting a serious child protection concern to the authorities, using variations of the following questions:

- What thoughts and feelings do you think you would experience if you had to report your loved one to the authorities?
- What could be lost by reporting?
- What could be gained?

Safeguarding counselling work with family members is only likely to add to safety if the family members involved are stable, provide a consistent protective influence, and have a reasonably good relationship with the parents and children; if they are part of the solution, not the problem. Family members also need to have the capacity to talk about difficult issues and sometimes this will go against the dominant family culture, and the habitual ways family members communicate with each other. For instance, some families rarely or never talk about difficult issues. Happily, Linda and Patrick were part of the solution. They were stable, had a good relationship with their adopted daughter, Zara, were open to Yasmin and had a long-standing nurturing bond with their granddaughters.

The counsellor began the safeguarding work with Linda and Patrick by asking how they felt about being involved in the proceedings. There is a certain desensitization that occurs with parents, subject to the necessarily intrusive nature of the child protection system. Most parents gradually become acclimatized to being under professional scrutiny although, as indicated elsewhere, this can be a painful and stigmatizing experience. When grandparents and other family members are suddenly brought into this process, it can be quite a shock. Hence, the practitioner should allow for this, and invest time respectfully inquiring how matters seem from the relatives' point of view.

As with non-offending partners, it is necessary for relatives to know what they are helping to protect children from. Thus, before any safeguarding work is agreed to be undertaken with family members, the person convicted and accused of sexual offending needs to be informed that part of the safeguarding work is to ensure that the family members involved in the safeguarding process know the basic details of the actual or alleged sexual offending, and the relevant authorities (usually Children's Services or the Family Court) have given permission for this information to be shared.

Sometimes the account given to family members by the offender or partner of the offender is a minimized account, shifting blame onto others. If so, this needs to be countered by the practitioner providing family members with a more balanced view. In the case of Linda and Patrick, Zara had provided her parents with an accurate picture of Yasmin's previous offending.

Once the above, initial tasks were completed, the counsellor provided some basic safeguarding information to the grandparents about how sexual abuse occurs in families, how to identify common risks of this happening, and ways of responding should such signs of risk emerge, in addition to raising their awareness of the impact of sexual abuse on children. Psycho-educational material to complete this safeguarding work can be found in Chapter 7. The counsellor then went through with Linda and Patrick the specific signs of risk which might occur with regard to Yasmin, based on the work undertaken with her and her pathway towards sexual offending (discussed above) i.e.:

- Yasmin becoming depressed
- Yasmin becoming uncommunicative
- Yasmin being drawn into solitary excitement seeking

Safeguarding counselling with all family members

It is fairly easy to make plans with clients but it is usually much more difficult for clients to follow plans through. Developing new patterns of responding to conflict with a loved one, or maintaining appropriate boundaries in the family home, is challenging because of its emotional component. Attention should therefore be given to the roadblocks to motivation. Roadblocks might include the following:

- Limitations caused through social stigma or poverty
- Fear of social rejection because of the stigma of sexual abuse
- Loss of social confidence, self-esteem and assertiveness
- Lack of skills in a certain area
- Learnt helplessness
- Secondary gains of maintaining problematic behaviour (e.g. staying angry to avoid feeling vulnerable)
- Taking up power in self-defeating ways through passive/aggressive resistance or open oppositional hostility

My experience of facilitating family safeguarding sessions is that often people are somewhat embarrassed about talking to each other in a formal way, in front of a professional. Often there can be a nervous, slightly forced jocularity at first. When this occurs, I usually respond with humour, to help put people at their ease.

Usually, if the respective family members have come this far, agreed to the work in the first place and gone through their individual safeguarding sessions, then the individuals involved will have a degree of maturity, and the relationships in the family will be fairly amicable. The fact that a family unit is prepared to talk about difficult issues, pertaining to risk and sexual offending, is a sign of safety in itself.

Facilitating a family session is more akin to running a group than one-to-one counselling. Similar skills are required in terms of the core Rogerian conditions of empathy, congruence and unconditional regard, but the facilitator also needs to be proactive, allowing everyone to have their say, and re-focusing the group back onto psychologically threatening issues from which the group may sometimes want to take flight.

The counsellor started by asking how everybody was feeling and inquiring about people's anxieties and best hopes for the session. She then clarified that the purpose of the session was to agree the New Life

Safety Plan with everybody, and to trouble-shoot the Plan for any potential problems.

The counsellor had previously agreed with Yasmin and Zara that they would read out the draft New Life Safety Plan which they had agreed in their joint session, together. The counsellor asked Yasmin and Zara to take it in turns to read out each point of the Plan, beginning with Yasmin. The grandparents were then asked to make any comments about each point and at the end of each of the three sections - Signs of Safety, Signs of Risk, Responses to Signs of Risk - to add anything they thought would be important.

The session proceeded amicably. There was clearly a culture of respect and politeness in the way the family members related to each other, although Zara was the most obviously outspoken. Below is the Plan agreed:

New Life Safety Plan

<u>Signs of Safety</u>

- Yasmin not being left at home with the children
- Yasmin not being on her own in the car with the children
- The children continuing to thrive at school and socially, with friends
- Zara continuing to be attuned to the children's emotional life
- Yasmin feeling fulfilled in her work life
- Yasmin being able to assert herself with Zara
- Zara not browbeating Yasmin into expressing her thoughts and feelings
- Zara having passwords to the children's internet devices, being aware of what is on the children's devices and who they are talking to online
- Zara continuing to have time with the children on her own
- Zara and Yasmin having fun with the children

- Zara taking prime responsibility for disciplining the children
- Yasmin and Zara continuing to have their own friends
- Linda and Patrick continuing to have their grandchildren to stay every other weekend until the girls no longer want to do this
- Linda and Patrick continuing to take their grandchildren on an annual holiday for as long as the girls want to do this
- All the family members to have a meal together at least once a month

<u>Signs of Risk</u>

- If the above boundaries are broken
- Yasmin having contact with the children which is kept secret
- Yasmin going out in the car at night on her own
- Yasmin becoming depressed
- Yasmin and Zara having increasing conflict
- Yasmin drinking more and/or losing pride in her appearance
- Yasmin distancing herself from family members

In addition, below are some common Signs of Risk with regard to sexual abuse:

- Sudden, unexplained changes in the children's behaviour: becoming withdrawn, self-harming and/or aggressive
- Children having gifts or money and being unable to explain where they came from
- Children being overly embarrassed or unusually ashamed of their bodies for their stage of development
- Children continuing bedwetting beyond the usual developmental stage
- Children displaying age-inappropriate sexualized behaviour/language, and not stopping when told to do so

- Children behaving sexually abusively towards younger or weaker children
- Injuries/soreness/unusual marks/discharges around sexual areas of children's bodies, loss of appetite, nightmares

Responses to Signs of Risk

If signs of risk or breaches of boundaries emerge in the home, this may not mean that children have been sexually abused. However, the adults in the family have a responsibility to fully check out any concerns.

- Zara talking to the children about any concerning behaviour
- Linda and Patrick talking to Zara about any concerning behaviour
- Linda and Patrick talking to the children about any concerns
- The above adults checking out concerns with the health visitor, GP, teachers etc.
- Zara contacting the GP and a counselling service if she feels distressed
- Ringing the Lucy Faithfull Helpline for advice: Stop It Now (Freephone 08081000900)
- Contacting Children's Services by both phone and email
- Contacting the police

The counsellor decided to get beneath the politeness, and problematize the capacity of the family to adhere to the above Plan.

Counsellor: OK, Linda and Patrick, what would you do, for instance, if you suspected that conflict was breaking out between Yasmin and Zara, and Yasmin was becoming more withdrawn and depressed?

Linda: I'd probably ask Zara if Yasmin was OK; maybe ask Yasmin.

Counsellor: And Patrick, how about you?

Patrick: I would talk to Linda about it, and probably Linda would have a word.

Zara: (Good humouredly) Typical man. Leave the emotional labour to the women.

Counsellor: (Playing devil's advocate) OK, so you've had a word, but nothing happens, the problems seem to continue. What do you do? Everybody gets depressed and most couples go through sticky patches. But Yasmin being depressed and increasing conflict with Zara are risk factors on the Safety Plan, because this is the sort of thing that happened in Yasmin's relationship with her husband, before she offended.

Linda: But that's different surely, that was back then. Yasmin's different now.

Zara: (Impatiently) But that's not the point Mum, it's in the Safety Plan.

Patrick: (Soberly) That's right, Linda. We are getting to be very fond of Yasmin, but that sort of behaviour is flagged up as a risk factor. Risk protocols work like that - it was the same when I worked at the nuclear power station.

Zara: (Laughing) That's completely bizarre, Dad, to connect the two.

Patrick: Well, I was just saying.

Counsellor: Yasmin, how is this for you, having people talk about you in this way?

Yasmin: Fine. I would expect Linda and Patrick to do whatever to protect the children. I know I would never harm them, but Linda and Patrick, or Zara for that matter - they can't take any chances.

Counsellor: Well, what should they do?

Yasmin: Ask the children if they are all right, and if everything is OK at home. If they still have concerns, maybe phone the LFF Stop It Now helpline for advice.

Counsellor: All right, let's suppose the kids tell them that they're fine, but that their mother works away on a Tuesday night and Yasmin looks after them.

Yasmin: They should definitely confront Zara and me about this, as this would be a flagrant breach of the Safety Plan.

Counsellor: And if they had a word, and Zara said that it was none of their business - what happened with Yasmin was years ago?

Yasmin: Zara would never say that, but if we didn't take any notice then they would have to report us to Social Services.

Counsellor: Zara, what would you say?

Zara: Yep, it would never happen but if it did, Mum and Dad would have to report us.

Counsellor: Linda and Patrick, what would you do?

Patrick: Like the girls say, we would have to report them.

Counsellor: Linda?

Linda: The same.

Counsellor: But what if Zara never spoke to you again? What if Children's Services were so concerned, they ended up taking the children into care?

Linda: It wouldn't come to that, as the children would come to live with us. But even if Zara never spoke to us again, we would have to put the children first.

Conclusion

Significantly, the counsellor above was able to facilitate Yasmin (the person posing the risk) and Zara (the children's mother) to give family members their permission to report them to the authorities if they were flagrantly breaking the New Life Safety Plan and they considered the children were being put at risk. Of course, there is no guarantee the family will abide by the Safety Plan. There are usually no guarantees about most things in life. However, as is hopefully made clear throughout this book, it is the interactional process that is the key matter, rather than simply words on a page. A New Life Safety Plan is a means by which the preceding safeguarding work can be integrated. It provides the focus for family members to talk about difficult issues involving risk. The family safeguarding process also allows family members, other than the parents, to play their part in risk management and to contribute to safety within the family system.

Practice points from this chapter

- As with counselling individuals and couples, working with families in a safeguarding context requires transparency with regard to confidentiality and goal setting, and working within the individual's motivational frame of reference
- Providing safeguarding counselling to different members of a family is not for all practitioners
- The responsibility for sexual abuse should not be shifted from the offender onto other members of the family
- Practitioners should be alert to becoming enmeshed in the chaotic dynamics of different family members, privileging the perspective of adults and losing sight of the child's best interests
- However, the parents' and child's interests are often not mutually exclusive
- Sexual offending is not a mental illness
- Similar criminogenic factors can be found in the lives of sex offenders with a mental illness and those without mental health problems
- If a client is psychotic, then the psychosis will have to be stabilized before rehabilitative work can be undertaken with the client
- Female offending is under-reported and the impact is often underestimated or minimized
- Females tend to be stereotyped as passive victims and not choice making offenders in their own right
- When working with female offenders, it is important to bear

in mind that men and women may commit similar sexual offences in comparable ways, but may do so for different reasons

- Safety planning should be informed by the prior safeguarding work completed with the different family members
- Contributing to safety is about the negotiation process that takes place with the respective family members, which should underscore the Safety Plan
- It is important to trouble-shoot the Safety Plan in order to prepare family members for the emotional cost of challenging loved ones if signs of risk emerge and if they have to report a loved one to the authorities

References

Beech, A.R. and Ward, T. (2004) 'The integration of etiology and risk in sexual offenders: A theoretical framework', *Journal of Aggression and Violent Behaviour*, 10 (1): pp. 31-63.

Bentovim, A. (1996) 'Trauma-organized systems in practice: Implications for work with abused and abusing children and young people', *Clinical Child Psychology and Psychiatry*, 1 (4): pp. 513-524.

Bentovim A., Cox, A., Bingley Miller, L. and Pizzey S. (2009) *Safeguarding children living with trauma and family violence: Evidence-based assessment, analysis and planning interventions*, London: Jessica Kingsley Publishers.

Berg, I.K. (1991) *Family preservation: A brief therapy workbook.* London: BT Press.

Cortoni, F., Hanson, R.K. and Coache, M. (2010) 'The recidivism rates of female sex offenders are low: A meta-analysis', *Sexual Abuse*, 22 (4): pp. 387-401.

Cortoni, F. and Gannon, T.A. (2013) 'What works with female sex offenders', in L.A. Craig, L. Dixon and T.A. Gannon (eds.) *What works in offender rehabilitation: An evidence based approach to assessment and treatment.* Chichester: Wiley Blackwell, pp. 271-284.

Cortoni, F., Babchishin, K.M. and Rat, C. (2016) 'The proportion of sexual offenders who are female is higher than thought: A meta-analysis', *Criminal Justice and Behavior*, 44 (2): pp. 145-162.

Davies, M. (2016) *Therapeutic assessment and intervention in childcare legal proceedings: Engaging families in successful rehabilitation*. London and New York: Routledge.

Dube, S.R., Anda, R.F., Whitfield, C.L., Brown, D.W., Felitti, V.J., Dong, M. and Giles, W.H. (2005) 'Long-term consequences of child sexual abuse by gender of victim', *American Journal of Preventive Medicine*, 28 (5): pp. 430-438.

Eldridge, H. J., Elliott, I.A. and Ashfield, S. (2009) 'Assessment of women who sexually abuse children', in M.C. Calder (ed.) *Sexual abuse assessments*. Lyme Regis, UK: Russell House, pp. 213-227.

Garrett, T. and Thomas-Peter, B.A. (2009) 'Interventions with sex offenders with mental illness', in A.R. Beech, L.A. Craig and K.D. Browne (eds.) *Assessment and treatment of sex offenders: A handbook*. Chichester, UK: Wiley, pp. 393-408.

Green, A.H. (1999) 'Female sex offenders', in J.A. Shaw (ed.) *Sexual aggression*. Washington, DC: American Psychiatric Press, pp. 195-210.

Hackett, S. (2001) *Facing the future: A guide for parents of young people who have sexually abused*. Lyme Regis, UK: Russell House.

Harris, D.A. (2010) 'Theories of female sexual offending', in T.A. Gannon and F. Cortoni (eds.) *Female sexual offending: Theory, assessment and treatment*. Chichester, UK: Wiley, pp. 31-51.

Hilarski, C. and Wodarski, J. (2006) *Comprehensive Mental Health Practice with Sex Offenders and their Families*. Binghamton, NY: The Haworth Press.

Ironside, V. (2004) *The huge bag of worries*. London: Hodder Children's Books.

Jenkins, A. (1990) *Invitations to responsibility: The therapeutic engagement of men who are violent and abusive*. Adelaide: Dulwich Centre Publications.

Jones, L. (2009) 'Working with sex offenders with personality disorder diagnoses', in A.R. Beech, L.A. Craig and K.D. Browne (eds.)

Assessment and treatment of sex offenders: A handbook. Chichester, UK: Wiley, pp. 409-430.

Matthews, R., Matthews, J.K. and Speltz, K. (1989) *Female sexual offenders: An exploratory study.* Brandon, VT: Safer Society Press.

Milner, J. and Bateman, J. (2011) *Working with children and teenagers, using solution focused approaches: Enabling children to overcome challenges and achieve their potential.* London and Philadelphia: Jessica Kingsley Publishers.

Milner, J. and O'Byrne, P. (2002) *Assessment in social work,* 2nd edition. Basingstoke: Palgrave Macmillan.

MoJ, HO, ONS Statistics Bulletin (2013) *An overview of sexual offending in England and Wales.* Available from: www.gov.uk/government/statistics/an-overview-of-sexual-offending-in-england-and-wales [22 February 2022]

Moore-Malinos, J. (2005) *Do you have a secret?* UK: Barron's Educational Series.

Parton, N., Thorpe, D. and Wattam, C. (1997) *Child protection: Risk and the moral order,* 2nd edition. London: Palgrave Macmillan.

Sanders, J. (2016) *My body! What I say goes.* Australia: Educate2Empower Publishing.

Sandler, J.C. and Freeman, N.J. (2009) 'Female sex offender recidivism: A large-scale empirical analysis', in *Annals of Sex Research,* 21 (4): pp. 455-473.

Saradjian, J. (1997) *Women who sexually abuse children: From research to clinical practice,* 2nd edition. Chichester: Wiley.

Selekman, M.D. (1997) *Solution focused therapy with children: Harnessing family strengths for systemic change.* New York: Guilford Press.

Smith, A. (2017) *Counselling male sexual offenders: A strengths-focused approach.* London: Routledge.

Turnell, A. and Edwards, S. (1999) *Signs of safety: A solution and safety oriented approach to child protection casework.* New York: Norton.

Turnell, A. and Essex, S. (2006) *Working with 'denied' child abuse: The resolutions approach.* Maidenhead: Open University Press.

Valença, A.M., Nascimento, I., Nardi, A.E. (2013) 'Relationship between sexual offences and mental and developmental disorders: A review', *Archives of Clinical Psychiatry*, 40 (3): pp. 97-104.

Ward, T. and Stewart, C.A. (2003a) 'The treatment of sex offenders: Risk management and good lives', *Professional Psychology: Research and Practice*, 34 (4): pp. 353-360.

Ward, T. and Stewart, C. (2003b) 'Good lives and the rehabilitation of sex offenders', in T. Ward, R. Laws and S.M. Hudson (eds.) *Sexual deviance: Issues and controversies*. London: Sage Publications, pp. 21-44.

Williams, K.S. and Bierie, D.M. (2015) 'An incident-based comparison of female and male sexual offenders', *Sexual Abuse*, 27 (3): pp. 235-257.

Winnicott, D. (1957) *The child and the family*. London: Tavistock.

Winnicott, D. (1958) *Collected papers: Through paediatrics to psychoanalysis*. London: Tavistock.

Woods, J. (2003) *Boys who have abused: Psychoanalytic psychotherapy with victim perpetrators of sexual abuse*. London: Jessica Kingsley Publishers.

NINE

THE ROBERTS FAMILY

Introduction

This final chapter features the Roberts family. The father, who is a military veteran, has recently been released from prison where he was serving a sentence for the rape of an adult female. Specific issues with regard to military veterans and rape are discussed, before the counsellor's systemic work with the family is depicted. As with the previous chapter, the safeguarding counselling with the Roberts family included many of the process tasks, strengths-focused questions and interventions illustrated in previous chapters. Again, to avoid repetition, only safeguarding issues specifically pertinent to the Roberts family are explored.

Case study: The Roberts Family
Viv (40) has been married to Rhys (44) for 17 years. They have 14-year-old twins: Rose and Alfie. Rhys has been in the Army since he was 18. He was dishonourably discharged after being found guilty of raping an 18-year-old woman on a drunken night out when home on leave to attend his mother's funeral. He

maintains that she consented to sex. Viv thinks there has been a miscarriage of justice. She says that Rhys has 'always been a bit of a womanizer' but 'he would never do anything like that'. Viv adds that she knows the young woman (the victim) in question, and she is a 'trouble maker'. Viv explains that she, herself, has had some one-night stands when Rhys has been away on service, and both of them have experimented sexually within their marriage with other couples. She says that both she and Rhys are risk takers and have a *carpe diem* attitude to life, but they have always been responsible with the children and have kept their alternative sex life completely separate from the twins. Rhys has been known to drink to excess on occasion, including over the period of his mother's funeral, when the rape occurred. He has seen action and has been diagnosed as having PTSD from his experiences of war. He has received trauma therapy from a prison psychologist. He appears stable, but does not like to talk about the past or the future.

Rhys has now been released from prison and is living with his wife's parents (Bob, 70, and Jean, 65), as he is not allowed to return to the family home because Children's Services think he is a risk to his children, particularly Rose. Both Rhys's parents are deceased.

Rhys and Viv have been referred to a counsellor who specializes in assessing parents and children within the child protection system. After assessing the parents, the therapist concluded that risk cannot be ruled out, but the risk Rhys poses to his own children is low. The therapist suggested a course of therapeutic safeguarding for all family members. Children's Services and the family members have agreed to this work. The schedule of the work is as follows:

- Eight two-hour sessions with Rhys
- Six two-hour sessions with Viv
- Two two-hour joint sessions with Rose and Alfie

- Two two-hour sessions with all family members

The purpose of this work was as follows:

- To address with Rhys how his sexual conviction may impact on any risk he may pose to his own children, and to women
- To raise Viv's awareness of how sexual abuse occurs in family settings, and how to identify and appropriately respond to such risk
- To ensure that Rhys and Viv are risk aware and can maintain safe boundaries between their sexual lives and family life with their children, Rose and Alfie
- To explore with Rose and Alfie what a safe family home would look like and how they would respond to feeling uncomfortable with anything happening in the home
- To agree with all four family members a New Life Safety Plan consisting of Signs of Safety, Signs of Risk and Responses to Signs of Risk

Therapeutic issues discussed in supervision

The male therapist considered himself non-judgemental but his ego ideal was tested by this couple. He was a pacifist, and did not have much natural sympathy with military values. He had also not worked with 'swingers' before, and found the concept troubling. Aware of his judgementalism about the military, he did not want to exacerbate this by being overly judgemental about the couple's periodic open relationship and partner swapping. At the same time, he did not want to collude with the maintenance of loose sexual boundaries within the home, which could have a detrimental effect on the children, although there seemed to be no indication of this. The counsellor also considered that the couple's liberal views about sex may have led to their downplaying the significance of power dynamics within sexual relationships and encounters, and he did not want to let that possibility go unexamined.

Aside from the safeguarding problems in this family, both parents liked spending money they often did not have on meals, holidays and good wine. They were both pleasure seekers and risk takers and, in fact, were compatible in these respects. This also irked the counsellor, who had always been careful with money.

The counsellor's supervisor congratulated him on understanding the importance of examining power and boundaries in safeguarding work, and also on his awareness of his personal biases. They agreed that each time he became aware of his belly tightening up with disapproval, he would resist the temptation to confront or challenge the couple there and then in the session. Rather, he would not say anything, but instead would focus on envisioning a therapeutic atmosphere in the room, which bathed both himself and his clients in acceptance and compassion. Only when the counsellor felt genuinely positive towards the couple, would he challenge them.

The counsellor recognized that, from a child, he had liked to put people right. He recalled how at infant school he had told teachers when other children misbehaved, until he learnt that this was making him unpopular. He had always been a stickler for detail. When he had worked as a psychology lecturer previously, he had once been told by a colleague that he was disheartening some students by marking in red ink every minute grammar error (some of which were subjective). This level of correction was unnecessary in an essay on psychology, in which the ideas and argument were the main thing.

The supervisor asked the counsellor if one part of him, perhaps a repressed part of his psyche, might be envious of the couple's carefree, pleasure-seeking attitude to life. The counsellor reflected that this was a possibility. He further reflected that when he goes on holiday, this is the one time he feels free to let his hair down, and he will deliberately go away with friends who like to party. The supervisor complimented the counsellor on finding a constructive way to let off steam, and asked if he could use this holiday experience to empathize with his clients' experience of life in the everyday. The supervisor suggested that if the counsellor were able to stop seeing pleasure-seeking irresponsibility as unconscionable and totally alien to him (consigned to his shadow), he would be more likely to enable the couple to explore the downsides of their pleasure-seeking behaviour without their feeling unduly judged, and reacting with resistance.

Military veterans who offend sexually

A veteran is a term denoting anybody who has ever served in the armed forces, no matter for how short a time. I will summarize some common themes of working with veterans generally, and with those who have sexually offended, as this will provide a wider context to the case study. Therapists working in the area of sexual offending are likely to encounter veterans as clients at some time, as although veterans are less likely than the general population to commit other offences, they are more likely to commit violent and sexual offences than non-veterans (MacManus and Wood, 2017).

Each veteran is obviously unique, but Caddick et al. (2017) and O'Neill (2017) make various useful general observations about veterans and military culture, which are consistent with my experience of working with veterans and their families impacted by sexual offending. It is generally observed that veterans who leave the forces after a short period have a higher incidence of attachment and trauma problems in their backgrounds, particularly lower ranked veterans from disadvantaged backgrounds.

Arguably, it is inevitable that there should be a culture in the armed forces of legitimizing violence as, in the final analysis, the military exists in order to fight. Veterans are used to taking risks, and pornography is particularly rife in military circles. The majority of veterans, even those who have seen action, adjust well to civilian life. However, those who do not tend to bottle up feelings and self-medicate through alcohol.

In my experience of working with veterans, the very compartmentalizing of emotions which is encourage and allows individuals to manage hardship, pain and life-threatening situations, can also block off empathy for others and compassion for self. When emotions are repressed in this manner, they are likely to surface in uncontrolled and destructive ways, especially under the influence of alcohol, resulting in violent and sexual crime being committed. Using alcohol to cope with negative emotions is also a cultural norm in the military.

On leaving the armed forces, veterans can find it difficult to come to terms with loss of role, structure and status. These difficulties are seriously compounded if an individual is dishonourably discharged, especially if it is due to committing a sexual offence. Many of these themes are apparent in the case study featuring the Roberts family.

With regard to the children and partners of veterans, they can build up resilience through having to cope with changing schools and moving to different situations, as the military partner is moved to different postings. This can help family members cope with resettlement and adversity. However, children and partners can also become used to being accepted as part of a community, with a strong sense of shared values and identity. Losing this security can be distressing. Hence, being a veteran's partner or the child of a veteran can be both a protective and an exacerbating factor, in trying to cope with the fear and social rejection when a parent has offended sexually.

Rape

The crime of rape is another feature of the Roberts family case study. Again, I will provide some brief information about rape, in order to offer background context.

The conviction rate for rape, as for all sexual offences, is far lower than the actual prevalence of offending. The Rape Crisis England and Wales website handled over 341,823 online and telephone helpline contacts in the year 2020-2021, an increase of 75% on 2019-2020. Specialist Rape Crisis services were accessed by 74,995 people (compared to 66,045 in the previous year) of whom 90% self-defined as female and 32% as disabled (Rape Crisis, England and Wales).

There is a lack of research about male rape, but it is estimated that 3% of UK males will be a victim of sexual assault (Coxell et al., 1999).

Men are 1.5 times less likely to report a rape by a male perpetrator than women (Pino and Meier, 1999), and the rate is probably lower again when sexual abuse is perpetrated by a female.

The maximum sentence for rape is life imprisonment, but frequently offenders are sentenced to between 5 and 7 years in custody. If victims do not give evidence, individuals can still be charged, but lack of evidence and the persistence of rape myths, discussed below, often make prosecution and conviction difficult. There are different forms of rape:

- Ritualistic sexual assault and rape, as occurs in anti-social gangs and wars, in order to humiliate and establish hierarchy
- Stranger sexual assault and rape, sometimes called grabbing
- Date sexual assault and rape
- Marital or relationship sexual assault and rape
- Male sexually assaulting and raping males
- Male sexually assaulting and raping females
- Female sexually assaulting and raping males
- Female sexually assaulting and raping females

There are various theories about why rape occurs. Ellis's (1989) sociobiological theory of sexual assault and rape posits that, unlike women, men maximize their reproductive potential by copulating with numerous sexual partners and are hard-wired to aggressively pursue this aim. Ellis suggests that, more than women, men experience a drive to possess and control, triggered by higher levels of testosterone. Higher levels of androgens (especially testosterone) make men more risk-taking and less empathetic to their victim's suffering. The biological explanation for rape is controversial, as it has been seen to normalize and to excuse rape, as a natural male inclination.

The psychodynamic explanation for rape suggests that, for some individuals, infantile sexual desires (especially for omnipotence) continue into adulthood (Freud, 2001, first published 1905). Feelings of inadequacy and anxiety can produce aggression towards victims, as substitute objects for mother. High levels of aggression also overcome the superego the ego control mechanisms (Groth et al., 1977). Psychodynamic theory posits that it is not uncommon for males who sexually assault and rape women to have missed out on healthy maternal nurturing experiences. When they subsequently find themselves in relationships and encounters with women, past maternal deficits can distort their perception, making them acutely sensitive and destructively reactive to being denied respect, affirmation, empowerment or sex. Unconscious rage can then be triggered, resulting in rape: major motivations being the drive to humiliate in order to compensate for a felt lack of power, or simply a sadistic pleasure in disempowering, frightening and hurting another.

The sociological perspective (Sanday, 1981) has interestingly identified certain characteristics of rape-free societies:

- Women are treated with greater respect
- Women are viewed as influential
- Women contribute equally with men
- Women are economically independent
- Women experience no limits on mobility

Conversely, characteristics of rape-prone societies have also been identified by Blanchard (1995):

- There is worship of a male creator deity
- Women are primarily nurturers of children, while men primarily assume the role of disciplinarian
- Husbands are positioned as head of the household
- Boys are taught to be rough and aggressive
- Competition is valued as a way to demonstrate superiority, dominance and self-esteem
- Warfare is glorified

Brownmiller's (1975) and Burt's (1980) 'rape myths' can be seen as one reason so many rape allegations never reach court or, if they do, tend not to result in convictions. The 'rape myths' are summarized as follows:

- Blame the victim
- Exonerate the perpetrator
- Only certain types of women get raped
- Claims of rape are not to be believed

Brownmiller (1975) contends that the central problem inherent to rape is one of patriarchy and male entitlement in relation to getting sexual gratification from females. Sexual abuse should be seen as part of a patriarchal continuum of male violence in order to maintain power and control. Maxwell and Scott (2014) argue that this radical feminist position does not account for female violence and for females raping women and also men (see Chapter 8 for a discussion of female sexual offending).

In their research, however, Maxwell and Scott (2014) did find that a vast number of studies show that men are more likely to endorse rape myths than women. Women who are anti-feminist are also more likely to believe rape myths. Men viewed male victims more negatively if they were sexually assaulted by a woman, especially if the man was heterosexual. The researchers concluded that rape myths are more apparent when victims violate traditional gender roles, when the perpetrator is female and the victim is male, or when the victim is homosexual.

Safeguarding counselling with Viv

In the work with the therapist, Viv voiced some traditional rape myths, discussed above. She stated that she had known the victim, and that she was 'trouble', having made allegations against other men. She added that the victim had been 'dragged up' and had been placed in care at one point. Rather than confronting these prejudices head on, the counsellor asked Viv if she would undertake some educational work, beginning with a case study to demonstrate how victims of neglect and

abuse of all kinds, including sexual abuse, can go on to be re-victim-
ized. The counsellor added that, regardless of whether or not Viv
changed her mind about her husband's accuser, she would be able to
demonstrate to Children's Services that she understood how repeat
victimization occurs. Viv agreed to undertake the exercise.

Case study: Victoria

Victoria (34) has one sister, Annie, two years younger than she
is. Victoria was always the more outgoing sister. Her sister was
well-behaved and more responsible, while Victoria was called a
drama queen by Annie and her mother. She spent hours reading
vampire novels and was always dressing up as famous
actresses, writing plays and poetry and acting out scripts on her
own. The girls' mother suffered domestic violence from their
father. Victoria worshipped her father and enjoyed being his
favourite child, although she would get frightened and feel
sorry for her mother when he lost his temper. At these times,
she would escape into a fantasy world of her own.

When Victoria was 9 years old, her father started to sexually
abuse her, after having to leave a high-ranking post in the Civil
Service because of a charge of gross misconduct. The abuse
eventually led to full intercourse. Victoria told her mother, but
she seemed too frightened to do anything. Instead, she would
encourage Victoria to spend time with her father, as this seemed
to pacify him. Victoria thought it was something bad inside her
that attracted her father, as she had always felt that she was a
wicked person. She knew herself to be self-centred and prone to
jealousy, unlike her sister. She also felt bad because a part of
her liked the fact that her father was not interested in Annie, but
only in her (Victoria).

Victoria had given up on her school work soon after her father
started abusing her, and despised the way her sister worked so
hard. Victoria was more interested in the attention she got from
boys at school. After the abuse started, Victoria put on more of

a show to the outside world, always talking about how great her family was. When her father died suddenly of a heart attack when she was 15, she was devastated, and started to idealize him. She began experimenting with drink and drugs, became promiscuous, getting into relationships with men who were controlling and abusive. Victoria fell pregnant and gave birth to a boy, Ollie. Victoria felt isolated as a single mother and at times couldn't cope, having to be sectioned on one occasion. Her sister Annie helped to look after Ollie as their mother's poor mental health meant that she could not help out with her grandson.

Victoria would go out when she received her benefits, seeking to escape the stress of her life by getting drunk and sleeping with men. She gained a reputation. One night, she was raped by a guy who insisted on coming in for coffee. She did not want to have intercourse, as she was not keen on the man, but he said she had 'done it with everyone else so why not him' and then forced himself on her. Victoria did not go to the police because she did not think she would be believed.

Counsellor: OK Viv, let's start at the beginning. What was Victoria's early life like?

Viv: Pretty shit, her mother was a victim of domestic violence and Victoria escaped into a fantasy world.

Counsellor: Yes, so she was disadvantaged from the start. How else was she disadvantaged?

Viv: Well, her father abused her.

Counsellor: Viv, what do you know about the long-term impact of sexual abuse upon victims?

Viv: Not much, really. I haven't ever thought about it but it can ruin your life, can't it?

Counsellor: Would it be OK if I could give you some information about the long-term impact of sexual abuse?

Viv: Why do I need to know that?

Counsellor: Good question. Well, the purpose of the work is for you to protect your children. Now I know you don't think that there is any risk to protect your children from, but you know that Children's Services see it differently. So, if they are to allow you guys to live as a family again, they will want to know that you have more understanding than the average person in the street about how victims generally, and your children in particular, could suffer if they ever became victims of sexual abuse.

Viv agreed to be given information about the consequences for victims of sexual abuse. The counsellor had various safeguarding aims, here. He was trying to raise Viv's awareness of the consequences of sexual abuse in general. He was also trying to deepen Viv's sensibility with regard to victims of sexual abuse being doubly victimized and, in the process, challenge the rape myth that 'only certain types of women get raped'.

The counsellor explained to Viv that when a person is sexually abused, they can try to survive the trauma by denying their sexuality: covering their body in baggy clothes, overeating to make themselves obese and unattractive, not eating to make themselves invisible, avoiding social and sexual contact. However, victims can have an opposite reaction to abuse. They can feel sexually commodified by the abuse and the grooming process, internalizing the message that what is valuable about them is their sexuality. If victims have suffered abuse or neglect by caregivers, they can be especially vulnerable to the exploitative attentions of older men, as they seek the nurture they have missed out on in childhood. They can thus present as sexually promiscuous, using sex, and frequently substances, to self-medicate traumatic symptomatology. Previous trauma can also result in the victim developing a problematic attachment style, desperate for the security of a relationship but hyper-sensitive to any sign that this security, or the promise of this security, may be threatened. This profound insecurity then results in volatile behaviour. For victims who develop promiscuous lifestyles, there can also be a compensatory sense of power in choosing to have sex with partners rather than having no choice, as was the case when they were abused. Hence, victims of abuse can be perceived as being 'bad' women (or men) who are asking to be sexually assaulted or raped, who are chaotic, unreliable, and likely to make false allegations of abuse. The counsellor suggested to Viv that those who commit sexual crimes often dehumanize victims as sexual objects: not acknowledging, through choice or ignorance, the humanity and vulnerability of the people they exploit or abuse. When helping clients to delve backstage, as it were, into the above vulnerability of victims, the exercises and the case studies in this book, particularly the psycho-educational material in Chapter 7, can be of significant use.

> *Viv:* So, what you're basically saying is that the woman who made the allegation of rape may have been abused?
> *Counsellor:* Not necessarily, but people are rarely just trouble makers, there's usually some sort of back story.

Viv said nothing, but looked thoughtful. The counsellor did not know how much of the information Viv took on board about how victims of abuse, disempowerment and neglect can be vulnerable to repeat victimization, but Viv never dismissed the victim of her husband's offence as a 'trouble maker' again. The counsellor then went on to explore what makes sexual relationships and encounters abusive.

> *Counsellor:* You and I both know that Children's Services have had concerns about yours and Rhys's sexual lifestyle.
> *Viv:* I don't know what that's got to do with protecting the kids. We've always kept our sex life away from the kids.
> *Counsellor:* Well, I don't know exactly what Children's Services have in mind but from what I've read in reports, and what is typically the case, professionals may have concerns. Would you like to hear what I think?
> *Viv:* Go ahead.
> *Counsellor:* Well, many people live alternative lifestyles and that's up to them, as long as it doesn't lead to exploitation, abuse, or criminal behaviour. However, where parents have

been involved in a swinging lifestyle and then one of the parents has also been convicted of a sexual offence, professionals will be concerned that the parent who has offended might be prone to crossing safe sexual boundaries, sexually objectifying others, or misusing power in relationships. So, part of the work I'm undertaking with you and Rhys is to give you both an opportunity to demonstrate that you know the difference between abusive sex and non-abusive sexual behaviour.
Viv: We do!
Counselling: OK, can you tell me what makes sex exploitative or abusive, whether it's in a long-term committed relationship, or a one-night-stand or casual sexual encounter?

The counsellor and Viv discussed the above, and came up with the following features of a non-exploitative, non-abusive relationship or casual sexual encounter:

- Sexual participants are above the age of consent
- Consent is given freely
- It is accepted by parties that consent can be withdrawn at any point
- Individuals are respectfully aware of power differences in relationships
- There is no misuse of power or status to gain sexual consent or to coerce anybody into sexual contact
- Vulnerability (i.e. one party being drunk, emotionally needy, dependent, impressionable) should not be taken advantage of
- Individuals are honest and transparent about their sexual intentions, in terms of not promising or implying relational commitment they are unwilling to make
- Participants are sensitive to what is in the best interests of the other
- Sex occurs within the context of respectful relating

- Safe boundaries between adult sexual behaviour and children are always observed

After exploration and reflection, Viv stated that there was a power difference between her husband and the victim. She was an 18-year-old girl, and he was a middle-aged man. He had far more life experience. Viv considered that, in his drunken and grieving state, it was unlikely that Rhys had had the young girl's best interests at heart, and he had probably sexually objectified her.

The counsellor explored with Viv the sexually alternative lifestyle she and her husband had adopted. In exploring the pros and cons of this lifestyle, Viv acknowledged that they had both sexually objectified other people and that to perceive casual sexual partners holistically, as rounded people, would take the fun out of the impersonal encounters.

Counsellor: So, a significant reward of sexually objectifying people is fun, sexual excitement with no strings.
Viv: That's exactly it. Doing it with a stranger is so - so animalistic, an escape from the drudgery of life. I don't want to know about the people and their problems, their kids, what they do for a living, their elderly parents who they got to look after (laughs), their arthritis. I just want it to be two animals fucking in the night.
Counsellor: … and the down side?
Viv: A bit of guilt afterwards. Sometimes I used to feel dirty, but never jealous about who Rhys had been with. In fact, the thought of him with somebody else was a bit of a turn-on, but yeah, I guess, as you say, you do objectify people and whether or not Rhys did rape the girl - and I still don't think he did by the way - he probably did objectify her (tears in her eyes), saw her as a piece of meat, I suppose, to take his mind off the death of his mother. He was also pissed at the time, of course. He's never been good at talking about his emotions - didn't need to in the Army. I'm a bit crap at talking about things as well.

Gradually, as the safeguarding counselling work with Viv continued, she was able to reflect at more depth on the pros and cons of her lifestyle. Crucial in this was the counsellor's ability to maintain a non-judgemental stance, creating a safe space in which Viv felt valued. As a result, no energy had to go into defending herself against the counsellor's attacks, real or imagined, and this created the atmosphere for in-depth, critical but compassionate self-scrutiny. The safeguarding work with Viv culminated in the following Signs of Risk of which to be aware:

- She and Rhys sexually objectifying others
- She and Rhys not communicating
- Rhys suffering from grief or any other strong emotion he is not talking about
- Rhys having encounters or relationships with younger women who clearly have less power than he has and who are vulnerable in some way

Safeguarding counselling with Rhys

In the work with Rhys, it became apparent that his history and values were, or had been, consistent with many pro-offending themes apparent in the sections above, both about veterans and about rape. He was in the habit of compartmentalizing his emotions, which served him well when he was involved in military action. He would then blot out troubling feelings with alcohol. He acknowledged that pornography was ubiquitous in the Army, and admitted to having sex with prostitutes when on overseas postings. He thought that his wife guessed he would do so, but would turn a blind eye as long as he made sure that he did not pass on any sexually transmitted diseases to her.

The counsellor took Rhys through the events of the day, leading up to his conviction for rape. Rhys said he had been on a rehabilitation course in prison, so was used to 'talking about this stuff'. However, he would not admit to raping the girl, insisting that he would never do anything like that, adding, with a touch of bravado, that he had never needed to force himself on any woman.

In my previous book (Smith, 2017), there are copious examples of how to work with individuals who are in various stages of denial with regard to their sexual offending and the risk they pose. However, below are a few examples of helpful questions a practitioner can ask if conducting safeguarding work with an alleged or convicted sexual offender who is denying his sexual offending:

- On a scale from 0-10, if 0 is no risk at all to children and 10 is very high risk, where would you put yourself on this scale?
- Can you say why you put yourself at this point on the scale?
- Where do you think other professionals or family members would put you on this scale?
- Where do you think that you need to be on the scale for people to think you are safe to be with your children? (Think, in turn, of various professionals and significant others)
- What do you think needs to happen in order for you to reach this point on the scale of being safe enough?
- What do other people think must happen, before you are considered safe?
- Imagine you have been living in the community safely for two years and you are living an offence-free, satisfying life, what sort of life would you be living?
- How would you be thinking about your offending?
- Who would you be seeing and not seeing?
- How would you be managing your relationships?

Counsellor: OK Rhys, I'm not going to try to make you admit anything, but if we go through the day of the offence you were convicted of, what could you have done differently to avoid being accused of the offence?

Rhys: Fine, I can work with that. That's looking forward, not looking back, that's more like the Army's way of doing things.

Counsellor: Let's start with what you did first when you got out of bed that day.

Rhys: Well, it was a couple of days before the funeral. Viv was out at work, and I had the day to myself. I got up, had some breakfast (pause).

Counsellor: What did you do next?

Rhys: I think I looked at some porn on the internet.

Counsellor: I appreciate your honesty.

Rhys: What you see is what you get, with me.

Counsellor: Can you recall your feelings and thoughts before you decided to look at pornography?

Rhys: I was feeling lonely, I guess, not looking forward to the funeral, at a loose end, I suppose.

Counsellor: Anything else?

Rhys: I was feeling guilty.

Counsellor: Can you say more?

Rhys: I was angry with my mother. She was dead, and the last time I saw her she seemed so pathetic. The cancer had shrunk her to nothing. She was never very big, but she was the matriarch of the family, a strong woman in a way. Hard-working. I respected that about her. She also had a right mouth on her, wouldn't take bullshit from anyone - a tongue like a whip (pause, tears in his eyes).

Counsellor: (Leaving space to honour the moment) Tell me more about her.

Rhys: She had all her teeth out when she was about forty, and she didn't persevere with her dentures because she said they made her gums sore. She was a bit of a martyr, always attended the local Catholic church. Her favourite saying was 'I haven't had a morsel to eat all day'. I can't remember a time when she wasn't on 'nerve tablets', as she called them. In her latter days, she would crush them up with all the rest of the tablets she was on - she kept this small hammer in her handbag to crush them with.

Counsellor: … and your father?

Rhys: He died a while ago (pause). He was completely under her thumb. He used to work as a waiter. He was effeminate, camp really, where my mother was hard, masculine almost. I could never imagine them having sex. I know most people can't imagine their parents going at it but with my mother and father, you really couldn't. Another one of her favourite sayings was 'your father is soft as shit'. She brought me up to despise him. I joined the Army when I was 18 to get out of it.

*Counsello*r: Why the guilt about your mother? Can we go back to that?

Rhys: I was thinking about the last time I took her out in the car when she was alive. She used to love being driven around, we'd go for miles and miles. It was a new car I had just bought. I tucked her into the front seat, putting the seat belt around her. There seemed to be hardly any of her body left to wrap the belt around. I said 'how do you like my new car, Mum?' She completely ignored me and said 'have you picked up my tablets from the kitchen table?' I had this urge to put my hand over her face, to squeeze her cheeks until they met in the middle, so that she looked like that famous painting by that guy from Norway.

Counsellor: Munch, The Scream, do you mean?

Rhys: Yeah, I think that's the one. My daughter Rose would know, she's really into art. I think she was trying to copy it once, that's why it stuck in my mind.

Counsellor: That's a very violent image.

Rhys: (In tears) I know, but I loved her. She looked so pathetic.

Often when a loved one dies, the relatives do not just grieve the loss of the person, but the final loss of what the relationship could potentially have been, but never was. Whilst the parent is still alive the hope, or the magical thinking, that one day the parent will be the parent the adult child wants, can endure. Death finally dashes this hope, producing a powerful emotional cocktail of anger, guilt and grief.

As the counselling progressed, Rhys gained insight into how he had always tended to project repressed anger towards his mother onto women with whom he was not in an intimate relationship. With Viv, the part of himself that loved his mother was in ascendancy, with his anger against womankind assigned to his shadow.

He had chosen a free-loving, liberated wife, completely unlike his asexual mother as, for Rhys, his mother was symbolically associated with curtailment of the life force. Sex for Rhys was not only about erotic and sensual pleasure but was also a psychological flight from the endless, tedious drudgery and suffering he associated with his family of origin. Rhys could not admit to the rape. However, he could agree with the counsellor that the following factors would make it more likely that he would end up in a similar frame of mind and situation, leading to his being accused and convicted of rape. There was a distinct cross-over between these risk factors and the ones which his wife, Viv, had identified (see above):

- Rhys sexually objectifying others
- Rhys not sharing troubling thoughts and feelings
- Rhys feeling anger and resentment towards women which seems out of proportion to what is occurring
- Rhys having encounters or relationships with younger women who clearly have less power than he does and who are vulnerable in some way

In addition, the counsellor and Rhys came up with the following Signs of Safety:

- Restricting his sexual life to his relationship with his wife
- Not looking at internet pornography
- Telling his wife if he lapses and looks at internet pornography

- Restricting his alcohol intake to three pints of beer, or three glasses of wine
- Keeping his distance from any female friends of his teenage children
- Imagining any woman, he finds sexually attractive as a human being, who has people who love her, who has hopes for the future, and who experiences similar trials and tribulations to his own
- If he sees a young woman, he finds sexually attractive, saying a quick blessing in his head, wishing her a long, happy and safe life

The above, last two Signs of Safety were designed to rehumanize potential female victims, if Rhys were ever in danger of dehumanizing somebody through sexual objectification. In order to commit an act of violence or abuse, offenders need to objectify victims. To empathize with a victim's humanity usually puts a hand-brake on causing harm. The exception is when offenders are sadistically inclined, and gain pleasure from causing fear and pain. The counsellor did not consider that Rhys was sadistic. In order to cause harm to his victim, he had needed to distance himself from the suffering, seeing her as 'other' and sexually objectifying her.

In addition to the above safeguarding work, the counsellor also employed the psycho-educational work completed with Viv, and illustrated comprehensively in Chapter 7. Having completed this safeguarding work with Rhys and Viv separately, the counsellor then saw them together as a couple.

Safeguarding counselling with both parents, Rhys and Viv

In earlier chapters, I have illustrated how safeguarding counselling work can be conducted with partners, using a strengths-focused approach. Here, I will focus on issues that are particularly pertinent to family work.

Offending behaviour is sometimes not talked about by adults in a family because of a genuine, if misguided, effort to protect children. However, sometimes not talking to and listening to a child can be due to the adult's own difficulties in processing and talking about what has happened, when a family member has been accused or convicted of sexual offending.

If children are left in the dark, they can make wrong assumptions, drawing unhelpful conclusions in the absence of proper explanations. These thinking errors or 'distortions' can be taken into adulthood if not addressed, and become part of a person's problematic belief system. Examples include:

- It's my fault that Dad left
- It happened because Social Services want to take people's children away from them
- It was the victim's fault
- The family broke up due to another reason, rather than the parent's offending
- We should never talk about him (the parent who left the home) for some unexplained and distressing reason
- The child can also idealize the absent parent and sometimes seek secret contact, putting the child at risk

The above examples of problematic thinking can result in the child having a low regard for authority figures, leading to self-defeating anti-social behaviour. Repressed rage can also be shifted away from the parent who has committed the sexual abuse onto others, such as the victim and professionals seeking to support the family and make the family safe. Not talking openly about what has happened can also lead to the child catastrophizing, discerning (rightly or wrongly) that the adults cannot cope, and prematurely taking on a rescuer role in the family. Moreover, sexual abuse is more likely to happen and not be disclosed in families where there is a history and culture of secrecy, and a lack of open communication.

Having said all this, the fact remains that it is usually very difficult for a non-offending partner to tell a child that the other parent has been convicted of a sexual offence and might pose a risk to them or other children. Adults are afraid of unduly frightening children, taking away their innocence, and alienating the child from the offending parent. There can also be concern that the child will talk about what has happened outside of the family, leading to the child and the family being victimized due to public fears about sexual offending. In my experience there is no pat 'out of the book' way of talking to children about such a sensitive matter, but there are broad principles, outlined below:

- The explanation should be age-appropriate
- The explanation should not denigrate the parent who has offended. To denigrate the parent is to denigrate the child
- The explanation should not blatantly minimize or shift responsibility for the offending onto others
- By words and attitude the child should be encouraged to ask any further questions and express feelings (including anger and fear) and to express any concerns
- If possible, safe persons should be identified to whom the child can talk, apart from the parents, with the child being encouraged to confide in these people about any concerns, rather than in people who have not been identified as safe
- Forms of words constituting explanations for children at different stages should be negotiated between parents and professionals

Below are various questions a counsellor or other child protection practitioner can ask parents to assist with communicating with children, when a parent or other loved one has committed a sexual offence:

- What does your child know about why their father is in prison or why contact with him is restricted?
- What do others say about this, such as Children's Services?
- What does your partner think?
- What do you want your child to know?

- What do you think can be gained from your child having a better understanding of what has happened?
- Have you any concerns about them knowing?
- How would you go about telling your child?
- What would help?
- When and where could you do it?
- You and the authorities have different views about what has happened. Do you think your child should know the different views?
- Can we come up with a form of words you could use to tell your child about what has happened? We can then see if other professionals are happy with this

Viv and Rhys told the counsellor that they had never really talked to the twins in detail about their father's offending or being in prison, but they considered that the twins 'knew the score'. The counsellor used some of above questions with Viv and Rhys, albeit not as a list, to help them reflect on the pros and cons of talking to the children about the abuse, with the counsellor chipping in about the positives of children having an age-appropriate explanation. Hence, the parents came up with ideas about how they wanted to talk to the children regarding Rhys's offending, agreeing that they should talk to the children together. The counsellor and the parents came up with the following form of words, to be delivered by Viv, with Rhys present when she spoke to the children:

Your father has been found guilty of having sex with an 18-year-old girl against her will, and had to go to prison for this. He was convicted of the offence of rape. He says that this girl agreed to have sex but the Court did not believe him, and found him guilty. Both of us (Viv and Rhys) agree with Social Services that we must respect the Court's decision. Like Social Services, we both want you to feel safe and comfortable with your father if he returns home to live, and this is why we are working with the counsellor to plan for this.

Once this form of words was agreed, it was passed on to the child protection social worker, to ensure that Children's Services were happy with the explanation, and to see whether they wanted to make any amendments. An invitation was also extended to the social worker to be present when the children were provided with this explanation.

Rose and Alfie were 14 years old, and were not naive children. They knew what rape meant. Both Viv and Rhys wanted to use this word, as it accurately reflected Rhys's conviction. With younger children, words such as 'hurt', 'harmed' or 'sexually assaulted' can be used. Individuals - professionals and non-professionals alike - are likely to have strong but differing opinions about the words to use when explaining to a child that a parent has sexually offended. I believe there is no one right way but, in each situation, those involved should be guided by the principles listed above. The form of words arrived at should, if possible, be agreeable to parents and professionals, but with professionals having the final say. This is in order to avoid families colluding to suggest that sexual offending did not happen and shifting the blame for the abuse onto the victim or others.

Safeguarding counselling with the Roberts children: Rose and Alfie

To work with family units is usually to involve oneself with strong familial attachments, bonds of culture and loyalty, and instinctive urges to protect loved ones and oneself from social stigma. Often, when a family member has been accused or convicted of sexual offending, the family group allies together against the outside world and professionals, as a defence against perceived or actual threat to the existing familial system. Sexual abuse can cause painful splits in families, with some family members choosing to believe that sexual abuse occurred, and other members insisting that it has not, preferring the explanation that there has been a miscarriage of justice or the loved one has been falsely accused. Sexual abuse usually evokes a maelstrom of painful emotions.

Engaging the children of a parent accused or convicted of sexual offending involves walking a tightrope between helping to make the children and young people more risk aware, but avoiding alienating or 'othering' the offending parent. If the latter happens, this can undermine the child's sense of identity through vicarious stigma. I believe the strengths-focused approach is ideally suited to help practitioners walk this safeguarding tightrope.

In my view, there are no set rules about the number of sessions a counsellor should have with children/young people in a family as there are so many variables: ages, levels of maturity, psychological functioning, motivation, relational dynamics between different children, financial resources available for the work. This list is not exhaustive. Hence, consideration must be given in each case as to how work with family members should be structured in terms of duration and sequencing.

In the case of the Roberts family the children were fairly stable, so did not need any significant therapeutic input, and they had a good relationship with each other. The focus was limited to including their voices in the New Life Family Safety Plan. The counsellor had a one-hour session with each twin alone, and two one-hour sessions with the twins together.

In the individual session with each twin, the counsellor began by building rapport and establishing the following:

- How they felt about attending the session
- Establishing confidentiality boundaries
- What they thought the work was about
- What they knew about what had happened with their father
- What they believed and how they felt about this
- What they wanted to happen with the family
- The good things about the family
- What they would like to change

In the joint sessions with the twins, the counsellor used a flip chart sheet to depict a happy, safe family, and an unhappy, unsafe family, asking them to complete the picture of the dysfunctional (unsafe) family first, and then working on the mirror image of a functional (safe) family. The twins did this together, with the counsellor asking them to focus on the following areas:

- How parents discipline their children
- How parents talk to each other
- How siblings talk to each other
- The state of the house
- How the family manages privacy boundaries, including sexual boundaries
- How parents spend time separately and with the children
- How children spend time separately and with the parents
- How family members use the internet
- The sort of visitors who come to the family home

Counsellor: OK, well done both. You've come up with two pretty clear pictures about what you think of as an unhappy, unsafe family and a happy, safe family. Can I keep what you've done on the flip chart and bring it into the last sessions, which will be attended by both of you and your parents?
Rose: Sure. (Alfie nods his head)
Counsellor: Having done this exercise, could I ask you what might sound like a dumb question? If you went to bed tonight and a miracle happened or somebody waved a magic wand and your family became how you would really like it to be, what would living in your family be like for you, beginning from when you got up the next morning?

The counsellor took Rose and Alfie through the details of each weekday, weekend and holiday times, focusing on the everyday, practical details of family life: getting up time, meal times, bed time, and various family routines. What came out of this exercise was that Rose and Alfie agreed they both wanted to do more fun, outdoor activities with their parents such as camping and cycling, and that they did not want their father to drink so much, or to smell alcohol on his breath. These suggestions were incorporated into the New Life

Safety Plan, the outdoor activities under the categories of Signs of Safety, and their father's drinking under the category of Signs of Risk, as drinking alcohol had also been a factor in their father's offending.

Throughout the above work, neither Rose nor Alfie mentioned anything which indicated that they were aware of their parents' previous swinging lifestyle. Family members are often very good at concealing embarrassing or shameful secrets. Nevertheless, the children's silence on this subject suggested that the parents had kept appropriate boundaries between their sexual life and family life with the children. Of course, if this had not been the case and the children had described loose sexual boundaries, this issue would have had to be worked through with the parents, and reflected in the Safety Plan.

Counsellor: You told me that you know what your father has been convicted of and this is why he is not living at home at present. What would you do if your father returned home and you found yourself feeling uncomfortable with him or if he touched you inappropriately?

Alfie: (Sullenly) What do you mean by inappropriate?
Counsellor: What do you think it means?
Alfie: Touching somebody's private areas.
Counsellor: Anything else?
Rose: We had it in school, any touching that you are not comfortable with.
Counsellor: Is feeling uncomfortable just about touching?
*Alfi*e: No, it could be talking about sex in front of kids.
Rose: He would never do that, but I would tell him to shut up or get off, and tell Mum.
Counsellor: Who else could you tell?
Alfie: We could phone Gran or Gramps, or ring Childline, but Dad's not like that.
Counsellor: Look, I've met your dad, and I like him, and I know that you guys love him and think he would never do anything to harm you. You may well be right, but if he did or you thought he might, could you make a list of everything you

could do, and we can add that to the New Life Safety Plan for your family.

Rose and Alfie came up with the following list:

- Tell him to get off
- Scream
- Leave the room or the house
- Tell Mum
- Tell Gran and Gramps
- Tell a teacher
- Phone Childline
- Tell a parent of a good friend
- Phone the police

This list was added to the New Life Safety Plan, under the heading Responses to Signs of Risk.

Safeguarding counselling with all family members

The session with the Roberts family followed the same format as the family session depicted in the last chapter, so I will not repeat similar material at this point. However, I will summarize the typical process of a family session, which comes at the end of a course of safeguarding work with family members:

- Put people at ease
- Ask how people are feeling about attending the family session
- Inquire about family members' worries and concerns
- Clarify that the purpose of the family session is to agree the contents of the New Life Safety Plan
- Hand out to all attendees copies of draft Safety Plans or other relevant materials used in previous sessions (such as Rose's and Alfie's flip chart sheet of an unhappy, unsafe

family and a happy, safe family) in order to aid the
discussion
- An example New Life Safety Plan (see Appendix) can also
  be used for the purpose of helping family members to
  discuss and agree what should go into the final Plan
- Provide the family with a blank New Life Safety Plan to
  complete while the counsellor leaves the room
- The counsellor returns to the room to trouble-shoot the
  agreed Safety Plan as the counsellor did in the last chapter

Sometimes the voices of children and young people are not
adequately heard in child protection proceedings, with professional and
adult discourses being privileged over the views of minors. The counsellor tried to redress this balance.

Counsellor: Rose and Alfie, would you be prepared to read out
what you put on these flip charts sheets, about what you
consider an unhappy, unsafe family and a happy, safe family
to be?

On this occasion, the teenage children in this family were sufficiently able and confident to talk to their parents directly about their
views. When this is not the case, the counsellor needs to be the voice
of the children. The counsellor, in this case, takes up this role with
regard to the father's drinking, and the children reporting any concerns.

Counsellor: Rhys, from what you heard, would you like to
change the way in which you behave in the family?
Rhys: Well, they clearly don't like me drinking - I never realized that before. I promise that they won't smell alcohol on my
breath again.
Counsellor: Rhys, Rose and Alfie clearly love you and it's clear
that you love them, but if they had any concerns about your
behaviour, what should they do?
Rhys: No brainer, they should tell their mother, and then I

should leave the house and Viv should inform Social Services (looks at the counsellor). When you told me in the last session about all the ways Rose and Alfie said they could protect themselves, I was proud of them, and all of what they say should go into the Safety Plan.

If the safeguarding work with a family has come as far as it did with the Roberts family, with all family members being able to sit in a room and talk about risk management issues connected to a parent's sexual offending, then risk of harm will have very likely been assessed as low, and the relationship between the parents, children and other family members will probably be amicable and open. Moreover, with the benefit of the safeguarding work completed with the counsellor, Rhys was giving his children clear permission to report any concern they might have about him in the future. This is a sign of safety. In riskier families, these positive, protective factors are not apparent. If this is the case, family reunification safeguarding work is unlikely to be feasible, and it will be too dangerous to allow an offending parent to return to the family home.

Risk assessment is an ongoing process, and if concerns arise about the way parents relate to children when in the same room (i.e. closing the child down, shifting responsibility etc.), then this should be recorded and reported to Children's Services, and the parents challenged about any such signs of risk at a later date. Child protection cases tend to take on a trajectory of their own, either away from or towards contact between the offending parent and children. However, this trajectory should never take precedence over any renewed consideration of emerging signs of risk and safety. Happily, in the case of the Roberts family no new signs of risk emerged in the joint family sessions.

Conclusion

The work with the Roberts family differed from the work with the family unit in the previous chapter, in that the issues were obviously different and the Roberts children were old enough to be directly involved in the final joint sessions, and have direct input into the formulation of the New Life Safety Plan. However, the same principles applied with regard to both families: the counsellor using strengths-focused techniques to negotiate with family members, separately and together, solutions to the problem of a parent-figure being convicted of a sexual offence and the related potential risk to the children. This was achieved by utilizing the strengths and resources in each family unit, in order to provide family members with a genuine say in their own destinies.

Practice points from this chapter

- Take any significant clash of values with clients to supervision
- Explore how unequal power dynamics and hedonistic tendencies have been factors in sexual offending
- The counsellor challenging a client is only liable to be effective if the counsellor is feeling compassionate towards the client and not disapproving at the time
- Military veterans are convicted of fewer general offences but more violent and sexual crimes than non-veterans
- Veterans have been trained to compartmentalize. This is an advantage in war, but can also be dysfunctional, allowing individuals to sexually offend in secret and to distance themselves from their offending
- The culture in the military of pornography use and repressing emotions through alcohol use can be triggers for sexual offending
- Being excluded from the close community of the military through the stigma attached to sexual offending can be particularly painful for military families
- Rape is often about offenders feeling sexually entitled, objectifying women and misusing power and control to act

out grievance towards women. This can sometimes be related to negative feelings about female caregivers

- Rape myths should be challenged in a supportive way
- Psycho-educational work is often the best way to challenge rape myths, and to raise awareness of repeat victimization issues
- The voice of the children should be heard in safeguarding work
- Children need to be old and mature enough to take part in family safeguarding work
- Sometimes the therapist has to be the voice of the children
- Assessment is an ongoing process, and any concerns arising out safeguarding work with families need to be thoroughly explored to prevent children being put at risk
- It should never be too late to call a halt to family reunification, if signs of risk emerge

References

Blanchard, G.T. (1995) *The difficult connection: The therapeutic relationship in sex offender treatment*. Brandon, Vermont: Safer Society Press.

Brownmiller, S. (1975) *Against our will: Men, women and rape*. New York: Simon and Schuster.

Burt, M.R. (1980) 'Cultural myths and supports for rape', *Journal of Personality and Social Psychology*, 38(2): pp. 217-230.

Caddick, N, Godier, L. and Fossey, M. (2017) 'Early service leavers: History, vulnerability and future research', in J. Hacker Hughes (ed.) *Military veteran psychological health and social care*. London: Routledge, pp. 27-44.

Coxell, A., King, M., Mezey, G., and Gordon, D. (1999) 'Lifetime prevalence, characteristics and associated problems of non-consensual sex in men: Cross sectional survey', *British Medical Journal*, 318 (7187): pp. 846-850.

Ellis, L. (1989) *Theories of rape: Inquiries into the causes of sexual aggression*. New York: Hemisphere.

Freud, S. (2001) 'Three essays on the theory of sexuality', in J. Strachey (ed.) *The Standard edition of the Complete Psychological Works of Sigmund Freud, Vol 7 (1901-1905)*. London: Vintage Books, pp. 135-243. First published 1905.

Groth, A. N., Burgess, A.W. and Holmstrom, L.L. (1977) 'Rape: power, anger and sexuality', *American Journal of Psychiatry*, 134 (11):1239-1243.

MacManus, D. and Wood, N. (2017) 'The ex-armed forces offender and the UK criminal justice system', in J. Hacker Hughes (ed.) *Military veteran psychological health and social care*. London: Routledge, pp. 62-80.

Maxwell, L. and Scott, G. (2014) 'A review of the role of radical feminist theories in the understanding of rape myth acceptance', *Journal of Sexual Aggression*, 20 (1): pp. 40-54.

O'Neill, J. (2017) 'Veterans' children', in J. Hacker Hughes (ed.) *Military veteran psychological health and social care*. London: Routledge, pp. 45-61.

Pino, N.W. and Meier, R.F. (1999) 'Gender differences in rape reporting', *Sex Roles*, 40 (11-12): pp. 979-990.

Rape Crisis England and Wales, https://rapecrisis.org.uk/get-informed/rcew-statistics/ [22 February 2022].

Sanday, P.R. (1981) *Female power and male dominance: On the origins of sexual inequality*. Cambridge: Cambridge University Press.

CONCLUSION

Hopefully, this book has demonstrated the complex issues involved in counselling partners and relatives of individuals who have committed sexual offences. Each case is different. However, there is a dividing line between cases where there are no child protection issues and cases where safeguarding children, and the client involvement in the child protection process, takes centre stage. The counselling depicted in this book has included working with partners on their own, working with couples and working with the larger family system.

Where there are no child protection concerns, the work has much in common with counselling partners of individuals who have sexual addiction/compulsivity problems. Partners will likely present with profound hurt and anger, often feeling humiliated by a loved one's secret sexual behaviour. Shame usually isolates such clients, and counselling can offer a safe space for the above painful experiences to be expressed, witnessed and honoured.

Often clients will want to know how they can ever trust partners again. In this book, unexamined notions of trust have been deconstructed, with magical thinking replaced with clear bottom lines of what non-offending partners are prepared and not prepared to put up with. Helping clients to understand the likely consequences of sticking to their bottom line has also featured. Through this process of exploration, clients have been seen to reclaim power, developing trust in themselves or an ultimately benign universe, rather than trust in an unreliable other. For each client, this growth has involved devising a unique set of solutions to presenting problems, co-constructed with the therapist, and earthed into everyday reality.

Some clients featured have had difficulties in breaking free from abusive or dysfunctional relationships, in which they have been disempowered. The limited re-parenting capacity of the therapeutic relationship has been shown to help clients reflect on the impact of poor attachments with main caregivers, and to help them see how resultant faulty scripts and belief systems have trapped them in toxic relationships. Increasing insight, developed within an affirming relationship with a therapist, enables clients to make informed choices about sex and partners. In order to maintain unconditional regard, therapists have had to be aware of their shifting ego needs in the here-and-now of each session and of the importance of compassionately reflecting, alone and with a supervisor, in order to prevent judgementalism and insecurity from contaminating relationships with clients.

In cases where non-offending partners and relatives are caught up in the child protection system, the counsellors have had to deal with initial resentment about child protection social workers, and about the State having so much power to intervene in the life of the family. Part of the work with non-offending partners is to enable them to envision what good ability to protect looks like, and to help them understand what they need to know in order to play their part in protecting their children from a partner who poses a risk to children. As explained, if a partner poses a risk deemed to be anything higher than low, then supervised contact or family reunification is unfeasible, as the risk would be too high to be managed.

The work featured with non-offending partners where there are child protection concerns features a great deal of psycho-educational work, perhaps unfamiliar to many counsellors. The art in using such educational interventions successfully is to avoid delivering information in a paternalistic way, but instead to pass on information in a way informed by talking therapy sensibilities. The combination can prove very effective.

Working with the family system to improve risk management might also be unfamiliar to some counsellors, and is not for everybody. This work requires the practitioner to be part counsellor, part mediator, part educator, and part advocate for children and young people, in order for them to have their voice heard in the matter of feeling safe and comfortable in families. As in all work with clients where a family member has sexually offended – be it with individual clients, couples, or family members – risk assessment needs to be an ongoing process going hand-in-hand with therapeutic interventions.

One way of conceptualizing what counsellors and therapists do for a living is to view their work activity as helping to process and reduce human distress, enabling clients to constructively use such distress as a doorway to transformative personal growth. This is sometimes a tall order, when a person's life has been devastated by a loved one's sexual offending, but it does offer a genuine hope in the midst of the most painful events. Clients cannot always change their circumstances, and counsellors and therapists rarely have the power to do so. However, therapists can be midwives, helping clients to conceive and bring to birth new ways of being and responding to 'what is'.

Discovering that a partner or relative has sexually offended, is seen as a risk to children, and that you have to a duty to protect children from this risk, feels like a catastrophe to most clients placed in this position through no choice of their own. Life can never be the same, can never go back to what it was. However, life will certainly reconfigure and continue. There is a desperate need to offer counselling support to non-offending partners and relatives placed in this situation, as such specialized support is currently thin on the ground and difficult to access. Counselling can help this neglected client group to make informed choices that will result, most importantly, in the better protection of children. Children are not only harmed by sexual abuse, but also by the break-up of families. Safeguarding counselling can enable otherwise well-functioning, or well-enough functioning, families to remain together. This can save children and adults from the misery and trauma of needless separation when the sexual risk to children is low and manageable.

Signs of Safety

- If mother had to be away overnight children will stay with maternal grandmother
- Both parents agree that father will not be in the bedroom or bathroom alone with children, and will help them with their homework in communal spaces in the home
- Father will not allow himself to be alone with friends of the children or other children
- Father will only attend school events with children's mother or maternal grandparents
- Both parents agree to continue to keep their sexual life private and separate from the children
- Both parents agree that parental controls should be activated on all internet devices children will use when they get older
- Both parents agree that mother should have access to all

passwords on online equipment used by father and she should regularly check his history on devices
- Both parents agree that adults will be appropriately dressed when with the children
- Both parents agree that all members of the household will knock on bedroom and bathroom doors before entering
- Both parents agree that they will try to be open and honest with each other, and talk more about their private thoughts and feelings
- Father will try in the future to just listen to his partner's feelings, and try not to give advice, problem solve, and prematurely point out the positive
- Father will be more sensitive to his partner's feelings, desisting from making it obvious that he is looking at attractive women

Signs of Risk

- The above principles and boundaries being broken or seriously compromised
- Father engaging with illegal online material
- Father resuming pornography use
- Father becoming increasingly depressed and isolated over a significant period
- Father losing his job and suffering a loss of employment status
- The relationship between the parents deteriorating

In addition to the above, the following are common signs of risk with regard to sexual abuse:

- Father being close to a child who is vulnerable and looking for attention
- Forming a close/special relationship with a child behind the mother's back

- Children being afraid of or intimidated by the father
- Children desperately wanting to please the father
- Children being overly involved with the father to the exclusion of the mother
- Children not wanting to be left alone with father
- Children displaying a fear of men
- Sudden unexplained change of behaviour
- Children having gifts/money and being unable to explain where/how they got them
- Children being overly embarrassed or ashamed of their bodies for the stage of their development
- Bedwetting
- Children displaying age-inappropriate sexualised behaviour/language and not stopping when told to
- Children behaving sexually abusively towards younger/weaker children
- Unexplained injuries/soreness/marks/discharge around sexual areas of the children's bodies, loss of appetite, nightmares

Responses to Signs of Risk

- If any of the signs of safety are broken, a discussion should take place about how to get back on track, initiated by either partner
- Parents talking to each other
- Mother talking to children, when father is not present
- Mother talking to maternal grandparents
- Either parent or maternal grandparents to contact the LFF 'Stop it Now' helpline for advice: 0808 1000 900
- Either parent or grandparent to contact StopSo (counsellors who work with sexual offending issues): info@stopso.org.uk
- Mother or maternal grandparents to contact duty social worker or Police

INDEX